Voices of the Civil War

Voices of the Civil War · First Manassas

By the Editors of Time-Life Books, Alexandria, Virginia

Contents

THE FIELD AT FIRST MANASSAS

The Battle of First Manassas was fought on the hills and ridges west of Bull Run. An artist's rendering depicts the ground where the battle took place.

Groveton-Sudle Road

Warrenton Turnpike

Groveton

Young's Branch

Chinn Ridge

Chinn House

Sudley Ford

Sudley
Church

Bull Run

Matthews House

Matthews Hill

Dogan Ridge

Buck Hill

Van Pelt House

Stone Bridge

Dogan House

Stone House

Robinson
House

Henry
House

Henry House Hill

Lewis Ford

Bull Run

Lewis House
"Portici"

Manassas-Sudley
Road

Conrad House

GENERAL SCOTT.

THE HERCULES OF THE UNION,

SLAYING THE GREAT DRAGON OF SECESSION.

Chaotic Beginnings of the Conflict

The shots that ignited America's Civil War were fired on April 12, 1861, at the order of a vain, dapper, 43-year-old Louisianan with the sonorous name of Pierre Gustave Toutant Beauregard. Newly promoted to brigadier general by the almost equally new government of the Confederacy, Beauregard had been put in command of the 6,000 or so Rebel militiamen who had gathered in and around Charleston, South Carolina, along with a formidable array of nearly 60 heavy guns and mortars, most of them recently seized by Confederate forces from Federal arsenals and navy yards.

The target of Beauregard's cannon was the powerful Federal bastion in Charleston harbor, Fort Sumter. Four months before, on December 20, 1860, South Carolina had formally seceded from the Union, the first Southern state to do so. Now, according to

....

An idealized version of the massive and aged Winfield Scott, general in chief of the U.S. Army, takes up the Unionist cudgel against the multiheaded Confederacy in an 1861 lithograph. Each of the beast's seven heads is that of a prominent Rebel.

fire-eating South Carolinian anti-Unionists, Sumter was no longer the property of the U.S. government but belonged by right to their new independent state. The garrison there must be ordered by its government to pack up and get out—or else.

That was an order the newly inaugurated President Abraham Lincoln would not give. To do so, as he saw it, would be to recognize the Southern states' right to disunite, to concede that the nation was shattered and the great American experiment in democracy a failure. He refused the Rebel ultimatum but continued to make conciliatory statements to the South. The Confederate government, fearing that failure to act might compromise the independent status of the new nation, and concerned by news of a Federal supply expedition bound for the fortress, decided that it could wait no longer. Accordingly, on April 12, at 4:30 a.m., the bombardment began, a mortar shell arching above the fort, its fuse fizzing brightly in the night sky.

As a battle, the fight for Fort Sumter was no great military affair. Vastly outgunned, the fort and its tiny 68-man garrison commanded by Major Robert Anderson—who, ironically, had been Beauregard's artillery instructor at

West Point in the 1830s—managed to hold out for a day and a half despite a rain of 3,341 enemy projectiles that made a shambles of Sumter's interior. On April 14 Anderson surrendered. Miraculously, not a single soldier on either side had been killed by shellfire.

But the muzzle blasts at Charleston, like the musketry at Concord in 1775, were shots heard round the country and the world. Rebelling Southerners had fired on Federal troops and property. The long-threatened war between North and South was finally on—a deadly fratricidal conflict that would kill more than half a million American men before guttering out four years later, and would become the defining event in the nation's history.

With Sumter conquered, Beauregard's star flared as brightly as the fuse of the bombardment's first shell. He was hailed as a hero throughout the South, and a few weeks later was put in command of the Confederate army gathering in northern Virginia. Beauregard would lead that army during the war's first great clash, a confused daylong battle called Manassas by the Confederates, for the nearest town, and Bull Run by the Federals, for the closest natural feature, a sluggish little stream bordering the battlefield. Desperate and bloody, the battle would have huge consequences, guaranteeing by its ferocity that the war would continue and serving notice to both sides that it would be a long, grim, deadly ordeal.

The firing on Sumter produced an immediate reaction in Washington. The day before the fort's surrender, on April 13, President Lincoln issued a proclamation asking the states to muster 75,000 militiamen to serve against what he termed, with fine understatement, "combinations too powerful to be suppressed by the ordinary course of judicial proceedings." Five days later he proclaimed

a Federal blockade of all Southern ports.

The shelling of Fort Sumter and Lincoln's call to arms had immediate repercussions in the South as well, most important in the state of Virginia. Back in January, following South Carolina's lead, Mississippi, Florida, Alabama, Georgia, and Louisiana had also seceded from the Union; Texas had done the same on February 1. One week later the seven defecting states had banded together, forming the Confederate States of America. Ten days after that they had chosen a president for their new republic, a dour, West Point-trained soldier and longtime senator from Mississippi, Jefferson Davis.

But Virginia, birthplace of so many of the nation's founders and early presidents, had held back, torn between fealty to the Union and loyalty to its fellow slave-holding states. Lincoln's call for troops, perceived by Virginians as a threat of war, abruptly ended the uncertainty. On April 17 a convention in Richmond hastily passed an ordinance of secession, which was then submitted to the citizenry for approval. This act aligned the Old Dominion, the richest and most populous state in the South, with the young Confederacy. By late May, after a majority of voters had ratified secession, Richmond would become the Confederate seat of government, President Davis and the legislature moving there from the previous Rebel capital in Montgomery, Alabama.

Well before the government settled in Richmond, however, intrepid Virginia militiamen wasted no time in striking their state's first blow against the Yankees, pulling off one of the most important and shocking coups of the war. This was the capture on April 20 of the valuable Gosport Navy Yard near Norfolk, in the Tidewater region.

Gosport fell largely because its commander, the elderly Commodore Charles S. McCauley, panicked when the yard was threatened by a contingent of local troops. He tried to send out to sea every ship capable of sailing and ordered all those remaining at anchor burned and scuttled. As it happened, only three ships got under way. The rest were soon lying half submerged in the shallow waters of the Elizabeth River. One of the charred hulks, the *Merrimack,* would be salvaged by the Confederate navy and given a suit of armor and a new name, the *Virginia.* Ten months later it would fight the Union's *Monitor* in the historic first-ever battle of ironclad warships at Hampton Roads. Left behind, too, were most of Gosport's equipment, naval stores, and more than 1,000 heavy guns, which the Confederates would use to fortify ports all around the South.

With Norfolk gone, the Union high command quickly took steps to save the strategic bastion of Fort Monroe, sitting 15 miles to the north on the tip of Virginia's Peninsula. The fort in future could, and would, become a staging point for a Federal thrust up the Peninsula toward Richmond. Even as it was, in Union hands it posed an immediate threat to waterborne commerce on the York and James Rivers.

The fort's garrison was reinforced first by two Massachusetts regiments shipped south from Boston, then by more troops from New York and Vermont. The Massachusetts units were among four regiments raised some months earlier in the expectation that the secession of South Carolina, Mississippi, and the other original Rebel states would inevitably lead to war. The regiments had been organized and were commanded by Benjamin F. Butler, a brilliant and energetic but unpredictable Massachusetts lawyer and politician who had never led troops in battle. He was one of the first of the so-called political generals appointed by Lincoln's government who would more often than not prove a curse to the Union cause as the war progressed.

Fort Monroe was now secure thanks to Butler's quick action, but the same could not be said for the nation's capital itself. With good reason, Virginia's impending secession profoundly alarmed Washington. The enemy would now be only a few hundred yards away across the Potomac River. For its defense the city had at most 1,000 Regular Army troops backed by about 1,500 militia—and many of the latter were thought to be Southern sympathizers and thus unreliable as defenders of the capital.

There was as yet no real threat, but wild rumors nevertheless swept through the city, causing near panic. A flotilla of ships was said to be steaming up the Potomac packed with Rebel cutthroats. Other reports had 5,000 or even 10,000 secessionists advancing overland to capture President Lincoln and hijack the entire government. The Treasury Building was hastily turned into an armed bastion where Lincoln and his cabinet could take refuge if one of the rumored attacks took place.

The Federal capital remained virtually defenseless for days—though not for lack of would-be protectors. Thousands upon thousands of young Ohioans and Rhode Islanders, Minnesotans, and Illinoisans, outraged by the Southern rebellion and sharing Lincoln's profound belief that the Union must be saved, had flocked to join up. Michigan, one observer said, "is one vast recruiting station." Sixteen of the states quickly exceeded their quotas of volunteers. But getting the troops to Washington was another matter.

The only quick way was to ship them by railroad, and the only practical route, as the tracks then ran, was through Baltimore. But Maryland was a slave state, and many of its people were militant, not to say violent, secessionists. A token contingent of five companies of Federal militia from nearby Pennsylvania, most with little training and few weapons, managed to traverse Baltimore largely unscathed despite a jeering, rock-throwing mob that had tried to stop them as they moved through the city's streets. The next contingent was not so lucky.

This was the 6th Massachusetts Infantry, which was one of Butler's regiments. He dispatched the unit southward from Boston by train, bound via New York and Baltimore to Washington. Commanding the regiment en route was another inexperienced officer, Colonel Edward F. Jones, a former Utica, New York, businessman.

The 6th Massachusetts arrived in New York on April 18, marching down Broadway through cheering crowds, then boarded a train for Philadelphia. There Colonel Jones heard of the mob in Baltimore that had harassed the Pennsylvanians. Piling his men on 10 coaches, he distributed ammunition and told the troops to load their weapons.

Once the train arrived at Baltimore's President Street Station, which was the terminus of the Philadelphia, Wilmington & Baltimore Railroad, the cars would have to be pulled by teams of horses, slowly making their way through the city to the Baltimore & Ohio's Camden Street Station, before being hooked up to another locomotive for the trip to Washington.

At President Street the 6th Massachusetts ran into a mob far larger and more prone to violence than the Pennsylvanians had experienced earlier. With the cars blocked, the troops were forced to dismount and march through the streets. When the column was fired upon, the regiment's front rank fired a volley into the mob.

By the time the regiment had fought its way to the Camden Street Station and was once again rolling toward Washington, three young soldiers had been killed and 20 injured; 130 were unaccounted for. In addition, 20 civilians lay dead or dying. Nevertheless, the troops at last reached the capital, and Lincoln himself was waiting at the station. Grabbing Colonel Jones' hand, he exclaimed, "Thank God you have come!"

The tragic fracas by no means ended the Federal government's problems with Maryland. Gangs of secessionists, mostly young men from the Baltimore city militias, given their head by Governor Thomas H. Hicks, soon thereafter demolished four railroad bridges, severing the Baltimore route. The best remaining alternative was to ship troops to Annapolis, 20 miles south of Baltimore, then move them overland from there 40 miles to Washington.

This plan also outraged Maryland's Southern sympathizers, who sent a delegation to the White House to protest to the president. The feet of Yankee troops, they said, would never be allowed to defile what they referred to as their state's sacred soil. Lincoln quickly turned them away. "I *must* have troops for the defense of the capital," he said. "Our men are not moles and can't dig under the earth; they are not birds and can't fly through the air. There is no way but to march them across, and that they must do."

First to make the new route work was the resourceful Ben Butler. He had already started south from Boston on April 20 with his last regiment, the 8th Massachusetts, when he heard of the trouble in Baltimore. Judging the city impassable, he immediately took the regiment by train to Perryville, Maryland, where the Susquehanna River empties into the Chesapeake Bay, and, commandeering a big ferry boat, floated the troops to Annapolis. From there he would move the regiment to Washington by rail.

Butler soon discovered, however, that local secessionists had chugged off with all the usable locomotives of the Annapolis & Elk Ridge Railroad, hiding them on distant sidings. Gangs of Southern sympathizers had also ripped up long stretches of track.

These obstacles proved not to be a problem. Butler quickly found an old broken-down engine in a shed—along with a Massachusetts private who had worked in a locomotive manufacturing shop and could repair it. With almost equal speed, a crew of veteran railroad workers arrived and began repairing the track. About noon on April 25 a train full of men from the 8th Massachusetts Infantry reached Washington, to the city's almost hysterical relief. More trains soon chuffed in, bringing the 7th New York and a contingent of 1,200 Rhode Islanders. The bottleneck was broken. From early May onward, it would now be possible to transport as many as 15,000 men a day from Annapolis to reinforce the capital.

General Butler was not quite finished with Maryland. A danger remained that the state's hotheads might push through a vote of secession. This would leave Washington a helpless Federal raft in a Rebel sea. Butler, acting on his own initiative, decided to discourage any such move. He ran a trainload of his troops into Baltimore's Camden Street Station and, under cover of an evening thunderstorm, oc-

cupied one of the city's high spots, Federal Hill. When the citizens woke the next morning they were astonished to find nearly 1,000 Union troops and a battery of guns staring down at them. In the weeks ahead work crews repaired the wrecked railroad bridges, and the once rebellious, dangerous Baltimore became a smooth-flowing conduit for Federal troops and supplies.

With several thousand soldiers now on hand, Lincoln and the army's commander in chief, the aged but exceedingly acute General Winfield Scott, were able to launch a first small offensive. They were goaded into action when on May 23 the voters of Virginia overwhelmingly ratified the Article of Secession drawn up weeks before, confirming that the state was now enemy territory. At 2:00 a.m. on May 24, 11 regiments of Federal troops moved to flush Confederate militiamen from their outposts just across the Potomac and occupy Alexandria and nearby Arlington Heights.

These strikes proceeded with surprising speed and efficiency, considering the inexperience of the troops and their officers. Three New York regiments crossed the Potomac upstream from Washington by a roadway that ran atop an old aqueduct connecting Georgetown, in the District of Columbia, with the northern end of Arlington. The troops pushed two miles into Virginia and cut the Leesburg & Hampshire Railroad linking Alexandria and Leesburg. Two more columns crossed the Potomac by the old, wooden Long Bridge. One, turning right, occupied Arlington Heights, chasing away some Virginia pickets and occupying the handsome pillared mansion belonging to Robert E. Lee, who had left for Richmond some time earlier with his family.

At the Long Bridge, Colonel Orlando B. Willcox's 1st Michigan wheeled left and headed for Alexandria, which was held by about 700 locally recruited state militiamen. To help surprise the Virginians and take the old port with its valuable rail yard, another regiment, the 11th New York, was to be landed at the town docks by three river steamers. The 11th was one of the numerous regiments, North and South, that called themselves Zouaves and wore gaudy uniforms of billowing pantaloons and short jackets modeled after those of French auxiliaries in Algeria. The unit was led by a handsome young Chicagoan and former Lincoln business partner, Colonel Elmer E. Ellsworth, who had organized crack drill teams before the war and was thought to be one of the North's most promising officers.

All went according to schedule—except when Commander Stephen C. Rowan, captain of the sloop of war *Pawnee*, sent an officer ashore ahead of time and alerted the Confederate garrison. Rowan wanted, the lieutenant said, to spare the town's women and children any unpleasant gunfire. The alarm given, the Virginia militiamen managed to assemble, scramble aboard a train, and escape before Ellsworth's Zouaves could round them up.

Ellsworth himself, intent on seizing the town's telegraph office, hurried up Alexandria's main avenue, King Street. On the way he spotted a large Confederate flag flying atop a hotel, the Marshall House. He rushed inside, ran up the stairs, and managed to cut down the flag, but on his way down he was shot dead by the hotel's proprietor. Ellsworth was to be mourned by President Lincoln and by people all across the North as the first Union martyr.

Despite the death of Ellsworth, his Zouaves and the Michigan infantrymen easily secured Alexandria. Soon they and the troops in Arlington were set to work building the first parts of a ring of forts that would offer Washington some measure of security against attack throughout the war.

With a solid foothold established across the Potomac and more and more regiments pouring into Washington, General Scott and his deputy, Major General Joseph Mansfield, began organizing a full-fledged army able to make a deeper thrust into the Old Dominion. Put in charge of that force, which would soon reach 35,000 men, was a newly minted brigadier general named Irvin McDowell.

A 42-year-old West Point classmate of Beauregard's, McDowell had served in the Mexican War, but he had no more experience of battlefield command than most of the other officers in either army. He was six feet tall and heavyset, however, and looked bluff, hearty, and capable. And he had the wholehearted backing of the politically powerful William Dennison, the governor of his home state of Ohio.

Forming up west of Washington not far from Harpers Ferry was a second Union army under the overall command of 69-year-old Major General Robert Patterson, a veteran of the War of 1812, whose forces guarded the Potomac River crossings and posed a threat to the northern end of Virginia's Shenandoah Valley. Still another Federal force was organizing west of Patterson's, in southern Ohio, led by Brigadier General George B. McClellan. Considered a brilliant officer, McClellan had topped the class of 1846 at West Point and then, after resigning his commission, had quickly risen to become president of a railroad. Back in uniform by April 1861, he was full of grandiose plans to conquer the

South—and would manage in his first campaign to quite neatly gain the Union a small but vital victory.

Guarding Virginia against Patterson's and McDowell's forces were a pair of fast-growing Confederate armies. President Davis, stealing a march on Lincoln, had called for 100,000 volunteers as early as March 6. Since then thousands of young Southerners had stormed the recruiting stations, rabid to repel any incursions by what they considered the villainous Lincoln government. "So impatient did I become for starting," said one recruit, "that I felt like ten thousand pins were pricking me in every part of my body." Forming into rough-and-ready local companies, they gave them names like the Ready Rifles or the Barbour County Yankee Hunters.

By June more than 30,000 of these raw but wildly enthusiastic recruits had flooded through the Richmond area, eager to fight what they thought would be a single, decisive battle in which the Yankees would be so thoroughly whipped that they would never again try to force their wishes upon the South. The Rebels' state regiments were organized into brigades, most commanded by West Point-trained Regular Army officers who, more loyal to their home states than to the Federal Union, had defected to the South. In all, 313 officers, about one-third of all the U.S. Army's experienced regulars—and among them many of the most brilliant and combative—took up arms against the United States.

By early July about 23,000 of these Confederates were assembled around Manassas, about 25 miles west-southwest of Washington, ready to protect the little town and its vital junction of railroad lines running south to Richmond and west to the Shenandoah. Taking command, the already famous Gener-

al Beauregard vowed defiance of what he called the "abolition hosts" of a "reckless and unprincipled tyrant."

In the Shenandoah itself another Confederate army was forming—and in fact had already been in action. On April 18 hastily recruited militiamen led by an exceedingly daring young cavalry captain named Turner Ashby had chased Union forces from Harpers Ferry, capturing the Federal arsenal there and bagging 5,000 rifles and the armory's machinery for making many more.

Harpers Ferry had then become a collecting point for militia recruits from the Shenandoah region—men who were soon drilling hard under the stern gaze of a 36-year-old colonel named Thomas Jonathan Jackson. Reinforced by regiments primarily from Alabama and Mississippi, as well as a battalion of exiled Marylanders, Confederate forces around Harpers Ferry would eventually number about 10,000 men. In command of the whole force guarding Virginia's western flank was 53-year-old Major General Joseph E. Johnston, formerly one of the Regular Army's top officers. From his headquarters in Winchester, Johnston planned to meet any Union invasion of the Valley—or to move his troops rapidly eastward through Ashby's Gap in the Blue Ridge and by the Manassas Gap Railroad to help Beauregard if he were attacked.

And it looked as though he would be, as General McDowell marshaled his host around Washington and Arlington. But first there would be a small and almost comical fracas well to the east near Virginia's Chesapeake coast—the first land battle of the war—and yet another to the west, in the distant Virginia mountains, that together would provide a frame, so to speak, for the much larger action yet to come.

CHRONOLOGY

April 12, 1861	*Confederates fire on Fort Sumter*
April 13	*Lincoln calls for 75,000 militia volunteers*
April 17	*Virginia convention votes for secession*
April 18	*Five companies of Pennsylvania troops reach Washington*
April 19	*Baltimore riots; Lincoln declares blockade of Southern ports*
April 20	*U.S. Navy evacuates and destroys Gosport Navy Yard at Norfolk, Virginia; Federals begin to reinforce Fort Monroe*
May 3	*Lincoln calls for three-year volunteers*
May 13	*Federal troops occupy Baltimore*
May 15	*Butler takes command at Fort Monroe*
May 23	*Virginia approves Ordinance of Secession*
May 24	*Federals occupy Alexandria*
May 26	*McClellan invades western Virginia*
June 3	*Battle of Phillipi*
June 10	*Engagement at Big Bethel*
July 2	*Patterson enters Virginia at Williamsport, engages Johnston's force*
July 11	*Battle of Rich Mountain*
July 13	*General Garnett killed at Corrick's Ford*
July 17	*McDowell's army advances on Fairfax Court House and Centreville; Johnston begins to shift troops from the Shenandoah Valley to Manassas*
July 18	*Engagement at Blackburn's Ford*
July 21	*Battle of First Manassas*

When the Virginia legislature voted to secede in April 1861, the most immediate effect was to put the lightly garrisoned Washington, D.C., just across the Potomac River, in acute jeopardy. By the time Virginia's voters ratified secession on May 23, however, Washington was secure and would itself soon pose a threat to the Old Dominion. Within weeks, the aggressive Union general Benjamin Butler took command at Fort Monroe on the southern tip of the Peninsula, compromising both Norfolk and Richmond. To the west, troops under General George B. McClellan advanced into western Virginia. Most dangerous of all, a Federal force under Brigadier General Irvin McDowell was massing for a strike southward from Washington.

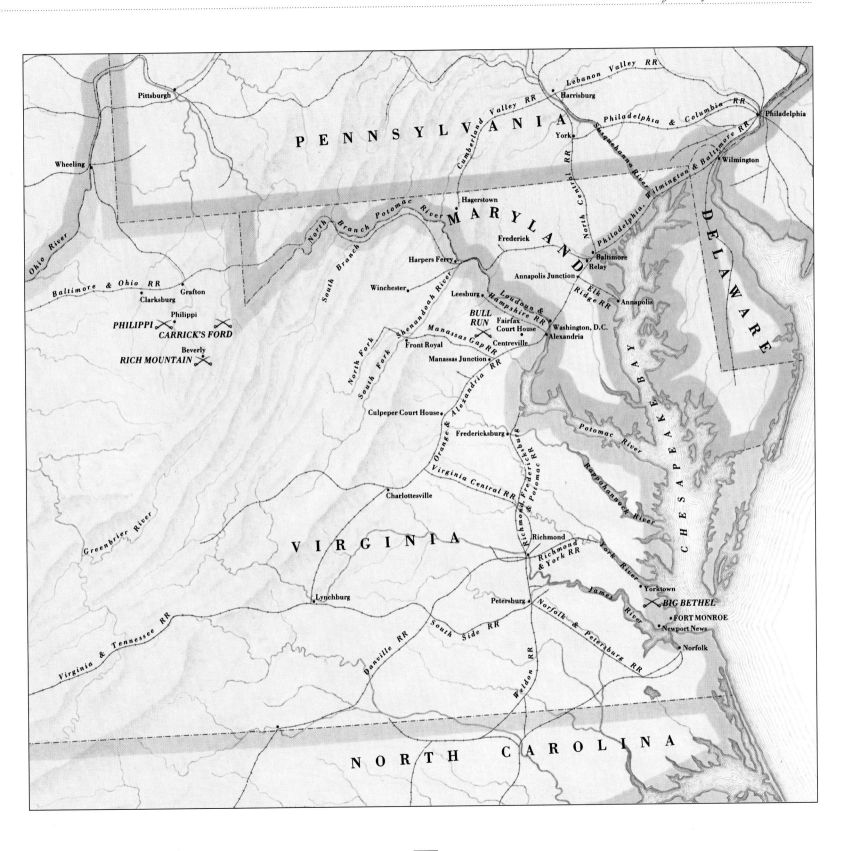

Dignitaries orate from a tented shelter while newly minted volunteer troops stand at present arms as the U.S. flag is raised over the south lawn of the White House. Such ceremonies as this one, sketched by Alfred R. Waud on June 29, 1861, helped maintain Northern morale during a period of confusion and uncertainty.

The Ringgold Light Artillery, a Pennsylvania militia unit, poses at the Washington Navy Yard in April 1861 (right). The first troops to reach the beleaguered District of Columbia, these gunners were outfitted as infantrymen and put to work erecting fortifications.

LUCIUS E. CHITTENDEN
REGISTER OF THE U.S. TREASURY

A noted Vermont attorney, Chittenden accepted his Treasury position at the urging of Secretary Salmon P. Chase. His diary entry below reflects the rumormongering present in the capital after Virginia passed an Ordinance of Secession on April 17. Despite Chittenden's jaundiced view of the upcoming referendum on the ordinance, the Lincoln administration waited to see which way Virginia would go.

Thursday April 18, 1861

The town is filled with rumors today. It is said, and is no doubt true, that Virginia has seceded and that the Union men in the convention were obliged last night to flee from Richmond for their lives. It is also reported that the Virginia troops have seized the arsenal at Harper's Ferry, and that a body of 5000 armed men are on the way to attack this city from Richmond—that the channel at Norfolk has been obstructed and preparations are being made by Gov. Letcher to seize the government property at that place. At two o'clock the heads of the Bureaus were called to the Assistant Secretary's office and requested to have their clerks report themselves at their desks at 5 o'clock to ascertain how many would arm for the defense of the buildings in the event of an attack. At 5 o'clock we met again and ordered our clerks in case of a night alarm to repair at once to the Treasury Building and report to Captains Shiras or Franklin by whom they would be furnished with arms and ammunition. All my clerks who were present signified a gratifying willingness to do so. Two were absent under pretense of sickness. I took immediate measures to learn whether their sickness was real or feigned.

In the six o'clock train from Baltimore between five and six hundred Pennsylvania troops arrived—the first volunteer forces which have come to the defense of the national capital.

During the evening the falsity of many of the rumors of the morning became apparent. Com. Paulding arrived from Norfolk & states that there is no disturbance there and that he has two ships in a position to repel any attempt upon the govt. property. It is now certain that the Ordinance of Secession passed the Virginia Convention in secret session and that the submission of it to the people is under restrictions that render their action a mere sham. All the cars and engines from Alexandria have been taken down to Richmond to be used in the conveyance of troops. Nothing reliable from Harper's Ferry.

PRIVATE EDGAR WARFIELD

17TH VIRGINIA INFANTRY

Warfield left a position as an apothecary clerk to join the 17th, a regiment raised in Alexandria. The young man celebrated four birthdays while in the Rebel army and was still bearing arms for the Confederacy when he was paroled at Appomattox on April 9, 1865. The humorous account below showed that soldiers sometimes faced dangers from unexpected quarters.

During our service in this city permission was frequently granted for the men to sleep at their homes at night. In case of an emergency call the town bell would be rung, sounding the military call and summoning the men to their armories. To my recollection this alarm was given only once. I was caught at home. The alarm was caused by a report that the enemy was crossing into Virginia at the Chain Bridge, above Georgetown. The report proved to be false, but we were not allowed to return to our homes, being kept under arms until daylight.

Guard duty at that time was rather pleasant. Certain posts were very desirable, especially those near which some of our popular young ladies lived. The post most sought by the boys was that on the south side of King Street between Henry and Fayette, and many were the tricks and maneuvers resorted to in order to get posted on that and other desirable stations.

On this particular post eatables and drinkables were plentiful at all times, and until a late hour there was also the company of bright and pretty girls. As an added attraction a Mr. Martin, who owned a brewery at the corner of Fayette and Commerce Streets (No. 802) and who lived just opposite at the southeast corner of King and Fayette Streets, kept a keg of ale on tap in his front vestibule for the benefit of those who cared to indulge.

Many are the stories told by the boys in the service at that time of adventures they met with while on guard duty around the city.

I call to mind one little incident that occurred while I was standing guard on North Washington Street. My post extended from the corner of Princess Street (where the rectory of Christ Church now stands) to the north end of the cotton-factory block, where I was met by the other sentry, whose post extended from that point to beyond the old canal basin.

This post was held by Billie Wright, of the Alexandria Riflemen, a comrade somewhat older than myself. While we were talking a fight occurred in one of a row of houses (still in existence) across the commons, between an Irishman and his wife. At that time there were a great many Irish in the city, drawn by the coal trade, which was very large and employed many hands.

The fight continued so long that Billie thought it was our duty to go across the square and try to put an end to it. I argued that we should not leave our posts for such a purpose but Billie, who was a lively sort of fellow and always ready for fun and frolic, thought this was a golden opportunity for a little excitement. I finally yielded and went with him. In the meantime the fight had grown warmer and a number of others, both men and women, were taking sides, some with the old man and others with the old woman. It began to look like a free-for-all.

I tried again to persuade my comrade not to interfere, but no, nothing would do but he must go in. Well, he went. In the twinkling of an eye the participants on both sides quit fighting each other, and making common cause turned on him. With a clean pitch on their part, out came Billie, gun and all, on to the sidewalk, nearly upsetting me in his hasty exit. It took but very little more argument on my part to convince him that we had no business there; and so the military beat a hasty retreat.

PRIVATE
JOHN B. DENNIS
6TH MASSACHUSETTS INFANTRY

Dennis, shown in this postwar photograph proudly wearing his veteran's uniform and medals, describes in detail the struggle of his regiment to pass through a violent mob of Baltimore's pro-secessionist plug uglies, as they were called, to resume its train ride to the isolated and defenseless nation's capital.

When we reached President Street depot we were met by the Mayor of the city and Chief of Police, Marshal Kane, who said to Colonel Jones: "You take care of your regiment and we will take care of our rowdies." You will remember that at the time of which I write the cars were drawn through the city of Baltimore by horses.

Before the Colonel had time to give his orders for the regiment to file out of the cars horses were hitched on and the cars were again in motion. The train, being a long one, was divided into four or five sections. The mob had begun to gather and we could see the companies in their armories equipping. We had not proceeded far when we were assailed with bricks, paving stones and firearms. They did not know to what state we belonged, but had somehow obtained the idea that it was the 7th New York National Guards, I suppose, probably, from the promptness with which we had moved, and we were greeted with howls and imprecations, and some of them said: "You damned 7th New York, you are the fellows that said you would not fight against the south!" referring, I presume, to some statements made when the 7th visited Richmond the year before. As we reached Pratt street the mob had increased to such an extent that it was with difficulty the horses could be made to draw the cars, and the shower of stones and bricks came the faster. Rifles and pistols were also brought into use and we were frequently, with an oath hurled at us, told that we were a little too early for them, alluding to the fact, I presume, of our having left Philadelphia at midnight instead of waiting until morning, as they expected we would and as we at first intended doing.

The men in our car, where the Colonel was a part of the time, were ordered to lie down, and to this some of us objected, not knowing at the time that lying down was a part of the tactics of war, and but for this precaution, in all probability, many more would have been killed or wounded, for as we went along the mob rapidly increased in numbers and violence, and they were armed with every conceivable weapon, from a scythe fastened to a long pole to an improved rifle. Heavy stones were carried and placed upon the bridges that we had to pass under, and they were rolled down upon the roofs of the cars with the intention of breaking through the roof and demolishing all within, and in this way the cars all got through to the Mt. Claire depot without anyone being killed or seriously wounded, except the last section of the train, which had to wait awhile at the President Street depot before starting on account of there not being horses enough to take the whole train at once. . . .

. . . When Captain Folansbee saw the first sections of the train moving away he also came to the conclusion that the Colonel had changed his mind about marching through the city, and when he was told by some of the railroad men that horses would be provided in a few minutes to take the remaining section through he felt no apprehensions regarding the matter, but waited patiently until the horses came and were attached to the cars and commenced to move. The mob then turned its whole attention to his little detachment, trying to impede the progress of the horses and even battering the cars and until Captain Folansbee saw that the only salvation for himself and his command was in filing out of the cars and fighting his way on foot; he therefore gave the orders for the detachment to form in line by the side of the track. This was just as they reached Pratt street, which is by the side of the bay, and, at the point where the railway runs into it, is very narrow. The mob had torn up some rails and had, from the ships lying at the wharves, procured heavy anchors and chains, which they put across the track, completely barricading the passage of the cars.

Obeying the order to leave the cars and form in line, our men seemed to throw themselves right into the arms of that howling mass of hungry rebel wolves, as they appeared to be. It was with the greatest difficulty that the men could file out of the cars, and to form a line was a much more difficult task. It was however, done, although it was hard to distinguish the orders of the commanding officer above the howls of the mob, which at the time acted and looked much more like a pack of wild beasts than human beings. The troops pressed the crowd backward a little and, notwithstanding all the boys had put up with, the officers disliked to give the order to fire. When Mayor Brown of Baltimore had worked his way through the crowd in some way to the side of Captain Folansbee, he snatched a rifle from the hands of one of the soldiers, turned it and deliberately fired right into the crowd, which for an instant seemed to recoil. This firing of the mayor acted as the signal for the officers and the command was given to fire.

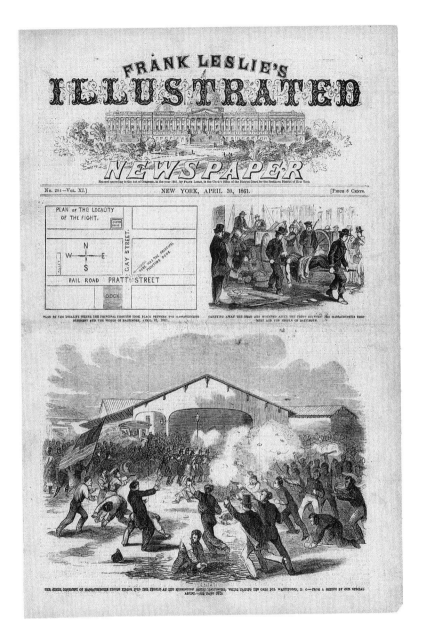

A volunteer named Luther Ladd (above) was one of three Massachusetts militiamen who were killed, along with 12 civilians, when the struggle between his regiment and the Baltimore mob escalated from oaths and flying rocks to gunfire.

The "fight in the streets of Baltimore" quickly became front-page news in both the North and the South. These engravings illustrate the chaotic nature of the melee, as enraged Southern sympathizers hurl bricks and rush upon the militiamen, who have hastily formed a defensive line next to one of their rail cars.

CAPTAIN CHARLES WILKES
U.S. NAVY

In mid–April 1861 the Navy high command, determining that the important Gosport Navy Yard at Norfolk, Virginia, could not be held, ordered Wilkes to sail there and destroy anything that might be of value to the Confederates. Despite all the actions described here, the Confederates reaped a bounty of cannon, naval stores, and even ships from Gosport.

The *Pawnee* reached the navy yard wharf without any opposition or disturbance whatever. The crews of the *Pennsylvania* and *Cumberland* received us with many hearty cheers, which were patriotically returned from those on board the *Pawnee*. In obedience to your order, I waited upon Commodore McCauley, with Captain Wright, of the Engineer Corps of the Army, reported your arrival with assistance, and introduced Captain Wright as the officer charged with the defense of the yard. Commodore McCauley informed me that he had been deserted by all his officers, including an officer of marines, and that the yard was without defense; that he had not one to rely upon, and desired me to report that he had scuttled all the ships about 4 o'clock p.m. and had destroyed a large amount of property to prevent them from falling into the hands of the disaffected. . . . One hundred men were sent by Commodore Pendergrast from the *Cumberland* to assist, divided into several gangs, to render the new guns unserviceable; but after some time spent therein it was found that the metal of the guns was so superior as to resist all and the most powerful efforts to break off the trunnions. They were spiked and rendered, as far as the time would permit, unserviceable. Commander Rodgers and Captain Wright, of the Engineer Corps, volunteered for the destruction of the dry dock, and the powder and necessary tools were transported by a detachment of forty men of the Massachusetts troops, detailed by Colonel Wardrop for this purpose. Lieutenant Russell was sent, under orders of Commander Rodgers, to act as his aid, by which communication could be kept open. Mr. King, engineer in chief, also volunteered for this service. Commander Alden was directed to prepare for the destruction of the storehouse, shops, buildings, etc., around the yard, including the barracks; Commander Sands, to prepare for the destruction of the ship houses and their contents, and, when ready, to report; Lieutenants Wise, Phelps, Gibson, McGary, and Morris, to prepare the several vessels of the Navy for destruction and to distribute the material provided for that purpose on board the several vessels designated by you; and trains were laid on the *Plymouth, Merrimack, Germantown, Raritan, Columbia,* brig *Dolphin,* and *Pennsylvania,* in the order in which they lay moored. The ship *Delaware* was left out in consequence of the distance she lay off, and the frigate *United States* was in so decayed a condition that it was deemed unnecessary to waste the material of turpentine upon her. At 1:45 a.m. it was reported to me by Commanders Rodgers, Alden, and Sands that all was ready, and directions were given that all the men that could be spared should be sent on board immediately, retaining only those necessary to ignite the material, and that the signal would be a rocket from the *Pawnee,* to be ordered by yourself. The troops and marines were rapidly embarked, when it was reported to you by the youngest son of Commodore McCauley, tears streaming down his cheeks, that his father refused to vacate his post, and declined all inducement to do so. Commander Alden was selected by you to make the endeavor to induce him to yield, and to state that it was your intention speedily to fire the buildings and his life must be lost. This last effort succeeded, and he was induced, with great reluctance, to remove to the *Cumberland*. All the shore parties having been withdrawn, two boats belonging to the *Cumberland* were alongside. One was put under the direction of Lieutenant Wise, with Lieutenant Phelps, to fire the trains on the appointed signal being given. The other I embarked in with Lieutenant Russell to await the signal and bring off those who were left, viz, Commander Rodgers and Captain Wright, of the Engineer Corps, and John Reynolds, ordinary seaman; Commander Alden and Samuel Williams, Commander Sands, Samuel Watson, and John Noble; in all, eight persons. The rendezvous was carefully pointed out and made known to all of them. The *Pawnee* left the wharf at 2:25 a.m., winded, and hawsers were passed from the *Cumberland* for the purpose of towing her out. At 4 o'clock, after a detention of nearly two hours, the *Cumberland* slipped her moorings, and both vessels stood out and down the harbor. At 4:20 the signal was made and the torch applied, and in a few minutes the whole area of the yard was one sheet of flame.

"One of the most cowardly and disgraceful acts which has ever disgraced the Government of a civilized people."

This drawing of the Gosport Navy Yard action shows flames roaring through warehouses and dry docks. The Pawnee heads to sea with the Cumberland in tow, while a vessel that could not be got under way lists to starboard after being scuttled.

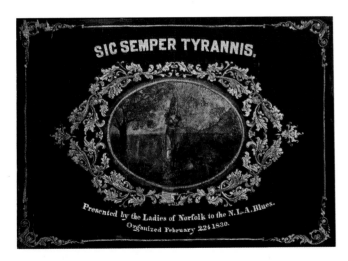

This flag was flown by the Norfolk Light Artillery Blues, one of the militia units commanded by Taliaferro. The Blues constructed earthworks on the Elizabeth River that threatened Gosport Navy Yard.

MAJOR GENERAL WILLIAM B. TALIAFERRO
VIRGINIA STATE MILITIA

Taliaferro ordered his troops to remove what powder and ammunition they could from the magazines of Fort Norfolk and the Navy Yard. His bitter disappointment at watching the Federals destroy vast amounts of matériel reached the improbable level of moral outrage, as is evident in the passage below. The Gloucester County, Virginia, native, a graduate of William and Mary College, received two wounds in the war and rose to divisional command in the Army of Northern Virginia.

Knowing how important it was to secure a supply of powder for the State, I determined to seize the powder magazine at old Fort Norfolk, and accordingly, on the night of the 19th, I directed Captain Terry Sinclair, of the Navy, to proceed to the magazine with Captain Taylor's company of infantry, to be so disposed as to prevent attack; and I directed Captain Harrison, of the Navy, to impress the Glen Cove steamer, and with Captain Vickery's company of artillery and two 6-pounder pieces to watch the harbor and fire into any boats from the navy yard which might attempt to land at the magazine.

This duty was performed without any attempt at resistance, and about 1,300 barrels of powder transferred to lighters and vessels, and sent to Richmond on the 20th. The residue, estimated at over 1,500 barrels, was transported in carts to a point beyond the range of the guns from the water.

To accomplish this it was necessary to press into the service of the State all the carts and horses which could be procured.

The whole volunteer force of Norfolk, under Major Taylor, was ordered out to aid in removing the powder from the magazine, all of whom worked with extraordinary zeal and uncomplaining patience, notwithstanding the severe labor and danger they encountered. A quantity of ordnance stores were removed at the same time.

Ascertaining that one 32-pounder and ten 18-pounder pieces had been found in the old custom-house, I directed carriages to be immediately constructed for them, and ordered them to be placed in battery at old Fort Norfolk as soon as the powder was removed. The guns were transported to the fort on the 20th, but were not put into battery until next day.

I did not think it prudent at that time to throw up earthworks at Craney Island or any other point, because in answer to my telegrams I was informed that the freshet in James River rendered it impossible to transport the guns from Bellona Arsenal, and it was useless to expose the working parties to attack until I had pieces to mount, when the works could be speedily erected under cover of night, and without loss.

Such was the condition of affairs when, on the night of the 20th, the sloop of war *Pawnee,* passing the obstructions in the harbor, steamed up to the navy yard with a force of 500 men, shortly after which, under the orders of Flag-Officer Paulding, was inaugurated and in part consummated one of the most cowardly and disgraceful acts which has ever disgraced the Government of a civilized people. The ships of war were sunk, and most of them burned at anchor; the ship houses and some other property fired; and to render the atrocity of the act still greater, the dry dock was mined, and a slow match, which was so arranged as not to ignite the train until our people should have filled the yard and the works in their efforts to save the Government property, set fire to and left burning.

When this diabolical act had been committed, the steamer, with the *Cumberland* frigate in tow and the whole command of sailors and marines on board, passed down the river, and in the course of that evening anchored under Fort Monroe.

LIEUTENANT H. SEYMOUR HALL
27TH NEW YORK INFANTRY

While males of the splintered nation hurried to join military organizations, women on both sides of the looming conflict eagerly made their contribution by providing items of comfort and martial ardor to the neophyte warriors. Hall describes the efforts of one such group on the eve of his regiment's departure for Elmira, New York, a rendezvous area for troops of that state before they were sent south.

The ladies made a beautiful United States flag and presented it to the company in the Methodist church, which, large as it is, was much too small to hold the audience that gathered to witness the scene and hear the service of religious and patriotic prayer, songs, and speeches. As the ensign was supposed to have something to do with the colors, and for other reasons, it devolved upon me to receive the beautiful emblem from the hands of the ladies and to respond to the presentation speech. We soon learned that our company color could not be carried, but

I kept it with the boys in every campaign and adorned our company headquarters with it in every camp, as long as I served with the company.

The ladies also made havelocks out of fine white flannel and gave each of us one to protect our heads from the hot sun, and they supplied each soldier boy with an elegant pocket needle-book of their own handiwork, so liberally furnished with pins, buttons, needles, and thread that if we could have caught the Rebels asleep, we could have sewed them up so tight that they could not have fired a gun. The committee gave each man a blanket, which was trimmed and bound by the same fair hands.

PRIVATE HARRISON H. COMINGS
11TH NEW YORK INFANTRY

Though the presence of Federal troops in Washington rapidly became commonplace, the arrival of a new regiment still merited a personal viewing by President Lincoln in the war's early weeks. So unsettled was the Union during this period that the men of Comings' regiment assumed that setting foot in Maryland meant that they were in enemy territory. The 11th was raised from several New York City fire companies and soon had a chance to show its mettle in a fashion familiar to it.

Some few days prior to our departure, orders were issued from Col. Ellsworth that each man should have his hair cut to one-eighth of an inch in length. Every design was thought of and one member of the company to which I was attached had his so cut that it represented an eagle on his head, he being perhaps more patriotic than the rest. It was a common thing for his comrades to knock his cap off and exclaim, "We have the American eagle in Co. E." On the morning of April 29th orders came to fall in and prepare to leave New York for Washington. All were eager to go through Baltimore, but wiser heads prevailed, and we left on the steamship "Baltic" for Washington, as we supposed, but next day we found that Annapolis was our destination. On the following day, about noon, we anchored opposite the Naval Academy. Upon landing we found the 8th N.Y. Militia in line to receive us, and that being a city regiment many of us found friends among them. After the usual form the first rations on secession soil—as we supposed—were served us, hard tack, cheese and herring with a bountiful supply of cold water. After dismissal a run over the entire grounds and buildings was in order. At about 5 P.M. the roll was beaten to fall in, and after the usual confusion peculiar to raw recruits we marched to the cars that had been put into proper shape by members of the 8th Mass. Vols. On the sides of the railroad we found soldiers of the 69th and 7th N.Y. doing duty as sentries to prevent the destruction of the track and switches. We arrived in Washington at about 8 P.M. Line was formed, and I doubt if any body of men ever felt the importance of the responsibility resting upon them when marching up Pennsylvania avenue more than we did. Our first call was at the White House, where President Lincoln stood on the steps, hat in hand, bowing to each company as it passed by, each company cheering in return. We finally brought up in the Hall of Representatives, where in a short time we turned in as best we could. I remember making a couch on a bench in the gallery, while many sought rest upon the floor. At about daylight next day, I with several others started on a tour of observation to see what the prospect was for breakfast. In arches under the front of the Capitol we found a member of the 6th Mass. making what he called "bacon stew." Judging from the color of the stew one would think it might have been made of old shoes. The thought occurred to me that a better breakfast could be obtained than bacon stew in the arches of the Capitol. On the third day of May we were transferred to the Senate Chamber. On the morning of the 4th about 3 A.M., I heard a small bell ringing, and presently a cry of fire. We all knew what that meant, and you can readily imagine how those firemen arose from their slumber and rushed forth to fight the element of destruction—different from that for which they had been selected, but still what they knew better how to meet and subdue. As soldiers, down the avenue we went, with our colonel at the fore. On arriving at the engine house, next to the markethouse, we tried to enter, but found the doors secured in such a manner that entrance had to be forced. One of our number went into the market, and returning with a cleaver, chopped out the lock on the small door. The large doors were barricaded, but it took only a moment to remove them, for we pushed the engine against them with such force that they were torn from their hinges. It was but a short run, and in a brief time we were pouring water upon the burning building, which adjoined Willard's Hotel. At 8 o'clock, when the fire was about out, orders were issued to fall in and formed by companies in mass. Gen. Mansfield of West Point fame was introduced to the regiment from the balcony of the hotel. He made an enthusiastic speech. One remark which I remember very distinctly was that should the Fire Zouaves act as well in actual warfare as they had in battling with that fire they would render an excellent account of themselves. The proprietor of the hotel then invited the regiment to breakfast, and judging by the disappearance of food, ample justice was done.

This dramatic engraving shows the men of the 11th New York saving Willard's Hotel. Though the Fire Zouaves were initially welcomed as saviors, their behavior soon wore thin with Washingtonians. It was not unusual to see them careering drunkenly from bar to bar, or filching livestock for their suppers. But their quick suppression of the Willard's fire helped them regain a measure of public esteem.

In this drawing President Lincoln, with Winfield Scott seated to his right, doffs his hat as he reviews a passing regiment in the nation's capital.

PRIVATE CURTIS C. POLLACK
25TH PENNSYLVANIA INFANTRY (THREE MONTHS)

For many Northern soldiers, their stay in the nation's capital was their first visit. Like tourists of any era, Pollack admired the artifacts of America's past and the trappings of government as he wandered about. Unlike other tourists, however, he and his comrades actually had their living quarters in the Capitol building, which became, in effect, an army camp, one of many in the teeming District of Columbia.

Lincoln was up here this afternoon and was all over the capitol shaking hands with all the soldiers. He is very tall but not at all bad looking. Secretary Seward was along with him and he also shook hands all around. Mr Seward is quite small not much taller than Uncle Joseph. I went to church this morning with Geo. Hill & Ed Shippen. we went to Trinity Church and heard a good sermon from Dr Butler of Cincinatti. We had quite a heavy rain this morning but it is now very pleasant but quite windy. Yesterday afternoon I was up at Patent Office looking around and saw a great many different things of all kinds sorts & sizes and was only through one or two rooms. I saw Washingtons clothes which he wore during the Revolutionary war and his sword tea set water chairs &c which he used to use. I also saw the Printing Press which Franklin worked on. The Presents which the Japanes presented to Buchannan were also there and other interesting relics. I intend to go to the Smithsonian Institute tomorrow and I will give you an account of what I see in my letter. We are all getting along very well and are in very good spirits, though a few are complaining of not being well. There is now in the city between 15 & 20 thousand men and are not afraid of the biggest the Virginians can bring down on us, though no person in town now thinks there will be an attack made. We all got a blanket two pair of shoes and two pair of stockings last night from the government and are to get our uniforms on Tuesday. It seems very little like Sunday here it all noise and bustle the men are working downstairs rolling flour and there is several bricklayers at work putting up cooking aparatus for the men. The capitol large as it is, is completely filled up with soldiers and flour barrels and the other two stories have the soldiers while the cooking apartment is in the cellar. We also bake our own bread. I suppose you have heard that the government had seized 20000 bbls. of flour and it is nearly all stowed up here. The other day I was down stairs helping to barricade the windows and doors so as to have the lower story safe in case of an attack.

Militiamen in swallow-tailed coats stand guard outside the unfinished Capitol in May 1861. Visible through the trees on the right are construction materials.

In this stereograph, Federal militiamen guard the railroad bridge near the Relay House, an important rail junction southwest of Baltimore.

SERGEANT ABNER R. SMALL
3D MAINE INFANTRY

Not every soldier shared his comrades' enthusiasm for being in Washington. The unusually perceptive Small, who later served in the 16th Maine as a commissioned officer, looked beyond the imposing Federal city of monuments and government buildings and found precious little in the way of urban attractions. He was impressed, however, with the spreading view of distant Virginia.

As soon as I had a chance, I obtained a pass from Colonel Howard and went down to see the sights. I found that Washington was not really a city. The vast and showy public buildings were surrounded by mere scattered huddles of dingy brick houses and small shops. I saw few sightly homes. The White House attracted me; but that was a home, or ought to be treated like one, I thought, and I spared myself the impudent pleasure of intruding upon the President. I headed for the Capitol and walked easterly along Pennsylvania Avenue, a tedious thoroughfare lined with barrooms and other places of business and half-heartedly furbished with dusty green trees in whitewashed palings. The saloons were driving a roaring trade, and the sidewalks were noisy with promenading soldiers. The crowd thinned away near Capitol Hill; I went up almost alone to explore the huge edifice. The size of the building and its promise of magnificence impressed me, though it was not completed; where the dome was to rise, there was scaffolding and ropes and cranes, and the ground beyond the east front was tumbled with cut stone.

From camp we could see the Capitol, and the stump of the Washington Monument, and beyond that the Long Bridge over the Potomac, and perhaps we could discern, away down the other side of the river, the steeples of Alexandria. Somewhere beyond that farther shore were the rebels in arms. Their pickets had been on the heights across the water, in sight from Washington, hardly two weeks before we had come to the city. Union troops were there now.

"An almost unanimous vote for secession was taken."

Alexandria's buildings are outlined against the sky in this Waud rendering.
The peaceful scene belies the turmoil in the city on the eve of Federal occupation.

ANNE FROBEL
RESIDENT OF ALEXANDRIA

Initially, Frobel greeted her state's secession from the Union as a lark and enjoyed watching units such as the 17th Virginia drill on the local commons as a welcome break from the usual routine. The portent of more serious events, however, came when news of the Federal buildup of troops in Washington reached her hometown. Suddenly, the shock of the upheaval that was to come struck her, as neighbors and friends fled Alexandria in a state of near panic.

May 1861

But one Sunday morning in the early part of May we went into town as usual to church, services were at St. Pauls, Christ Church, our church, was closed, I do not remember why, I think perhaps the minister Dr Walker had left town with his family.

But as I entered St. Paul's I could but observe how exceedingly solemn and quiet every thing and every body looked, and before the sermon was half over the ladies were all in tears, the men looked stern and neither to the right or left—I could not understand it—I could not feel it—and as I rode home I thought how silly it was for people to put on such air but still it produced an uneasy sensation, and the next day we rode to town again, to see and hear all we could about it. When we got with in sight of the Orange depot we both exclaimed, "What on earth is the matter—what is going on," Such a dense crowd thronged the streets, carriages filled with people, wagons, carts drays, wheelbarrows all packed mountain high with baggage of every sort, men, women, and children streaming along to the cars, most of the women crying, almost every face we saw we recognized, and all looking as forlorn and wretched as if going to execution.

I believe every body from both town and country that could possibly get away left at this time, and for the first time it dawned upon me that it was something more than *pastime,* and O what a feeling of loneliness and utter despair came over us when we thought of every friend and acquaintance gone—and poor Lizzie and me being left entirely alone to battle it by ourselves. O how little we knew, or dreamed of what was going to befall.

LUCIUS E. CHITTENDEN
REGISTER OF THE U.S. TREASURY

Though Chittenden found his work as register exhausting—his responsibilities included dismissing "Southern sympathizers" from the Treasury's employ—he often found it difficult to sleep in the tense atmosphere of the District. As he fretted in his room during the evening of May 23, Chittenden became privy to the ominous, moonlit spectacle of Union troops stealthily embarking upon one of the first offensive actions against the Confederacy.

Sleep I could not. I arose, walked the room for a time—struck a light, and opened my Bible. I had just read a verse of two in the touching account by John of our Saviour's trial when I heard a faint noise in the distance. I went to the window and threw it open. The night was exquisitely lovely. The full moon shone serenely and soft out of an unclouded sky upon the quiet city. The silence was unbroken save by the barking of a dog in the distance—and—the regular measured sound which first arrested my attention—growing clearer now as if approaching and regular as the beating of a clock. It comes nearer now, and I am no longer in doubt. It is the tread of armed men! I hear it clearer now and the glistening of polished bayonets in the bright moonlight is seen distinctly. There was something indescribably impressive as they came nearer, and I saw the regular ranks and recognized the quick sharp steps of the New York Seventh Regiment. The men had their knapsacks and blankets and were evidently in regular marching order. They passed down the street, and the 12th. N.Y. filed in behind and moved off with them. After a few minutes I heard another column approaching and immediately the New Jersey Brigade, 3500 strong, followed after those who had preceded them. I knew well what their destination was. Calling up Mr. Jordan we had some conversation and both agreed that their destination was the shore of Virginia. An idea of the silence with which this movement was conducted, may be gained from the fact that this body of more than 5000 men passed the Rugby House filled with guests and the sleep of none of them but myself was disturbed. There was neither music nor conversation, nothing save that heavy regular solemn sound which I shall never forget—the tread of armed men.

CORPORAL GEORGE N. WISE
17TH VIRGINIA INFANTRY

The author of the 17th Virginia's regimental history, Wise served with this unit until paroled after Lee's surrender. He had a successful postwar career in Alexandria selling insurance until his death in 1923. This account describes the confusion surrounding the Confederate evacuation of his hometown, precipitated, he asserts, by a Federal violation of the surrender agreement.

The 23d of May arrived; the polls were opened, and an almost unanimous vote for secession was taken—night closed upon the city—the citizens, deep in slumber, dreamed not of what the morrow would bring—the sound of the sentinel's tread and the oft-repeated cry of "All's well," were the sole interruptions to the calm of the midnight hour.

Morrill, the sentinel on duty at Cazenove's wharf, keeping a sharp watch upon the movements of the "Pawnee," caught the sound of creaking oars, and, through the faint glimmer of the dawning day, beheld the outlines of a boat coming quietly towards him. The challenge, "Who comes there?" is thrice repeated, and the sharp report of the sentinel's rifle awakes the neighboring housetop pigeons, and gives the alarm to the soldiers on guard; a volley from the boat, aimed at the sentinel, drowned the rifle's echo, but did no further damage.

A flag of truce from the enemy was received by Colonel Terrett, then in command of the city, and, after consultation with the civil authorities, terms were agreed upon for its surrender; a specified time being promised for the withdrawal of the Confederate troops. Long, however, before the expiration of said time, the enemy's forces were landing upon the wharves. Orders were at once issued for our companies to assemble at the Lyceum Hall, the point previously designated as our "rendezvous."

The Battalion assembled, and there being no time for farewells to the numerous friends, most of whom were asleep in their beds, we marched out Duke street and took the Little River Turnpike westward, the enemy, at the same time, entering the city from transports lying at the wharves, and by column from the Washington and Alexandria Turnpike, down which they had marched during the night.

Through an oversight, the "Old Dominion Rifles" failed to receive the order to march, and came near sharing the fate of Captain Ball's Cavalry, who, acting as rear guard to our forces, were captured, and, after some months' close imprisonment, paroled as prisoners of war. Captain Herbert, hearing musketry below, called his men into line and started at once for the point from whence the sounds proceeded. The Battalion was marching out Duke as the company reached the intersection of King and West streets, where, the Major recognizing it, a halt was ordered, and the Old Dominions soon joined the column. . . .

. . . On reaching the tollgate, a mile or more from the city, [the Battalion] learned that a report was in circulation to the effect that a squadron of cavalry were in pursuit. Our Major immediately halted the column and gave the order to "fix bayonets;" after waiting a short time, the rumor proved false, and we again moved on.

Soon, the welcome sound of the car-whistle reached our ears, and striking for the O. and A. R. R. track, we had the pleasure of stopping the trains moving towards Alexandria. But little time was consumed in occupying the "Flats," and the Battalion was pushed back to Manassas where many friends from various quarters awaited us.

PRIVATE HARRISON H. COMINGS
11TH NEW YORK INFANTRY

Comings and his fellow New Yorkers were among the first Federal troops to venture onto the soil of Virginia. The shooting of their dashing and popular commander, Colonel Elmer Ellsworth, tempered their otherwise successful investment of Alexandria. The "Col. Wilcox" mentioned by Comings was Orlando Bolivar Willcox, who was later wounded and captured while leading a brigade at First Bull Run. In 1895 Willcox received the Medal of Honor for his actions in that battle.

At daylight a large steamboat stopped opposite our camp, and in short time we embarked, first by taking small boats, as there was no wharf or dock. As we steamed down the river, Alexandria came into view, with a secession flag floating from one of the buildings. On arriving at the dock my attention was attracted to two boat loads of sailors alongside the dock with pistols drawn. The officers were parleying with a soldier on the dock. The moment we stopped he discharged his musket and fled up the street. Co. E being near the gangway was the first to obey Col. Ellsworth's order to proceed on the double quick to the Orange & Alexandria railroad station and intercept or hold any train that might be going out. On getting in sight of the station we saw a train just going around a bend in the road, so we lost it. Capt. Leverich ordered us to destroy all switches so that the train could not return. Guards were posted in different places, presently one came in and reported that a company of cavalry was forming on the next street. The captain ordered all to fall in, which was done, and on the double quick we went. As we arrived at the corner of the street, a loud noise was heard as it appeared to me like the falling of buildings; in a moment I saw the pieces of artillery facing us, evidently with the intention of sending us to Kingdom Come without any warning. Our captain made the remark to us that we had better make our peace with God, as our time had come. You can imagine the sensation that was felt at that moment, not knowing what was in store for us. Col. Wilcox of the 1st Michigan rode up to us and asked what squad of men we were. Our captain replied by giving him the name of company and regiment. Col. Wilcox then ordered us to surround those cavalrymen, which was done, they in turn being ordered to throw down their arms, which they did instantly. I then strolled into the slave pen of Alexandria, where I found a negro chained to a ring in the floor. He was asked what he was doing there, and replied that he was a runaway. He asked who we were and we said we were Yankees. The negro said, "Golly, boss, glad you's come." He was released after some labor. We were soon ordered to Shuter's Hill, about half a mile distant, where Fort Ellsworth was afterwards built. We had been there but a short time when two civilians came to us and informed us that our colonel had been shot. We could hardly realize it, and while talking it over, a company of the 1st Michigan relieved us. I was sent with others to the Marshall House, under charge of our 2d Lieut., for information as to where the company should report. While awaiting for our lieutenant to return, I went up stairs and saw the assassin Jackson as he lay upon the landing of the stairs. Our lamented colonel had been conveyed to Washington. The excitement was intense, and I honestly believe that had precaution not been taken, and guards placed around the regiment, Alexandria would have been razed to the ground. Having no place or tents to lie under, our company was ordered to the locomotive or round house, where we were told to make ourselves as comfortable as we could.

LIEUTENANT EDWARD B. KNOX
11TH NEW YORK INFANTRY

Knox lived in Chicago and became acquainted with Elmer Ellsworth through the city's militia organizations. Though Ellsworth claimed Mechanicville, New York, as his birthplace, he had resided in Chicago and practiced law there in the years before 1861. When Ellsworth returned to his home state to obtain a regiment, Knox went with him. Knox eventually obtained the rank of major in the 44th New York; he survived the war to return home to Illinois, where he died in 1889.

I shall never forget that scene. The night was peculiarly still and clear, not a leaf stirring, and the moon so full and lustrous that objects were visible at a great distance. The men stood immovable as statues, listening attentively to the words that fell from the lips of their commander, who, in a low, clear voice, explained to them, so far as he could consistently with instructions, the nature of the service they were expected to perform. He endeavored to impress upon their minds the great necessity of obedience. I can call to mind but little of what he said, but I remember distinctly these words: "I will never order one of you to go where I fear to lead;" also, "Don't fire without orders." And he added, "Now go to your tents, and remain quiet until called."

At two o'clock the "Baltimore" and "Mount Vernon" (the steamers chartered to take the regiment to Alexandria) appeared off the shore, under charge of Captain Dahlgren, of the navy, who announced their arrival, whereupon the men were marched by company to the river bank, and the embarkation began. Owing to the absence of wharf or landing-place, and the shallowness of the river at that point, the men were conveyed to the steamers in small boats, which consumed nearly two hours' time. At length all was in readiness, and just before dawn we slowly and silently streamed down the river, the "Mount Vernon" leading.

As we approached the place of landing, the United States steamer "Pawnee" was discovered at anchor off the town, the ship being "cleared for action." At the same time a boat was seen to leave the vessel for the shore, filled with men, and bearing a flag of truce. This boat reached the wharf a few minutes before us. As we drew nearer, several Rebel sentinels were observed on shore, quietly walking their posts, apparently ignorant of our approach. Suddenly they discharged their pieces in the air and started away on the run, when some half-a-dozen men on our upper deck, in violation of orders, began a fusillade upon the retreating sentinels, which was promptly checked. The boat soon touched the wharf, and the regiment hastily landed and formed on Cameron Street in column of companies, my company (A) at the head, which rested at the intersection of Lee Street. During the formation, two companies were despatched to the Orange & Alexandria Railroad depot to take possession, cut off the retreat of the Rebels if possible, and tear up the track. These dispositions being made, the next matter of importance, it seems, was to cut off telegraphic communication with the interior. Leaving the regiment standing in the street, the Colonel, accompanied by two officers, a New York "Tribune" reporter, and a squad of four men under a sergeant, taken from the right of my company, started for the telegraph office, some two blocks distant.

"He dropped forward with that heavy, horrible, headlong weight which always comes of sudden death inflicted in this manner."

EDWARD H. HOUSE
Correspondent, New York Tribune

House had a long and varied career as a journalist, which included covering the trial of John Brown in 1859, and field assignments with Union armies in the eastern theater. This account of his progress with Elmer Ellsworth through the streets of Alexandria and of the colonel's death was recorded in his memoirs. During the 1870s, House served as the first official foreign correspondent in Japan.

After landing, the colonel gave some rapid directions for the interruption of railway traffic and then turned toward the center of the town, to destroy the means of communication southward by the telegraph; a measure which he appeared to regard as very seriously important. He was accompanied by Lieutenant H. J. Winser, military secretary of the regiment; the chaplain, Reverend E. W. Dodge; and myself. At first he summoned no guard to follow him, but he afterward turned and called forward a single squad with a sergeant from the 1st Company. We passed quickly through the streets, meeting a few bewildered travelers, when the colonel first of all caught sight of the secession flag, which has so long swung insolently in full view of the President's House. He immediately sent back the sergeant with an order for the advance of the entire 1st Company, and pushed on to the Marshall House, a second-class inn. On entering the open door, the colonel met a man in his shirt and trousers, of whom he demanded what sort of a flag it was that hung above the roof; the stranger who seemed greatly alarmed, declared he knew nothing of it, and that he was only a boarder there. The colonel then sprang up the stairs, and we all followed to the topmost story, whence, by means of a ladder, he clambered to the roof, cut down the flag with Winser's knife, and brought it from its staff. There were two men in bed in the garret whom he had not observed when we entered, who now rose in great apparent amazement. We at once turned to descend, Corporal Brownell leading the way, and Colonel Ellsworth immediately following with the flag. As Brownell reached

the first landing-place or entry, after a descent of some dozen steps, a man jumped from a dark passage, and hardly noticing Brownell, leveled a double-barreled gun square at the colonel's breast. Brownell made a quick pass to turn the weapon aside, but the fellow's hand was firm, and he discharged one barrel straight to its aim, the slugs or buck shot with which it was loaded entering the colonel's heart, and killing him at the instant. I think my arm was resting on poor Ellsworth's shoulder at the moment; at any rate, he seemed to fall almost from my grasp. He was on the second or third step from the landing, and he dropped forward with that heavy, horrible, headlong weight which always comes of sudden death inflicted in this manner.

His assailant had turned like a flash to give the contents of the other barrel to Brownell, but either he could not command his aim, or the Zouave was too quick for him, for the slugs went over his head, and passed through the panels and wainscot of a door which concealed some sleeping lodgers. Simultaneously with this second shot, and sounding like the echo of the first, Brownell's rifle was heard, and the assassin staggered backward; he was hit exactly in the middle of the face, and the wound, as I afterward saw it, was the most frightful I ever witnessed. Brownell did not know how fatal his shot had been, and so before the man dropped, he thrust his saber-bayonet through and through the body, the force of the blow sending the dead man violently down the upper section of the second flight of stairs, at the foot of which he lay with his face to the floor. Winser ran from above crying, "Who is hit?" but as he glanced downward by our feet, he needed no answer. Bewildered for an instant by the suddenness of this attack, and not knowing what more might be in store, we forebore to proceed, and gathered together defensively. There were but seven of us altogether, and one was without a weapon of any kind. Brownell instantly reloaded, and while doing so perceived the door through which the assailant's shot had passed beginning to open; he brought his rifle to the shoulder and menaced the occupants, two travelers, with immediate death if they stirred. . . . From the opening doors, and through the passages, we discerned a sufficient number of forms to assure us that we were dreadfully in the minority. I think now that there was no danger, but it was certainly a doubtful question then.

Corporal Francis E. Brownell sits on a toppled column in this carte de visite, a pose intended to symbolize the subjugation of the plantation South. The Northern press applied the sobriquet Ellsworth's Avenger to Brownell for his shooting of his colonel's killer.

Americans viewed the incident at the Marshall House as a romantic example of either "Northern pluck" or "Southern grit." In reality, the bloody struggle acted out inside the hostelry, idealistically portrayed on this song sheet cover, served as a harbinger of the violence to come.

JUDITH MCGUIRE
RESIDENT OF FAIRFAX COUNTY

Descended from Carter Braxton, a Virginia signer of the Declaration of Independence, McGuire presents the killing of Ellsworth from the Southern point of view in this passage from her journal and ends the passage with a bit of true prophecy. McGuire and her husband, John, an Episcopal clergyman, soon fled to Richmond. There, he worked as a post-office clerk and she found employment with the Commissary Department.

Yesterday morning, at an early hour, as I was in my pantry, putting up refreshments for the barracks preparatory to a ride to Alexandria, the door was suddenly thrown open by a servant, looking wild with excitement, exclaiming, "Oh, madam, do you know?" "Know what, Henry?" "Alexandria is filled with Yankees." "Are you sure, Henry?" said I, trembling in every limb. "Sure, madam! I saw them myself. Before I got up I heard soldiers rushing by the door; went out, and saw our men going to the cars." "Did they get off?" I asked, afraid to hear the answer. "Oh, yes, the cars went off full of them, and some marched out; and then I went to King Street, and saw such crowds of Yankees coming in! They came down the turnpike, and some came down the river; and presently I heard such noise and confusion, and they said they were fighting, so I came home as fast I could." I lost no time in seeking Mr. ——, who hurried out to hear the truth of the story. He soon met Dr. ——, who was bearing off one of the editors in his buggy. He more than confirmed Henry's report, and gave an account of the tragedy at the Marshall House. Poor Jackson (the proprietor) had always said that the Confederate flag which floated from the top of his house should never be taken down but over his dead body. It was known that he was a devoted patriot, but his friends had amused themselves at this rash speech. He was suddenly aroused by the noise of men rushing by his room-door, ran to the window, and seeing at once what was going on, he seized his gun, his wife trying in vain to stop him; as he reached the passage he saw Colonel Ellsworth coming from the third story, waving the flag. As he passed Jackson he said, "I have a trophy." Jackson immediately raised his gun, and in an instant Ellsworth fell dead. One of the party immediately killed poor Jackson. The Federals then proceeded down the street, taking possession of public houses, etc. I am mortified to write that a party of our cavalry, thirty-five in number, was captured. It can scarcely be accounted for. It is said that the Federals notified the authorities in Alexandria that they would enter the city at eight, and the captain was so credulous as to believe them. Poor fellow, he is now a prisoner, but it will be a lesson to him and to our troops generally. Jackson leaves a wife and children. I know the country will take care of them. He is the first martyr. I shudder to think how many more there may be.

Jackson, who proudly signed his letters "James Jackson, Secessionist" and had been trying to organize an artillery unit for the Confederacy, was lionized in verse as a defender of Southern honor.

SONG.

JACKSON'S REQUIEM.

AIR——"Dearest Mae."

That noted burglar Ellsworth,
  We all remember well
How the rascal tore the flag down,
  And how righteously he fell.

CHORUS.
Then let each Father to his child,
  The noble story tell,
How boldly Jackson shot the thief,
  How gallantly he fell.

The leader of those blackguards,
  By Tories styled "pet lambs,"
Who for God and their country,
  Care no more than rams.
    Chorus—Then let, &c.

This Ellsworth from Chicago,
  The first Zouaves led forth,
But robbed them of their earnings,
  Before he joined the North.
    Chorus—Then let, &c.

A man more cursed and hated,
  Has never yet been found,
But as he's gone we'll leave him,
  May he rest under ground.
    Chorus—Then let, &c.

The late lamented JACKSON,
  We will remember well,
How he nobly shot the ruffian,
  Though murdered by Brownell.
    Chorus—Then let, &c.

B.

Havelocks are put to the test as members of the 7th New York labor to erect breastworks around wooden guide frames at Columbia Springs, Virginia. Supervising are the gesturing Brigadier General Joseph Mansfield and, to his left, Colonel Montgomery Meigs.

ANNE FROBEL
RESIDENT OF ALEXANDRIA

The use of thousands of green, ill-trained troops in the occupation of Alexandria contributed mightily to the existence of a period of lax discipline among Union officers as well as among enlisted men. A palpably vitriolic point of view toward the Yankees flowed from Frobel's pen as she described acts of theft and personal insult in a diary entry recorded a week after the Federal occupation had begun.

June 1st—1861 And now war fare between us and this vile refuse of the earth begins in earnest. They came day—and night—any all day long. The first thing in the morning, before I am up I hear their vile, abusive, scurilous, blasphemy, O how can we live through it to have our peaceful home thus invaded—and our ears pained and blasted by such . . . sounds. We kept all the lower part of the house shut up, every window and door, locked bolted and bared, and we ourselves shut up, and stationed at the upstairs windows, and with what heart sickening terror do we see their approach to the house—their guns and bayonets only showing above the top of the cedar hedge—all glittering and gleaming in the sun light. Sometimes one party will rush into the kitchen and snatch and take off whatever they find, to-day they took a dried shad hanging against the wall. Old mammy seized it and tried to wrest it from him but he very soon got the better of her. They got all the setting hens out of the coops. One party came to the front door, when they come there we think it best to confront them ourselves, one or both thinking we can better keep them out of the house than the servants can, and there

they stood using all manner of vituperative language, and calling us all the vile shocking names that could be thought of. They dance, hoop and yell, and make all manner of threats, They behave and look like demons. Nothing that I could say, no words could convey, an idea of the horror of these scenes, and all without any provocation. The officers are not a whit better than the men for these marauding parties are nearly always accompanied by one or two officers. I do not know how they can attend to their military duties when such throngs of them are constantly ranging all over the country in quest of plunder. I never was spoken roughly to, or encountered rudeness from a man before. One man who was particularly insolent I remonstrated with and asked if he was not ashamed to speak to a lady in that way, he turned upon me in the most contemptous manner and said I would like to know who in the h—— made you a lady. . . .

. . . and these are the people who we have been led to believe were so much in advance, and so much better, than *us poor ignorant* Southern people in morals, and manners, education, piety, sobriety, and every christian virtue I can only say deliver me from such.

Soldiers of the 71st New York appear like masters of all they survey as they lounge, smoke, and chat idly near rows of stacked muskets in a clearing in Alexandria's north end. Before long, 50 members of this regiment would be killed or wounded in the fields adjoining Bull Run.

PRIVATE FREDERICK S. DANIEL
RICHMOND HOWITZERS

Part of the Confederate strategy in abandoning Alexandria was to conserve its forces so that they would be available to protect the crucial, and more defensible, rail center of Manassas Junction. Soon troops, including portions of the Richmond Howitzers, were being rushed to this locale. In 1864 Daniel's bouts of "remittent fever" forced him into Richmond's Stuart Hospital. His health shattered, he served out his enlistment working in the Confederate Conscript Bureau.

This amateur style of soldiering terminated on the 31st of May, when the first company received orders to take the field in earnest at Manassas Junction, and the second and third companies kept back for the peninsula. About noon on that day the company was embarked, with their guns, on a long freight train at the Central, now Chesapeake and Ohio, railroad station, and, after several hours' delay in starting, left Richmond rejoining and amid enthusiastic hurrahs for their destination. At the principal stations by the wayside there were crowds to see and greet them—many young ladies, with refreshments in trays and baskets, lavishly supplied, with ice-water and lemonade in abundance. On the next day, June 1st, the Howitzers were landed on the hot plain of Manassas, when they speedily had their tents pitched and their guns parked. Their battery was the very nucleus of the artillery corps that was to contribute so effectively to the building up of the undying fame of the "Army of Northern Virginia." Things were found very quiet at Manassas; very few troops had reached there, Beauregard was in command, there were rumors of cavalry dashes towards Washington, the weather was extremely hot, the drills heavy and exhausting, but the messes were well supplied, and especially well patronized, thanks to the hard exercise and splendid appetites that foreshadowed a consuming drain on Virginia's commissary department. Foraging at that flush and dawn of hostilities was excellent, and the mess-tables, rough-board constructions under the broiling sun, were loaded with the delicacies of the season, over and above the bounteous ration of flour, bacon, beef, molasses, coffee and sugar, regularly issued.

"Each party is awaiting for the other to make the attack."

CAPTAIN THOMAS J. GOREE
STAFF, BRIGADIER GENERAL JAMES LONGSTREET

The 25-year-old Goree left his successful law practice in Montgomery County, Texas, after the bombardment of Fort Sumter, traveling to the Confederate camps near Manassas. Unrestrained optimism—fed partly by misinformation about Federal fortunes at Philippi and losses at Bethel—exudes from this passage of a letter he wrote to his mother.

As soon as we crossed the Tennessee & Virginia line, what a change!! At every depot the platform was crowded with men, women & children & negroes to welcome the troops. Every lady, almost, had a bouquet for a soldier. I received several.

In the country as we passed houses, the men would hurrah, and wave their hats, the ladies their handkerchiefs, and the children their flags. The negroes in the field would stop and wave something at us, and were equally as enthusiastic as the whites. Texas is a long way behind the times. You never saw such excitement & enthusiasm in your life as there is here.

Here, nine out of every ten men you see is dressed in a military suit. This is a perfect military camp. Thousands of troops are encamped here. Many are quartered in the different churches, and there are from 2 to 500 arriving daily.

We passed several hundred on the road (among them 2 companies from Eastern Texas) which have not yet reached here. While there are so many coming in, they send others out to the Seat of War. Most of the troops are now being sent to Manassas Gap, some to Yorktown, and some to Harpers Ferry. All seem to be anxious to go where seems the best prospect for a fight.

One cannot hear much more news here than in Texas. Our plans are all kept very secret, and it is impossible to tell what the movements are to be until they are about to be executed. At this time, everything seems to be in "status quo." Each party is awaiting for the other to make the attack.

The Yankees, after their little experience at Bethel, Phillippi & Vienna are not so keen to fight. In every fight and skirmish that has taken place they have ingloriously fled. I have seen men who were in the fight at Bethel, and from what they say the Yankees must have had 500 killed and wounded. At Vienna they had about 20 killed.

PRIVATE WILLIAM C. HARRIS
5TH SOUTH CAROLINA INFANTRY

Harris, a 28-year-old grocer from Unionville, South Carolina, also found Rich-mond to be overflowing with cheering crowds and patriotic vigor. Often South Carolina troops would proudly display their state symbol, the leaf of the palmetto tree, on their uniforms, caps, and buttons—items that quickly became coveted as keepsakes. Though Harris exaggerated the size of the Confederate presence in the Old Dominion, some 10 regiments from the Carolinas were at First Manassas.

This is a beautiful city. Lincoln can never take it. There are now over one hundred thousand Volunteers in Virginia. S C has five Regiments here numbering 4000 men, others coming in. The S C boys are almost taken whether willing or not by ladies. Boquets come in from every direction. Just present a lady with a palmetto button and she prefers it to all presents. The little boys along the streets beg for buttons. I have sewed on my cap (all the others boys having given there's away) a plaited palmetto leaf which is gazed by thousands of fair eyes. I have been begged for it but I expect to keep it and return home with it and lay it at the feet of my beloved. All along the . . . road through N C shouts for S C and waiving of handkerchiefs by the fair ones (the prettiest faces almost I ever saw) was continual.

PRIVATE ELI S. COBLE
11TH NORTH CAROLINA INFANTRY

In 1864 and 1865 Coble would suffer the hardships of being incarcerated in the Federal prison camps located at Point Lookout, Maryland, and Elmira, New York. But in the enthusiasm of the war's beginning, he was one of the many happy young men whose units sifted through Richmond on the way to the front. Some 30 years later, Coble could still recall the excitement caused by the presence of pretty girls and by his receiving the trappings of a soldier.

We moved on, the sidewalks and much of the available room was occupied by great throngs of people waving handker-chiefs & cheering us on. There were some exceedingly pretty young women in that throng, God bless them. I do not remember of breaking off to the right or left tho we may. We came to a section of the city where there was large square lot, hardly large enough for a fair ground, but about a for a wagon yard—4 or 5 acres of ground into this, we halted on the east side near N. E. corner of this year, which was on our right, we marched. And it was here in this yard, now Monroe Park and the site of the Davis monument, we were armed and equipped with old U.S. smooth board muskets and rifled. Changed from flint to percussion. I think some of them had been rifled. This yard I speak of at this time was a quarter to half mile east of a publick building. . . . Some of the men said it was a penitentiary. I think if it was not that it was an asylum. This building I and some of the boys strolled out to. It was a warm day and no shade in our camp this Saturday evening. . . . We meandered our way back till we came to where the—it was not the main post office building was situate and perhaps a few squares north west of the State Capitol. Here at this Post Office, I think it was on the street west of Broad and 7th, we halted several minutes. I had a letter ready and went to the door to mail it and it was then and there I seen a pretty Richmond girl. She was waiting to mail a letter just ahead of me.

CORPORAL GEORGE N. WISE

17TH VIRGINIA INFANTRY

As Federal strength coalesced in Alexandria, armed reconnaissances were sent out to probe the Confederate line. One 75-man foray, a force of Regular Army cavalrymen and dragoons commanded by Lieutenant Charles Tompkins, trotted west along the Little River Turnpike on May 31. At 3:00 the next morning, the horsemen entered the hamlet of Fairfax Court House. Here they encountered resistance from the Warrenton Rifles militia company and the Prince William Cavalry.

On the morning of June 1st, before daylight, a force of Federal cavalry made a rapid descent upon them, hoping, by the rapidity of the movement, to find the Confederates off their guard. In this, however, they were mistaken; in passing through the town at the rate described, firing to the right and left indiscriminately, they aroused the sleeping inhabitants, and by the time they had halted beyond and prepared for a return charge, the Rifles were ready to meet them. During the advance, Captain Marr had moved off a short distance, for the purpose of securing a position for his company; his voice was not heard thereafter, and from what information could be gathered, it is judged that he fell from the first fire of the enemy. In the meantime, General Ewell, who was severely wounded, and Ex-Gov. Wm. Smith, both of whom happened to be passing the night in the town, had taken charge of the Rifles, to all of whom they were well known, and deploying them along the main street in the Court House lot, met and repulsed the second charge of the enemy. Two other attempts were made to force a passage, neither of which, from the determination of our brave Fauquier boys, proved effectual. After the departure of the enemy, it was found that the beloved Marr had fallen.

LIEUTENANT TOMPKINS, AT THE HEAD OF B COMPANY, U. S. DRAGOONS, CHARGING INTO THE TOWN OF FAIRFAX COURTHOUSE, IN THE FACE OF 1,500 CONFEDERATE TROOPS, JUNE 1st, 1861.

On June 1st, 1861, there was a smart skirmish between B Company, U. S. Dragoons, under Lieutenant Tompkins, and a body of 1,500 Confederates, at Fairfax Courthouse, Va. The Federal cavalry charged into the town, meeting with a brisk fire from houses on both sides of the street and from all quarters of the town. Lieutenant Tompkins's horse was shot under him, and falling beneath the animal, he sprained his ankle. After being completely inclosed by the Confederates for a short time Lieutenant Tompkins and his men fought their way out, taking with them seventeen prisoners.

This engraving shows the climactic moment of the clash described above. Earlier, while halted in the village of Fairfax Court House, Union troopers dodged several potshots, possibly fired by civilians. Their commander, Lieutenant Charles H. Tompkins, ordered his men to the west end of the village, re-formed them, and raced back through the town in an effort to return to Alexandria. Alerted Rebel troops successfully repulsed two charges before Tompkins' men finally broke through and escaped.

John Quincy Marr, pictured above in a prewar photo, captained the Warrenton Rifles in the Fairfax Court House encounter. A native of Fauquier County and a graduate of VMI, Marr earned the dubious distinction of being perhaps the first Confederate soldier to die in battle. Despite the caption of the engraving opposite, Marr's was the sole fatality among a Confederate force of not 1,500 but 50.

The Federals' loss in killed at Fairfax Court House also amounted to one man, although Lieutenant Tompkins had two horses shot from under him and suffered a severely bruised foot in one fall. During the engagement Private Benjamin D. Merchant of the Prince William Cavalry captured this model 1840 "wristbreaker" dragoon saber, which bears the initials "J. L." scratched in the guard.

JUDITH MCGUIRE
RESIDENT OF FAIRFAX COUNTY

Her slumber disrupted by the sound of a battle involving cavalry, McGuire watched as the Union troopers repeatedly attempted to bludgeon their way through the stubborn Rebel line. Richard S. Ewell, who would later command a corps in the Army of Northern Virginia, earned the public and professional praise of Southerners for his command in this encounter, suffering a slight shoulder wound in the process.

About three o'clock in the night we were aroused by a volley of musketry not far from our windows. Every human being in the house sprang up at once. We soon saw by the moonlight a body of cavalry moving up the street, and as they passed below our window (we were in the upper end of the village) we distinctly heard the commander's order, "Halt." They again proceeded a few paces, turned and approached slowly, and as softly as though every horse were shod with velvet. In a few moments there was another volley, the firing rapid, and to my unpractised ear there seemed a discharge of a thousand muskets. Then came the same body of cavalry rushing by in wild disorder. Oaths loud and deep were heard from the commander. They again formed, and rode quite rapidly into the village. Another volley, and another, then such a rushing as I never witnessed. The cavalry strained by, the commander calling out "Halt, halt," with curses and imprecations. On, on they went, nor did they stop. While the balls were flying, I stood riveted to the window, unconscious of danger. When I was forced away, I took refuge in the front yard. Mrs. B. was there before me, and we witnessed the disorderly retreat of eighty-five of the Second United States Cavalry (regulars) before a much smaller body of our raw recruits. They had been sent from Arlington, we suppose, to reconnoitre. They advanced on the village at full speed, into the cross-street by the hotel and court-house, then wheeled to the right, down by the Episcopal church. We could only oppose them with the Warrenton Rifles, as for some reason the cavalry could not be rendered effective. Colonel Ewell, who happened to be there, arranged the Rifles, and I think a few dismounted cavalry on either side of the street, behind the fence, so as to make it a kind of breastwork, whence they returned the enemy's fire most effectively.

"Our comrades of the First had run into a 'masked battery,' and were cut up into mince-meat."

This Waud sketch shows Vienna, Virginia, the destination of a Yankee scouting foray. In order to determine the Confederates' positions the Federal high command ordered a probe down the Loudoun & Hampshire Railroad to Vienna on June 17. Selected for the mission were the 700 men of Colonel Alexander McCook's 1st Ohio Infantry, who traveled on several flatcars pushed by a locomotive. As the train neared the objective, the engineer blew the whistle, alerting a Confederate contingent of infantry and two cannons commanded by Colonel Maxcy Gregg. As the cars hove into view, the Rebel artillery opened fire on the exposed Union troops.

CAPTAIN GEORGE M. FINCH

2D OHIO INFANTRY

Though Finch appreciated the "original" technique of "a reconnaissance on a locomotive into the enemy's country," he expressed dismay at the fate that befell the 1st Ohio, which—with the 2d New York and a regular artillery company— belonged to the same brigade as his 2d Ohio. In this stage of the war, soldiers of both sides freely applied the term "masked battery" to any concealed artillery piece. At Vienna, the Confederates simply posted their guns on a tree-covered hillock.

After hearing the details of the advance to be made the next day by the Ohio boys, from the willing lips of the sympathizing Viennese, the graybacks concluded to give them "a hospitable welcome to bloody graves," so far as they were able, and I must say they made a neat job of it. They concealed their two cannon in a grove of trees, and trained them carefully on the railway track, in a curve, and when the First Regiment, which was gayly advancing into the enemy's country on flat gondola cars, pushed ahead of the engine, reached the right place, bang! bang!! went the cannon. The very first shots fired struck the leading car, and over it went, spilling the men off into the ditch. It was a complete surprise, and cost us a dozen lives, much mortification, and great loss of prestige. The brave engineer uncoupled his tender from the train, and, suddenly realizing that "he who runs away will live to run his engine another day," put on a full head of steam and lost no time in making his way to Alexandria, not forgetting, in his panic, to toot his whistle at each and every cross-road. He slackened speed at our camp, five miles away, long enough to tell us the direful news that our comrades of the First had run into a "masked battery," and were cut up into mince-meat. That gave the most of us chills. Again we thought of "home, sweet home," and were almost sorry we had volunteered, when we thought that we, too, might unawares come into collision with one of those confounded "masked batteries" as we made a night march to meet the First Regiment at Falls Church, to which point they had "retired with some slight confusion in their ranks," as one newspaper had it.

SERGEANT EDWARD S. DUFFY

ALEXANDRIA LIGHT ARTILLERY (KEMPER'S BATTERY)

Duffy, a watchmaker in civilian life, had a peripatetic career in the Confederate artillery. In July 1862 he transferred from Kemper's to Parker's battery as commissary sergeant. Captured at Fredericksburg while with this unit, Duffy was held in Washington's Old Capitol Prison and then Fort Delaware until paroled and exchanged in May 1863. He then served with Woolfolk's battery until the war's end. He describes frankly the effect of his battery's shots upon the packed railcars.

A muscular man often compared in appearance to General P. G. T. Beauregard, 27-year-old Delaware Kemper left his position as the headmaster of the Alexandria Academy to command the town's artillery company. The crews of the two six-pound howitzers he directed at Vienna executed ably, drumming solid shot and canister off the wooden surfaces of the platform cars, causing 12 casualties and forcing the Yankees to scramble for safety.

Monday we marched to the R.R. & in the afternoon reached Vienna where we halted for some time a detail of infantry tore up the track at the Station. After waiting for some time, we started for Fairfax C.H. but were halted and ordered to take position on a slight hill above the side of the R.R. with a pine woods in our rear. Both guns were loaded one with Solid Shot the other with Canister, in a few minutes the train made its appearance having a car in front of the engine they whistled Down Brakes and we commenced firing, they fired a few straggling shots and then our men went to the cars (I did not go, neither did Capt. Kemper) as he said he did not come to see his Dirty work. There were six dead soldiers in the car—30 or 40 muskets and about the same no of Blankets. A large pot pie was also found which our men soon devoured as we had had nothing to eat since coming and Green Corn wasn't in Season.

Bungling in the Virginia Tidewater

The busy Ben Butler, having earlier dispatched the troops that reinforced Fort Monroe and kept it out of Rebel hands, arrived on May 22 to take personal command of the stronghold. By this time Butler was already in bad odor with army chief Winfield Scott for having acted without authority when he occupied Baltimore with 1,000 soldiers on the night of May 13. Scott was exceedingly dubious about entrusting Fort Monroe to such a headstrong political general. Butler, however, had powerful friends in President Lincoln's cabinet who urged his appointment.

Scott finally gave in, doubtless figuring that in such an isolated post even Butler could not cause too much mischief. In a letter, Scott urged him to enjoy his stay on the Chesapeake. "It is just the season for soft shelled crabs," he wrote, "and the hogfish have just come in." Butler was not, however, to take any military action without express permission from army headquarters in Washington.

Butler may well have followed Scott's advice about the crabs, but he brazenly ignored the substance of the old general's orders, deciding to mount a wholly unauthorized attack on a forward Confederate outpost near the village of Big Bethel, about eight miles northeast of Fort Monroe. The result would be the first land battle of the Civil War—and the second Federal fiasco of the young war in the Virginia Tidewater.

Commanding the Rebel outpost was Colonel Daniel Harvey Hill, a cantankerous West Pointer who had won commendations for bravery in the Mexican War and was always ready for a fight. Hill had about 1,400 men—

the 1st North Carolina Infantry, a company of the 3d Virginia Infantry, a handful of militia cavalry, and five guns from an elite old artillery outfit, the Richmond Howitzers. Reaching the Big Bethel area on June 7, the troops had dug earthworks on both sides of the Back River near a bridge carrying the main road from Fort Monroe to Yorktown. On June 9, the digging done, Hill had deployed his infantry to cover the bridge as well as spots north and south where attackers might ford the stream.

The next night Butler, intending a surprise attack, sent about 4,400 of his men marching off at 1:00 a.m. in two columns. One column was made up of the 3d New York Infantry and the 5th New York, Colonel Abram Duryée's Zouaves. The other included the 7th New York and parts of the 1st Vermont and the 4th Massachusetts.

The columns of inexperienced troops promptly became lost in the dark, then blundered into one another and, mistaking friend for foe, opened fire. Before the shooting stopped, 21 soldiers had been killed or wounded and the Confederates, hearing the gunfire, were on full alert.

Colonel Duryée tried to call a halt, arguing that it made no sense to go on now that surprise was lost, but the expedition's commander, a stubborn Massachusetts colonel named Ebenezer Pierce, insisted on continuing. By 8:00 a.m. Union skirmishers had driven back Hill's pickets south of Big Bethel. Then, after some delay, the main body of Federals began advancing toward the enemy earthworks.

The column was hit immediately by heavy fire from the Richmond Howitzers. Pierce then

deployed his troops in line of battle on both sides of the road, the units on the ends spreading out in an attempt to turn the enemy flanks.

Duryée's men, making a charge on the right, were torn by musket fire from entrenched Confederates, then pinned down by more cannon fire. Units on the left made some headway until, in the confusion of battle, they again fired on their own men. Trying a second time on the right, companies from the 1st Vermont and the 4th Massachusetts led by Major Theodore Winthrop crossed a ford and made a head-on assault—until Winthrop was killed by an enemy bullet. Winthrop was, said the acid-tongued Rebel commander Hill, "the only one of the enemy who exhibited even an approximation of courage during the whole day."

With Winthrop's death the attack petered out, and Colonel Pierce, finding his entire force now wandering about in disarray, started the troops stumbling back toward Fort Monroe. Behind them they left 18 dead and about 80 wounded; only one Confederate had been killed and 10 wounded.

In the aftermath, Pierce lost his command —and reenlisted as a private. Butler, too, was roundly condemned for the defeat. The only hope, one of Duryée's men declared, was that the fiasco might "be the means of removing our New York troops at least from Massachusetts generals, who have been fledged in the foul nest of party politics, without the least military merit." Unfortunately for the Union, Butler was powerful enough to survive even such gross ineptitude and insubordination. He would go on to make far more costly mistakes elsewhere.

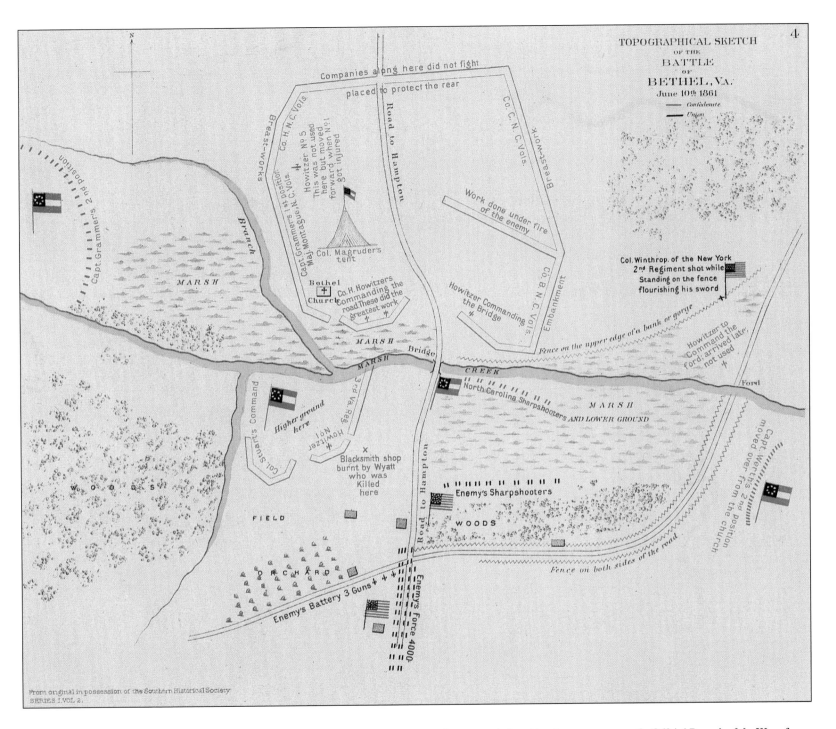

This map of the engagement at Big Bethel, copied from a Confederate original, was part of a set commissioned in 1891 to accompany the Official Records of the War of the Rebellion. It shows the Confederate earthworks around Bethel Church, which guarded the bridge over Marsh Creek, a swampy tributary of Back River. In the early morning of June 10, 1861, two columns of Federal infantry under Colonel Ebenezer Pierce converged on the bridge but were repulsed after a poorly managed attack.

PRIVATE ROBERT S. HUDGINS
3D Virginia Cavalry

The son of a wealthy plantation owner, Hudgins grew up on the family estate, Lambington, on the outskirts of Hampton, Virginia. Two weeks shy of his 19th birthday he left a local military school and enlisted in the Old Dominion Dragoons, which became Company B of the 3d Virginia Cavalry. Shortly before his death at 85, Hudgins recorded his memories of the first weeks of war on the Peninsula.

On about the first of June 1861, we received orders to move up to Yorktown, Virginia, where our regiment came under the overall command of Col. J. Bankhead Magruder, who was soon promoted to the rank of brigadier general. While here, we performed routine camp and picket duty. Occasionally we would scout toward Ft.

Monroe where we would run into Yankee patrols, driving them back to the protection of their large guns at Ft. Monroe, which they had continued to hold since the outbreak of the war. These raids and encounters were becoming so frequent that we all felt certain that the day was not far distant when there would be a try at strength between the two forces. We looked forward to the time when we could give the Yankees a taste of our steel, and we were confident that when the time came we would certainly be victorious.

One night in the week preceding the 10th of June 1861 we held a big dance at Yorktown. Col. Magruder had ordered the regimental band to furnish the music and the ballroom had been appropriately decorated with Confederate flags, bunting, and spring flowers, which were, at the time, in great profusion. Pretty girls attired in the conventional hoop skirts were in attendance from York, Gloucester, Warwick, and Elizabeth City counties, as well as many from Williamsburg and Richmond.

Frank Schell, an artist working for Frank Leslie's Illustrated, sketched soldiers of the 3d and 4th Massachusetts Militia standing guard while gunners of the naval brigade man a howitzer in the streets of Hampton, Virginia. Evacuated by its Confederate garrison along with most of the civilian population, the village was briefly occupied and vandalized by General Benjamin Butler's forces in the last week of May. "The pretty country town was deserted," one Yankee wrote, "not a white person in sight, only a large number of blacks." Hampton lay just outside th main Federal lines, where Butler readied for an advance up the Peninsula toward Yorktown.

Waited upon by runaway slaves, a convivial group of officers and visiting civilians dine in the camp of Colonel Abram Duryée's 5th New York Zouaves. The meal included champagne contributed by lawyer and noted Civil War diarist George Templeton Strong, who sits at the center of the table at left. The photograph was taken on June 4 by George Stacy, who left his Manhattan studio to record life in the camps at Fort Monroe. When viewed through a device called a stereoscope, the double image appeared three-dimensional.

It was a sight long to be remembered—the bright young faces of the dancers, the girls in lavender and old lace, the soldiers in their new uniforms (quite a contrast to those we would wear in years to come). The epaulets and gold lace of the officers mixed with the sparkling laughter from the girls until a burst of song would come forth from a young heart too full to contain itself. That night we thought little of the grim toll that death would take of those assembled—several would be laid low within the coming week. But it has ever been with soldiers, thinking of today and its pleasures, willing to let the morrow take care of itself. I remember how the mockingbirds sang in the lilacs outside the ballroom on that evening. The moon at its full shed a path of silver on the broad bosom of the York River where the French fleet had anchored seventy-five years earlier when the infant Republic was struggling for its existence. The old fortifications were still visible from where I stood, as were numbers of mounds in the little cemetery representing those who had made the supreme sacrifice.

SERGEANT ALFRED DAVENPORT
5TH NEW YORK INFANTRY

One of the Union's most colorful units, the 5th New York wore regalia modeled on the uniform worn by the French Zouaves. In his 1879 history of the regiment, Davenport recalled the Zouaves' first experiences on campaign with Butler's Peninsula expedition. A 24-year-old clerk from New York City, Davenport went to war as fourth sergeant of Company G but ran afoul of military authority. On June 14 he was demoted to private following an altercation with one of his officers.

On Tuesday, the 4th, only two companies were left in camp; the rest were sent on a scout to Fox Hill, about five miles distant. They were accompanied by the Troy regiment and others, and expected to have a fight. The night before had been a trying one; the regiment was out on parade, when a storm, which had been threatening to break at any moment, burst upon them in all its fury. The men were dismissed to their tents, but before reaching them were completely drenched. The tents were small, and not being water-proof, the rain soaked through so much that the inmates and the contents were thoroughly wet. The earth floors caught the drippings, and were soon turned into muddy beds. The men passed a sleepless and disagreeable night; the whole camp was flooded, and the next day blankets, overcoats, Bibles, and Prayer-books were spread out to dry, and the men waited patiently for their clothing to dry on their backs.

The provisions were scant at times, and the officers were disposed to be cross—a feature which did not make matters any more cheerful.

Much of the spare time of the men when off duty was occupied in cleaning their arms and accoutrements, and it was required of them that they be kept in prime order, or the guard-house or extra duty awaited the delinquent; and as nothing was allowed to rub them with, the men were compelled to use earth and old pieces of rags, if they could be procured. But all, both officers and privates, were held to a strict account in their various spheres of duty, and the discipline was very severe. It may have been rigorous, but it was the only way to make good soldiers of such a diversified body of men as composed this regiment.

"SOUTHRON"
1ST NORTH CAROLINA INFANTRY

An anonymous North Carolinian described his unit's baptism of fire in a letter to the Charlotte Western Democrat. On June 3 several companies of the 5th New York marched to Bethel Church, some 10 miles inland from the Union base of operations. Although casualties occurred, the action was merely a prelude to the clash at Big Bethel, in which Colonel Hill and the 1st North Carolina would play a key role.

About two weeks ago a part of three hundred Yankees came up from Hampton and occupied Bethel Church, which position they held a day or two and then retired, leaving written on the walls of the church several inscriptions, such as "Death to the Traitors!" "Down with the Rebels!" &c. To nearly all of these the names of the writers were defiantly signed, and all of the pensmen signed themselves as from New York except one, who was from "Boston, Mass., U.S." To these excursions into the interior, of which this was the boldest, General Magruder determined to put a stop, and accordingly filled the place after the Yankees left with a few companies of his own troops. In addition to this, he determined to carry the war into the enemy's country, and on Wednesday last Standard's battery, of the Howitzer battalion, was ordered down to the church, where it was soon joined by a portion of Brown's battery of the same corps. The North Carolina regiment, under Colonel Hill, was also there, making in all about eleven hundred men and seven howitzer guns.

On Saturday last the first excursion of considerable importance was made. A detachment of two hundred infantry and a howitzer gun under Major Randolph, and one of seventy infantry and another howitzer under Major Lane, of the North Carolina regiment, started, [by] different routes, to cut off a party which had left Hampton. The party was seen and fired at by Major Randolph's detachment, but made such fast time that they escaped. The troops under Major Lane passed within sight of Hampton, and as they turned up the road to return to Bethel encountered the Yankees, numbering about ninety, who were entrenched behind a fence in the field, protected by a high bank. Our advance guard fired on them, and in another moment the North Carolinians were dashing over the fence in regular French (not New York) zouave style, firing at them in regular squirrel-hunting style. The Yankees fled for their lives, after firing for about three minutes without effect, leaving behind them three dead and a prisoner. The fellow was a stout, ugly fellow from Troy, N.Y. He said that he had nothing against the South, but somebody must be soldiers, and he thought he had as well enlist. None of our men were hurt.

PRIVATE CHARLES F. JOHNSON
9TH NEW YORK INFANTRY

A Swedish-born bookbinder, 18-year-old Charles Johnson served his adopted country in the ranks of the 9th New York Zouaves. The regiment joined Butler's command on June 8, and the following night the fledgling soldiers had their first taste of picket duty guarding the perimeter of Colonel J. W. Phelps' brigade at Newport News. Johnson recorded his experiences in a diary.

Sunday, June 7th.

Our pickets were established along the line of a fence across the open space between the James and the woods, then following a road into these woods to the first cross-road where our advance picket was placed. It so happened that I was posted next to this advance pick-

"He said that he had nothing against the South, but somebody must be soldiers, and he thought he had as well enlist."

The camp of the 9th New York Infantry —shown here in a sketch by Alfred R. Waud—was located on a bluff overlooking the James River near Newport News. "It was an ideal location," Sergeant Matthew Graham recalled, "abundance of good water near at hand, and the ground smooth and with slope enough to secure good drainage." Commanded by Colonel Rush C. Hawkins—an ambitious New York lawyer and bibliophile—the colorful unit was popularly known as Hawkins' Zouaves. In late August the New Yorkers left their comfortable quarters to take part in the Federal amphibious invasion of Hatteras, North Carolina.

et, though the darkness was too intense to enable me to see him.

All was quiet until about eleven o'clock, I should think, when my companion hailed me in a whisper and informed me that he heard voices in the woods, and immediately disappeared in the darkness. I myself could hear nothing, and was getting used to the stillness again, when he challenged and fired. This, of course, being the signal, we rallied on the main guard, and while the "Long Roll" beat in camp, our hearts beat high, expecting an enemy, which, however, did not appear. Another relief was sent out and posted, while we were drawn up in line ready for any business at hand. This fresh relief had not been on their posts more than a few minutes before we all heard distinctly commands of "File Right and Left" issuing from the woods. Our sentinel's challenge followed immediately, one or more shots were fired and the pickets came in on us pell-mell.

The officer of the guard (Lieutenant Leahy, I think) now called upon the sentinel who had fired, to report. He said that as soon as he had been on his post a short time, he could hear not only voices, as we did, but the tramping of feet, and only when he saw a figure approach him, he challenged, and not being answered, he fired. He waited for some effect of the shot and heard curses from some one for not doing so and so. By this time two Companies arrived from the Regiment, scouts were sent out to reconnoiter, but as nothing could be found, seen or heard, they soon came back and returned to camp. After this our fellows became so possessed by excitement that it seemed as if every rustling leaf provoked a challenge and a shot; so that in an hour's time over a dozen shots were fired, I really believe, at nothing; for, with the one exception, I had certainly seen or heard nothing to fire at. And this voice giving the command that we heard, may have proceeded from some party of our own, some neighboring picket perhaps, or party returning from forage.

"Nobody would have thought that a large body of men were on the move, by the stillness that prevailed."

SERGEANT ALFRED DAVENPORT
5TH NEW YORK INFANTRY

Davenport's account of the opening moves of Butler's attack on the Rebel position at Big Bethel on June 9 describes a surprisingly successful night march by the green Federal column that set out from Hampton. The Zouaves of the 5th New York were able to surprise an enemy outpost, but Butler's plan began to go awry when the 3d and the 7th New York regiments fired upon each other in the darkness.

Taps were sounded as usual, and we were ordered to our tents. A few minutes after a man might be seen going to each tent, and whispering the words, "At half-past ten every man will be called; he will immediately, and without noise or light, arise, equip himself, and fall in line in front of the tents. He will be supplied with one day's rations; will also tie his turban around his left arm twice, as a distinguishing mark."

About an hour before the time I was outside of my tent, when I saw a body of men going by: they made so little noise that it seemed to me mysterious where they had come from. I learnt that they were two of our companies, who were to go ahead as skirmishers under the command of Captains Kilpatrick (now major-general of cavalry) and Bartlett. I now understood that we were to surprise a rebel camp about fifteen miles from here. It seems that a negro who had ran away from the rebels, being employed by them to help build their batteries, had given information of it, which led General Butler to determine to attack it. There were several secessionists who came down to Hampton for the purpose of shooting the negro. We were to act in conjunction with a regiment at Newport News, and others were to follow us.

We were finally on the march. Nobody would have thought that a large body of men were on the move, by the stillness that prevailed. After we had gone some five or six miles, we were ordered to halt. I looked through the woods and saw a bright light; it could not be mistaken, it was a rebel signal: it was in a house, and pointed directly in the line of their company. Further on we came in sight of another. Soon after we came to a slight halt, heard a volley of musketry, and were ordered on at a double-quick. Our company being on the right was ahead of the line, and I am near the head, so that I had a chance to see every thing. We halted, and found that we had come upon the extreme outpost. There was a camp-fire burning, and we had taken an officer prisoner. He was well mounted, with a fine revolver and sword, the edge of which was sharpened up to the handle. He was a fine looking man, over six feet high. We then heard rapid firing in the rear. We supposed that the rebels had come in contact with the Newport News regiment under Colonel Bendix.

Alfred Waud sketched the Yankee column, which included three cannons under the command of Regular Army lieutenant John T. Greble, advancing on Big Bethel. But by the time the Federal troops neared the Confederate position the defenders—alerted by the earlier firing—were ready and waiting. Greble unlimbered and opened fire but was outgunned by well-entrenched Rebel batteries.

PRIVATE ROBERT S. HUDGINS

3D VIRGINIA CAVALRY

Hudgins' company, the Old Dominion Dragoons, were among the first to make contact with the Yankee column moving toward Big Bethel. Rather than attempt to delay the enemy advance, the Rebel troopers galloped back to their entrenchments and brought word of the imminent attack to the senior Confederate officer, Colonel D. H. Hill. Hill's soldiers scrambled into line of battle behind the earthworks and watched the Federal units deploy half a mile to their front.

Early on the morning of June 10, a Mrs. Schmelz and her son Henry passed through our picket on their way to Hampton. They had not proceeded far when they encountered the Yankee advance. Mrs. Schmelz immediately wheeled her horse and buggy in the road and applied the whip. She raced back to our position and advised us of the advancing force.

Some interval passed, and the men on the outpost were quite nervous. One man would light his pipe only to take several puffs before knocking out the fire against his rifle butt. Horses sensed the growing tension and began to champ their bits and paw the ground. High in an old oak tree a squirrel broke a small branch which fell to the ground

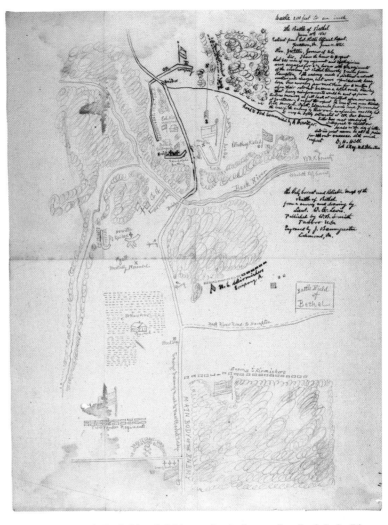

This map of the Big Bethel battlefield was sketched soon after the fight by Lieutenant William G. Lewis of the 1st North Carolina, a former railroad surveyor. It shows two companies supporting an entrenched howitzer south of the Back River, while most of Hill's 1,200 soldiers manned earthworks north of the stream.

Hatbands like this one, worn at the Battle of Big Bethel by Major John B. Cary of the Virginia Artillery, were used as distinguishing marks by both sides during the fighting. Telling friend from foe was a serious problem in the first months of the war, as many Yankee units were clad in gray and Rebels in blue. Some units even resorted to prearranged gestures or utterances to identify themselves.

and instantly drew all eyes toward the sound. Finally a large unbroken dust cloud was visible rising from the area of the intersection of the Sawyer Swamp Road. In another few minutes, the enemy's skirmishers were visible and the report of a rifle down the road could be distinctly heard as the Yankee's sighted our picket. Little time was lost in mounting, and with a farewell scattered volley, we put spur to horse and were shortly back within our position at Big Bethel, where our sergeant reported the enemy advance.

Veterans of the clash at Big Bethel, officers of the 5th New York (Duryée's Zouaves) posed for photographer George Stacy on the porch of regimental headquarters at the Segar plantation. Left to right: Major J. M. Davies, Lieutenant Colonel Gouverneur K. Warren (with telescope), Assistant Surgeon B. E. Martin, an unknown sentry, Chaplain Gordon Winslow, Adjutant Joseph E. Hamblin, Colonel Abram Duryée, and Surgeon Rufus Gilbert.

Very shortly, the enemy reached Buzzard's Roost, a distance of one-half mile from our breastworks where they deployed into line of battle. Between the wood and our line was an open field south of the creek and west of the Hampton Road near the Pressey home. Into this field advanced a howitzer and several hundred infantrymen in support. To drive us from our position, the enemy had either to cross this field or attack on our left after passing through the swamp previously described. The howitzers near the bridge, commanded by Capt. Randolph, had now gone into action and were throwing shells into the enemy ranks, which were in turn replying with a hand-drawn piece, shelling the road near the ford. Soon the infantry of both sides was engaged and the battle was now in full swing. Men were shooting the tops out of the small pines, shouting and swearing; frightened horses were bolting and running riderless to the rear.

Just then, an aide dashed up to Capt. Phillips and shouted "Col. Magruder's compliments, sir. You will take your company and capture the gun shelling the ford." We knew the next command given would be "charge." We also knew that the moment we topped the rise in our front we would receive the full brunt of the battle and not many of us would return. I, being in the first set of fours, knew my hour had come. At this moment, another aide galloped up to Capt. Phillips and countermanded the first order so as to enable the howitzers to draw the enemy's fire. We were then removed further to the rear to await our turn.

CHAPLAIN WALLACE W. THORPE
3D NEW YORK INFANTRY

Wallace W. Thorpe, who served 10 months as chaplain of the 3d New York, witnessed the blunder that cost needless bloodshed and deprived the Union of the element of surprise in its offensive at Big Bethel. When order was restored after fellow Federal soldiers loosed a volley against Thorpe's regiment and the 3d returned fire, it was found that 10 men had been wounded, two of them mortally.

Colonel Duryea and Colonel Townsend crossed the creek at Hampton by means of fishing boats manned by members of Bartlett's brigade, and took up their line of march. Simultaneously with this movement, the Massachusetts Fourth and Vermont regiments, located at Newport News, hastened forward to form a junction with the forces from Fortress Monroe before reaching the field of action. When about five miles from Hampton, Colonel Townsend's command met with a mishap. As they were advancing toward a narrow defile through a dense wood, marching by flank, in the rout-step, with "arms at will," and wholly unconscious of the proximity of an armed force, a heavy and well-sustained fire of cannon and small arms was suddenly opened upon them which told with terrible effect. So sudden was the attack that the men staggered backward, and, for a moment or two, the utmost confusion prevailed throughout the ranks, but they rallied immediately and fell into their places with the promptness and precision of well-disciplined troops. After remaining more than twenty minutes in the midst of this deadly fire, they withdrew in perfect order to a more favorable position, and, at the command of General Pierce, formed in line of battle and advanced once more to the conflict. But it was soon ascertained by our imagined foe that they had been foolishly firing upon their friends. The forces which opened the fire proved to be Colonel Bender's German regiment and a detachment of the Vermont regiment, having come from Newport News with two six-pounders to join the forces from Fortress Monroe.

In a drawing by Frank Schell, soldiers of John E. Bendix's 7th New York Infantry—a unit largely made up of German immigrants—pause during their march from Newport News to Big Bethel. The drawing depicts the troops moments after the regiment had fired into the 3d New York, which was advancing from Hampton.

PRIVATE GEORGE MELOY
5TH NEW YORK INFANTRY

On June 10 Duryée's Zouaves launched an attack on the Confederate defenses at Big Bethel, but the Federal ranks were quickly broken by Rebel artillery fire. Some Zouaves continued to advance, while others sought cover in the woods and roadside ditches. Two days after the battle, Private Meloy described the chaotic fight in a letter to his wife, Priscilla, who was expecting their first child.

About nine O'clock we halted in the woods for a rest and to prepare for what was coming. We were within half a mile of the enemy's camp and all very tired from marching all night, the distance of about eight miles without any sleep and but little rest. We had just stacked our arms and sat down when the bugle sounded to fall in line. Some of the Scouting party ahead came back with the news that the enemy was just ahead in full force of about Five Thousands. We

This gold-braided forage cap was worn by Major George Wythe Randolph, who commanded the Virginia Howitzer Battalion at Big Bethel. "He has no superior as an artillerist in any country," D. H. Hill reported, "and his men displayed the utmost skill and coolness." A grandson of Thomas Jefferson, Randolph was born in 1818 at the former president's estate, Monticello. Promoted to general in February 1862, Randolph was named Confederate secretary of war the following month.

came upon the field and had just time to form in line when the ball was opened by the enemy sending into our ranks a shower of balls. What followed after that I cannot give you any connected account but I give it incidentally.

The enemy were not in line of battle on the open field as we expected to find them but entrenched behind a thicket of brush and woods and when we came upon the field we could not see a man of the enemy's. They were completely in ambush and within the embankment of one of the strongest fortifications in this section of the country.

After forming in line the order came to take to the wood in companies and act as skirmishers. Four companies on the right of the line fell into the woods and worked themselves through to the fence where they halted and delivered their fire loading and firing again amid a shower of grape shot rifles and cannon balls.

What became of the left of the wing I cannot say for we left them out of sight. After a few rounds we drove the enemy from one of their batteries and silenced it and carried one of their cannons. We were now ordered to fall upon our faces and hold fire. We lay there resting for about twenty minutes while the left of the wing with some of the Albany boys and a company of German riflemen having got down to a fence under their guns peppered away until we rallied and went to their assistance. This was the worst of all. We had to cross a ploughed field within fifty yards of the enemy and open to their fire which came thick and fast. I can't begin to describe the scene which here met the eye. I will only tell a few instances. A Lieutenant of Artillery received a cannon ball shattering him to pieces and throwing him across one of his own pieces. A man behind him was shot in his breast and another in the heart, dyeing instantly. I saw another having his arm blown away just below the elbow, and Mr. Griggs the young man that went to see you, was cut in two by a cannon ball and Third Sergeant was killed and our First Corporal badly wounded.

PRIVATE REYNOLD M. KIRBY
Richmond Howitzers

The artillerists of the Richmond Howitzer Battalion sighted their guns with deadly accuracy and accounted for many of the 76 Federal casualties at Big Bethel. Kirby and his comrades lost the use of their gun when the priming wire, a thin metal spike used to pierce the flannel cartridge bag, broke off in its vent. Six weeks after describing the fight in a letter to his mother, Kirby succumbed to disease.

Early the next day I was awakened up by orders of the Capt. from where I was laying wrapped in my blanket under a tree, to accompany the rifled guns on an expieition upon which we were to be accompanied by some Infantry, we proceeded down the road about five miles when we received information that the enemy was approaching in superior numbers when we returned to our entrenchments and prepared for them, the rumor was one of those that we've become accustomed to hear so often that we paid little attention to it but as a precautionary measure prepared as fast as possible to receive them perfectly, when in entrenchment we received messenger after messenger that they were approaching rapidly estimating their numbers at various sizes, I suppose in proportion to the fear of each man still however we . . . could'nt bring ourselves to beleive that they were really coming, till between the two houses in our front we could see their glisting bayonets like a forest of steel, beautifully they came up in heavy column as if to sweep us from the earth, and we expected an instant charge but they halted in front of the houses on the road before spoken of when they planted one of their pieces and opened a heavy fire upon us, in reply to ours which had been opened at a distance of 600 yards by one of our rifle men who advanced down the road to meet them to within that distance, he fired at that distance upon them retiring immediately within our entrenchments, their reply to this our opening shot was a long huzzah to which we returned an answer in the shape of a minnie ball from a man on our far right, . . . the time occupied by them in forming their column of attack was empaired [employed] by our men in loading our pieces and making our casons and horses secure, soon the silence which had become almost painful was broken by the voice of Hughes gunner of our rifled piece whos loud voice might be easily heard to all parts of our works "fire" and the pecular singing of that gun assured us that the shot had been well aimed down the road . . . , again our gunner at Hughes gun tried his skill this time the shot was repeated but not with so much spirit and their answering canon spoke their acceptance of the challange, our gun that is the one at which I was stationed which was nearest to them, soon opened its mouth and constantly repeated its fire till unfortunitaly our priming wire was broken off in the vent of the gun totally disabling the piece for the day compleatly, great was our disapointment when the order was given to run

the gun into the swamp, which for my part I did with a heavy heart, we remainded however in the battery with a portion of the North Carolina men ordered into it for our support, where they all remaineded till the enemy charged over from in front of our gun, when they received from Capt Walker's company . . . which occupied our flanking battery a most beautiful discharge cupling [crippling] them considerably and causing them first to wane and then retreat to the cover of the house on the road. This charge was made by the Zouaves whose conspicuous red pantaloons made an admirable mark for our men and which you may well suppose we didn't fail to avail ourselves of.

"Our regiment is called the red-legged devils, and the terror to evil doers," Private George Tiebout wrote of the 5th New York Zouaves, shown in a stereoscopic view. The next day Tiebout fell in the charge at Big Bethel, his heart torn from his body by a Rebel shell.

PRIVATE JAMES E. WEIR
5TH NEW YORK INFANTRY

Weir describes the Rebel artillery fire that swept Duryée's charging column from the road that led toward the Confederate works along Back River and prevented the Federals from crossing. A native of Canada, Weir left his job as a soap boiler to enlist in the Zouaves. After his mustering out from the 5th New York he joined the U.S. Navy and served as a fireman aboard several vessels of the Atlantic fleet.

Everything got along very well until we got up to where the enemy was. Then we drew up in line of battle for to meet them but we found our mistake for instead of being a field fight it proved to be a battery. We had to attack so we got in four abreast and the order Right Shoulder Shift was given so we got at ready for double quick. Then the order was given for double quick march. Then the men made a grand charge for them but in going up the road they fired upon us and the balls went within two feet of the line. If it had been two feet closer there would have been upwards of one hundred killed besides as many more wounded but it was the mercy of God that saved us from it. They sent a second shot which cut one man's hand off besides taken another man's arm off close by the shoulder and the same shot come within an inch of taking my head off but thanks to God for his kind mercies to me for keeping me from harm. We commenced the fire about nine o'clock on Monday morning and kept the fire on steady for four hours then some more Regiments came to our relief and General Peirce said we could go back to the camp again for we had done our duty and if every other Regiment did as well as we did we would have the South in less than two weeks. There was 7 killed, 17 wounded and 2 missing. One of the missing is our 3rd Sergeant by the name of Hopper, as nice a sergeant as in the Regiment. He was the only one in our Company that is missing or killed or wounded. Sergeant Matthews had a very narrow escape from being shot in the head by a grape shot. It struck the barrel of his musket with such a force that it knock it out of his hands. One of our Captains by the name of Kilpatrick got shot twice in the same place in the thigh. It was only a flesh wound but it did not signify much as he was able to walk.

Alfred Waud's wash drawing of "Federal troops driving the rebels from one of their batteries" reflects artistic license. The only redoubt to fall to the Yankees had earlier been abandoned by its contingent of Rebel troops.

"If every other Regiment did as well as we did we would have the South in less than two weeks."

PRIVATE THOMAS P. SOUTHWICK

5TH NEW YORK INFANTRY

Only five feet one inch tall, South-wick, shown in a postwar photo-graph, was nicknamed Pony by his comrades in the 5th New York Zouaves. An orphan, he spent sev-eral years in an institution for des-titute children and worked as a newsboy. But his love of books—he went to war carrying a volume of Shakespeare—made him an astute chronicler of his unit's exploits.

LIEUTENANT BENJAMIN R. HUSKE

1ST NORTH CAROLINA INFANTRY

A lawyer from Cumberland Coun-ty, North Carolina, Huske went to war with the Fayetteville Light Infantry—the oldest militia unit in North Carolina. In 1862 he was pro-moted to major of the 48th North Carolina State Troops. Wounded during the Peninsula campaign, Huske died on July 15, 1862.

The fire of the enemy was so heavy and incessant that it was impossible to reform our ranks. Everybody seemed to be fight-ing on his own hook. In the midst of the wood, stretched out stiff and stark in death, was a member of our regiment. Over him someone had laid a blanket. I lifted the blanket but failed to recognize him, but read the white strap of his canteen, "Tibout, Company A." Off on the dusty road lay the mangled body of an officer in the uniform of the reg-ular army. It was the lifeless body of Major Theodore Winthrop, a gal-lant soldier from Massachusetts who had gone from the scene of strife with the humble Zouave private to the land of eternal rest.

I was granted permission to crawl up further in the wood to see the enemy's battery. I was stopped pretty soon by Captain Davies, who demanded where I was going and that I come back or he'd blow my infernal head off. After explaining,` he permitted me to proceed. On my hands and knees I went, drawing my musket after me. Presently I came to a field of growing corn, too high to see over. I tried here and there to peep through the corn and was just turning away when I per-ceived the chaplain of our regiment, Captain Winslow's father, stand-ing near the fence with a big cavalry pistol in his hand. I left him there and returned to the company.

I was at the main battery and had a fine view of the entire fight, having been detached from the Company with 30 men to sup-port them in case of a charge. They came up the Hampton Road and directly in range of this battery and only 1/2 or 3/4 mile off. Their muskets gleaming in the sunshine. The Battery commenced its work and it was not long before they found that we had quit "running" for they had to do some pretty scientific dodging. Very soon their first shell came in reply and then shot after shot from each side, our shots from one place were bad at first but from the other capital. And I could see precisely where each shot from us struck and the fellows, when it was a good one, scampering for their lives backwards & forward.

Very soon their files commenced flanking across the open space—between some houses that were there. These passed through an open-ing of about 30 yds and the batteries poured the shell and shot into them. After they had all passed across this opening which was a move-ment to flank us on the right—very soon a single musket shot was heard then another and then such a roar and the hissing of the shots and the striking trees, banks & everything, made us squat close I tell you behind our embankments. They are good things I assure you. Some of the boys lying down said Col. Hill knows more about good banks and ditches than we and I'll never grumble at pitching dirt again.

Well this kept up for some half-hour and our piece there got out of order, and the banks were abandoned on our right. That is the outer works. Very soon Col. McGruder who with Col. Hill was very much exposed and often at our battery said to one of our companies "This point must be retaken and maintained at all hazard, go Sir (to the Capt.) and tell them I say so." This backward movement originated from the piece gun getting out of order and as there were only 20 infantry to hold it they retired and the other companies through some misunderstanding as to orders also retired—and fell back towards us— But Col. McGruder's orders were hardly issued before the Yankees were double-quickly out of the entrenchments and our men into them and by this time the Gun which had gotten out of order was replaced and that, opening upon them scampering away the field. They then filed across the opening in front of us where they had passed at first and caught it from this battery too. Then for a time both parties remained quiet and for 15 or 20 minutes not a shot was fired.

We then threw a shell or two from the Battery and they returned it— and very soon commenced their march on our left flank. Here took place pretty much the same thing as in the right and Col. McGruder heard that this gun and the entrenchments had been carried. He came up to our company and said "By God they say the North Carolina boys are running—Go quick and help them out. If that point is carried we are lost." Here they went across the field under the musketry fire and soon got to the trenches. Major Randolph who commanded the artillery and is as cool as a cucumber and as calm as if eating his breakfast—at this juncture ran across under the fire and found all the men there

Captain William W. McDowell (left) led the Buncombe Rifles— Company E of the 1st Carolina—which defended the north-ern face of the earthwork at Big Bethel. In the fall of 1862 he became a major in the 60th North Caroli-na Infantry, a regiment command-ed by his brother. Both resigned early in 1863, following their unit's poor performance in the Battle of Murfreesboro, Tennessee.

down in the trenches, as quiet as lambs waiting to catch a glimpse of the rascals and our old Col.—just waiting for them as if he had been at his tent. Some of the boys sat smoking a small pipe—and also Lieut. Col. Lee with him, a brave and excellent officer, and it was not long before the Yankees found out somebody was there. Here it went bang pop bang then the continual crack and I felt just as secure knowing that Col. Hill was there as if we had a thousand pieces of artillery—for I for-got to say that Major Randolph soon came running back and said "Col. the North Carolina Boys are doing the prettiest sort of work." "By god Sir, then they are whipped, I thought N. Carolinians would never run!"

I with my 30 men jumped up to run along thinking we were includ-ed in the order—When McGruder said "Stay here Sir, and stand by those pieces"—Gracious how the balls did shower around us and 3 struck the piece we were next to. You can't form any idea of how they hissed and struck, just like a shower of hot stones falling into the water. . . .

Well very soon the musketry ceased on the left—and back to their batteries they fell again, and it looked as though they were throwing up embankments—we watched them awhile and then 4 shots, 2 from each of our guns were aimed with a precision that was perfectly surpris-ing—I saw them strike exactly in their midst and then they scampered and so closed the first pitched battle.

SERGEANT ALFRED DAVENPORT
5TH NEW YORK INFANTRY

The death of Union artillery commander John Greble, described here by Davenport, represented one of the last casualties of the Battle of Big Bethel. Davenport recalled how a group of Duryée's Zouaves rescued their wounded comrades when the rest of the Yankee force abandoned the field. Two of those, Lieutenant Colonel G. K. Warren and Adjutant Joseph E. Hamblin, later attained the rank of general.

Lieut. John T. Greble, with the regulars and a few of the Massa-chusetts men, as before stated, held the most dangerous post, on the road, with the three guns. The solid shot from the Confeder-ate batteries plowed their way straight up the road, from which there was no cover, except that occasionally some of the men took shelter in the edge of the wood on the right of the road. Lieut. Greble would not deign to leave his post for an instant, but coolly sighted the guns him-self and watched the effect of every shot. . . . When the troops left, he saw that he could not hold the position any longer, and was in the act of sighting or spiking his gun when a cannon ball struck him on the temple, carrying away half of his head. The ball passed through the body of a man standing near and took the leg off of a third. He had only five men left with him at this time. His Sergeant then spiked the gun. Four of the regulars were killed or wounded out of the eleven that came with him from the fort.

Greble's body was laid over a caisson, and was dragged off under the superintendence of Lieut.-Colonel Warren. . . .

A small number remained behind after the regiment moved, among whom were Philip L. Wilson and George L. Guthrie, to rescue the wounded, but the special mission of the former was to bring off Thomas Cartwright, already mentioned as having been shot through the thigh, and who was one of his messmates.

He asked the men guarding Greble's body to assist him, but they refused. He went into the woods and there met Guthrie, who was alone, and shouting for Tom, they were finally overjoyed to hear him answer their call. They carried him with much exertion to the edge of the wood by the road, and leaving Guthrie as companion, Phil went to find a conveyance. He succeeded in obtaining a hand cart, and went back with it to the place where Guthrie and Cartwright were waiting, having first handed the Lieut.-Colonel his rifle, who told him to make haste or he would be taken prisoner. In this way Cartwright's life was probably saved on this occasion. . . .

At a cross-road they met two of the Troy regiment who were driving a wagon they had seized. They got out and Cartwright was put in. A skirmish soon after ensued with the enemy, who were following, and was kept up all the way to Newmarket Bridge, Tom Cartwright also taking a hand in from the wagon. At the bridge they met Lieut.-Col. Warren, who had left them a little while before, and gone forward to hurry up the detail of the naval brigade, whom he had sent forward when he left camp with two guns. The old sea-dogs came pushing up the road, armed with clubs, dragging the cannon after them, crying out every now and then, "Heave hearty! Heave hearty, my lads!" All who were at Camp Hamilton will never forget the "sea-pirates." They were the wildest and most reckless set of men ever got together.

The rear guard, after crossing the bridge, pulled up the planks, and the enemy seeing the cannon, abandoned further pursuit. One of the latter was shot here by one of our men. The regiment, in the meantime, kept on their weary march back to camp, tired and footsore. Their giant Adjutant, Hamblin, at every short halt to rest, threw him-

self on the ground with the exclamation, "How I like the mud!" and when the men got up to resume the march, it was with considerable effort they could get their stiffened joints to obey their will. Finally they reached Hampton, and were rowed across the river by the naval brigade in flat-bottomed scows, in one of which lay the body of the lamented George H. Tiebout, of Company A, who was shot through the heart by a canister ball, and was the first martyr of the 5th Regiment, in the first battle of the war. Having arrived on the other side of the river, the march was resumed, and we arrived in camp about 8 P.M., all completely exhausted, after a march of thirty miles since leaving camp, besides standing the brunt of the battle, which lasted two hours and forty minutes.

A highly regarded graduate of the West Point class of 1854, John T. Greble returned to the academy as assistant professor of ethics and married the daughter of a fellow instructor. Just before starting on the expedition to Big Bethel he assured his wife, "There is not much danger to be incurred."

Sketched by Jasper Green

Union Victories in Western Virginia

While Ben Butler was bungling on Virginia's Peninsula, Federal forces in the Allegheny Mountains of the far western part of the state were achieving two small but significant successes. The people of the region were in any case largely pro-Union. Mostly small farmers, many were not susceptible to the economics of slavery—and they had long felt themselves at odds with the interests of Virginians in the more affluent counties east of the mountains. Indeed, on May 13, 1861, some of the area's leaders called a convention in Wheeling to consider opposing the state's Ordinance of Secession and establishing a rival pro-Union state government.

Nothing came of this initiative at first, although Lincoln's government found it to be a cheering sign. Of more immediate concern to the Federals was clearing Confederate troops from the area. This was done in smart fashion

Jubilant Yankee foragers, laden with struggling piglets, dodge an angry sow in front of the Greek Revival courthouse in Philippi, Virginia. The sketch was made by Pennsylvanian Jasper Green, an artist-correspondent for Harper's Weekly.

by the budding Young Napoleon—as he would soon be called—George McClellan, recently promoted to major general and placed in command of the Department of the Ohio.

McClellan's first job was to protect the Baltimore & Ohio Railroad, which ran from Harpers Ferry through western Virginia to Parkersburg and the Ohio River—the Union's all-important river-rail supply line for troops and goods coming from the West. The route was vulnerable to Rebel raiders, and on May 26 McClellan heard that some were congregating in the area.

McClellan sent two columns of troops hurrying to head them off. The first, commanded by Colonel Benjamin Kelly, moved south from Wheeling toward Grafton. The other, led by Brigadier General Thomas A. Morris, crossed the Ohio River at Parkersburg to drive eastward and link up with Kelly. With luck they would meet near Grafton and squeeze the Confederates between them.

Commander of the enemy force was Colonel George A. Porterfield, sent by Virginia's governor to organize some detachments of volunteers who had been gathering in the mountains. When assembled, Porterfield's little army totaled a mere 1,500 men, and they were a ragtag bunch, ill armed and undisciplined.

Porterfield knew he could not hold Grafton—plainly the Federals' first objective—with this poor force, so on June 2 he fell back some 30 miles to the town of Philippi. Hardly had he pitched camp there, however, when he heard that both Federal columns were on his coattails.

Quickly ordering his few supply wagons loaded up, Porterfield told his officers to start marching the troops farther south toward Beverly, about 40 hard miles away. The officers objected to such a hasty departure on a miserably rainy night. Porterfield unwisely let his officers sleep, comfortable and dry, in Philippi's only hotel. Unfortunately, the soldiers on picket duty also sought shelter in town, leaving Philippi unguarded when, at dawn, the Yankees attacked. Somehow Porterfield got most of his men moving, but only the fact that Colonel Kelly was shot and wounded by a Rebel straggler kept the Federals from pursuing and scooping up the entire Rebel contingent. The Virginians' headlong retreat was greeted with huzzahs by local Unionists. "The chivalry couldn't stand," crowed a Wheeling newspaper. "They scattered like rats from a burning barn."

A few weeks after this victory, news came that a highy respected West Point-trained brigadier general, Robert S. Garnett, had replaced Porterfield and was busy enlarging and reorganizing the Confederate force around Beverly. In response, McClellan himself moved into the field on June 21, marching with some fresh regiments into western Virginia and linking up with the Federals already camped in the Grafton-Philippi area. In all he had 27 regiments organized in four brigades, along with 24 field guns. Leaving 5,400 troops to guard the B & O tracks, he advanced with

the rest to find Garnett and his Confederates.

Garnett, knowing a Union force was coming, divided his army, stationing the main part on a promontory called Laurel Mountain. The rest he placed on nearby Rich Mountain under the command of a combative 29-year-old West Pointer, Lieutenant Colonel John Pegram.

McClellan also divided his force, sending one brigade under General Morris to hold Garnett on Laurel Mountain, then swinging widely to the right with the main body to hit the Rebels on Rich Mountain. McClellan's movements were slow, but by July 10 his troops were in position. Meanwhile General Morris was finding that his advance skirmishers were meeting stiff resistance, which argued that Garnett's main force must be on Laurel Mountain and the smaller detachment on Rich Mountain, rather than the other way around, as McClellan had thought.

Still, the Confederate defenses on Rich Mountain looked formidable enough to McClellan, and he hesitated to attack. At this point one of his subordinate commanders, Brigadier General William S. Rosecrans, proposed a flanking maneuver. A local Unionist, David Hart, had come into the lines saying he knew a little-used wagon trail that would provide the perfect route.

McClellan agreed, and at 4:00 a.m. on July 11 Rosecrans set out with a force of 1,900 men around a southern spur of the mountain. Pushing hard, the troops clambered up the steep rear slope and about 2:30 in the afternoon attacked the Confederate rear.

After a seesaw battle that lasted for three hours, Pegram was forced to retreat, hustling his men off the mountain toward the northeast to try to join up with Garnett. This proved impossible in the broken terrain, and after a day and a half of confused wandering Pegram's

famished, thirsty Confederates surrendered.

Garnett was not much better off. Hearing of Pegram's retreat and threatened in his turn by Rosecrans, he fell back off Laurel Hill—to find General Morris and his brigade in hot pursuit. Garnett and some of his men got across the Cheat River, but he was killed fighting a rearguard action—the first general on either side to die in battle.

With Garnett's death and the rout of his rear guard the fighting stopped. McClellan lost no time in informing Washington and the Northern press of his triumph—omitting to mention that Rosecrans deserved much of the credit for the victory. It had been, McClellan announced grandly, "a brief and brilliant campaign."

But regardless of who was responsible for it, a heartening and important Yankee victory had been achieved under McClellan's command, securing the region and ensuring that it would eventually join the Union as the new state of West Virginia. Even the hard-to-impress General Scott was enthusiastic and sent congratulations. McClellan was clearly a rising star.

This military map of the mountainous area south of Beverly, Virginia, was copied from one captured by Union troops in Camp Garnett after the Battle of Rich Mountain. The original was drawn by Confederate cartographer Jedediah Hotchkiss for Colonel John M. Heck of the 25th Virginia Infantry and shows the main routes through the Allegheny Mountains that were guarded by General Garnett's small Rebel army. The struggle for these mountain passes, begun in 1861, would continue throughout much of the war.

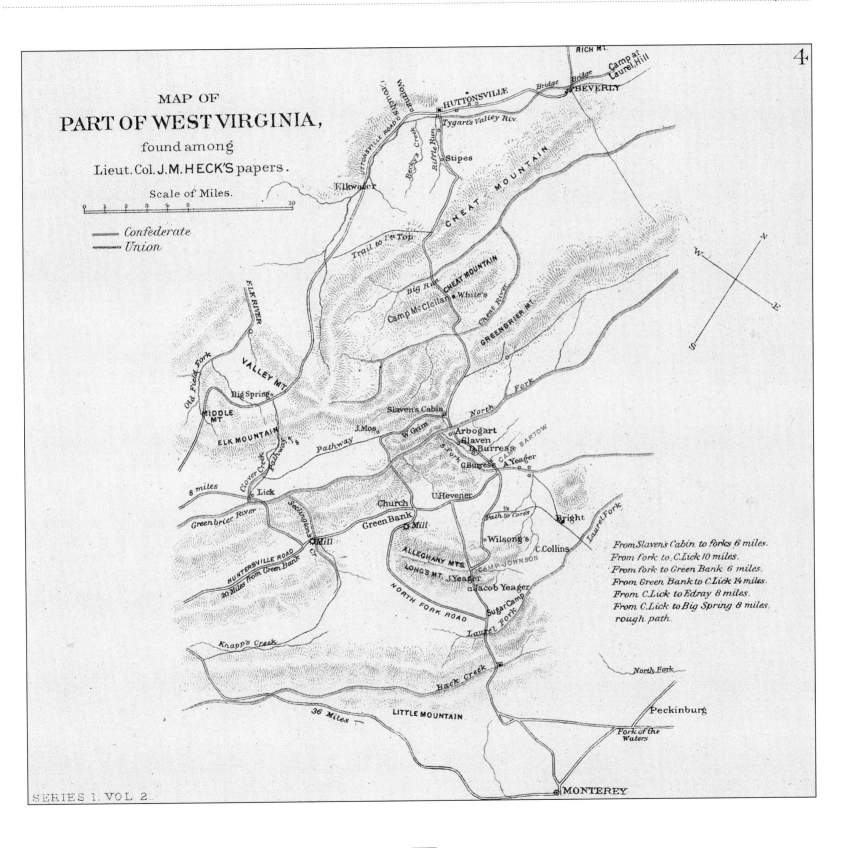

MAP OF
PART OF WEST VIRGINIA,
found among
Lieut. Col. J. M. HECK'S papers.

Scale of Miles.

Confederate
Union

From Slavens Cabin to forks 6 miles.
From fork to C. Lick 10 miles.
From fork to Green Bank 6 miles.
From Green Bank to C. Lick 14 miles.
From C. Lick to Edray 8 miles.
From C. Lick to Big Spring 8 miles.
rough path.

"I call upon you to fly to Arms and support the General Government. Sever the connection that binds you to traitors."

MAJOR GENERAL GEORGE B. MCCLELLAN

COMMANDER, DEPARTMENT OF THE OHIO

McClellan first came to public attention when he orchestrated a major troop incursion into western Virginia to help safeguard the vital Baltimore & Ohio rail line. In this grandiose proclamation, issued from his headquarters in Cincinnati before he joined his troops in the field, McClellan betrays two traits for which he would later become notorious—a lordly sense of self-importance and a penchant for making political pronouncements.

*H*ead-quarters Department of the Ohio
    Cincinnati, May 26, 1861
    To the Union Men of Western Virginia:
The General Government has long enough endured the machinations of a few factious Rebels in your midst. Armed Traitors have in vain endeavored to deter you from expressing your loyalty at the polls. Having failed in this attempt to deprive you of your dearest rights, they now seek to inaugurate a reign of terror, and thus force you to yield to their schemes, and submit to the yoke of the traitorous conspiracy dignified by the name of the Southern Confederacy. They are destroying the property of Citizens of your State, and ruining your magnificent Railways.

The General Government has heretofore carefully abstained from sending troops across the Ohio, or even from posting them along its banks, although frequently urged to do so, by many of your prominent citizens. It determined to await the result of the late election, desirous that no one might be able to say that the slightest effort had been made from this side to influence the free expression of your opinion, although the many agencies brought to bear upon you were well known. You have now shown, under the most adverse circumstances, that the great mass of the people of Western Virginia are true and loyal to that benificent Government under which we and our fathers have lived so long. As soon as the results of the election was known, the traitors commenced their work of destruction.

The General Government cannot close its ears to the demands you have made for assistance. I have ordered troops to cross the River. They come as your friends and brothers—as enemies only to the armed Rebels who are preying upon you. Your homes, your families, and your property are safe under our protection. All your rights shall be religiously respected. Notwithstanding all that has been said by the traitors to induce you to believe that our advent among you will be signalized by interference with your Slaves, understand one thing clearly—not only will we abstain from all such interference, but we will, on the contrary, with an active hand, crush any attempt at insurrection on their part.

Now that we are in your midst, I call upon you to fly to Arms and support the General Government. Sever the connection that binds you to traitors. Proclaim to the world that the faith and loyalty so long boasted by the Old Dominion are still preserved in Western Virginia, and that you remain true to the Stars and Stripes.

CARTOGRAPHER JEDEDIAH HOTCHKISS

STAFF, CONFEDERATE DEPARTMENT OF NORTH-WESTERN VIRGINIA

A New York State native, Hotchkiss relocated to Virginia in 1847. After the Battle of Philippi, he volunteered as a cartographer with the Confederate forces opposing the Union offensive. Hotchkiss later gained fame as Stonewall Jackson's mapmaker.

We had a very pleasant time after we left Monterey—saving the black gnats on Cheat Mnt. & at Greenbrier River. I slept on the floor, simply wrapped in my cloak, at Greenbrier river. . . . I found it a good deal of labor to take proper care of my horses the next night. Saturday, we slept on the wagons 1 1/2 miles from Beverly—had a good sleep, wrapped in my cloak on the top of the boxes, was only awakened once by Crawford, who was sleeping on the ground, crying out, in his sleep, dreaming that a snake was around his neck. We were up Sunday morning by 4 A.M. & by 5 were on the way to Beverly, in the rain, by the way at Hutonsville we found the 1st troops, Mountaineers, about as dirty as the ground & eating black victuals out of black dishes, tin, out in the hot sun—it gave a disgust for camp life. . . . We found the "boys" encamped in the yard & occupying the houses of a Mr. Crane who is in the Wheeling Tory Convention. the yard has a good sod & fine shade trees & is a nice place. They fare well there, have good bread, & good sleeping places, but their duties are severe & they are always on the alert being an advanced post & liable to be attacked at any time, though they cannot be surprised or cut off, for they have guards out 9 miles. It was noon Sunday when we got there & we were very tired & very dirty, got cleaned up & was resting some towards evening when, just after dark, news came that we were to be attacked in an hour—the wagons were hustled round, harness strung out, of course, & things tumbled in in a hurry, I waded around in the mud & rain, got my horses harnessed & was ready to start, but no enemy came & we slept on our arms, giving to rest at midnight.

LIEUTENANT CHARLES LEIB

11TH U.S. INFANTRY

Leib describes the early morning hours of June 3, when a Federal column that had marched from Grafton attacked the Confederate garrison at Philippi. The Rebel troops were caught off guard, despite the fact that sympathetic civilians had tried to warn them of the attack, and they soon began a precipitate flight. Northerners quickly derided this retreat as the Philippi Races. Leib had a checkered military career, being passed over for promotion several times before his death in 1865.

They had received information from Miss Abby Kerr, of Fairmont, whose father and two brothers were among their forces, that the day following they would be attacked. She had learned this from some source, and started on horseback, accompanied by a Miss McCloud, whose lover was also in the rebel army, eluded our pickets, and made their way to the camp. Their rout was complete. It was a continuation of Grafton races; but this time they left behind, arms, ammunition, clothing, horses, wagons, subsistence stores, and a very large number of letters, written by hands of fair rebels, congratulating them upon the spirit of patriotic devotion, which had induced them to volunteer in defense of "Southern Rights." When our forces arrived at Philippi, they were worn down from fatigue, having marched twenty-two miles from 11 o'clock at night. The roads were in a horrible condition, the mud ankle deep, the night so dark that the outlines of the forms of the men could not be discerned even at a few feet distant, and the rain descended in torrents. To enable them to bear up under such severe fatigue, they were ordered to throw away everything they had, except arms and ammunition. Some of the men, from exhaustion, were left by the way; but the troops pushed forward, and would have taken the whole camp by surprise, had not a woman, living within half a mile of it, hearing the tramp of the men, fired a pistol which alarmed the pickets, who roused the camp. When the charge was made, some ludicrous scenes occurred. Dozens of the flying soldiery were seen rushing along the road, with their coats in one hand, their pantaloons in the other, and the white flag streaming out behind. Others were bare-footed, while one fellow had only time to get one leg into his breeches, and in the hurry to get in the other, lost his balance, and fell to the ground.

Although the 25th Virginia lost most of its "clothing, provisions, ammunition, and guns" during the retreat from Philippi, it saved its regimental banner (above).

SERGEANT JOHN L. HILL
Virginia Militia Cavalry

Their sleep shattered by gunfire, Hill and his fellow troopers hastily mounted up as Union soldiers poured into their camp. Employed as a farmer and teacher in Rockingham and Augusta Counties in the prewar years, Hill eventually joined the 14th Virginia Cavalry and was promoted to lieutenant. He survived the conflict and was active in the United Confederate Veterans before his death in 1909.

As the gray dawn of morning appeared in the east, we were startled by a loud explosion which I at first supposed to be a musket over-charged. Another report with a terrible crash among the tents in our camp in which I was sleeping, with the cry "the enemy! the enemy!" made some twenty of us hasten to our horses in "double quick" time. But this time there was one constant roar and the balls were falling and skiping all around us. All was now confusion. Horses broke their bridles, and fled minus bridles, sadles, and riders. The infantry were marching toward "Dixie's Land" in great disorder. Order was finally restored and our retreat effected without the loss of a single man, strange to tell. Many volleys were fired into the rear of our retreating legion and with only three men wounded. All our Baggage, wagons, and about five hundred Va. muskets fell into the hands of the enemy. On the night of our retreat, our company camped in a certain meadow near Laural Hill. The rain fell in torrents; and to sleep was impossible. We sat on our horses until 1 o'clock in the morning.

THE FIGHT AT PHILIPPI, VA., JUNE 3D, 1861—THE UNITED ST...

Acting under instructions from Brigadier General Morris, the Federal troo
Kelley's command should proceed along the Beverly Turnpike, above Philippi,
the village. Colonel Kelley being delayed by a treacherous guide, Colonel D
Colonel Kelley then arrived and pursued the fugitives through the streets of P

The roar of cannon fire blankets the rugged landscape surrounding Philippi, as two guns of Ohio's Cleveland Artillery lob shells into the camp of Colonel George A. Porterfield's Confederate troops—whose orderly rows of pitched tents can be seen in the fields adjacent to the hamlet. Porterfield's problems were compounded by the fact that he had no cannon of his own. To the left, a Union column led by a mounted officer double-quicks toward the enemy.

UNDER COMMAND OF COLONEL DUMONT, SUPPORTED BY COLONELS KELLEY AND LANDER, AND THE
ATES UNDER COLONEL PORTERFIELD.

in two columns. one commanded by Colonel B. F. Kelley and the other by Colonel E. Dumont. It was agreed that Colonel
engaging Colonel Porterfield's rear, when Colonel Dumont's column would simultaneously open fire from the heights overlooking
dash upon the Confederate pickets, carrying consternation in their ranks and capturing the barricaded bridge across the river.
was badly wounded.

"Spring houses unsecured failed to retain their milk and butter, and poultry began mysteriously to disappear, even the ducks and geese."

SERGEANT PLEASANT S. HAGY
37TH VIRGINIA INFANTRY

The Confederacy rushed several regiments, including the 37th, to western Virginia to help offset the losses at Philippi. Referring to his unit by its old militia name—the Glade Spring Rifle Company—Hagy seemed most concerned with obtaining food and liquor, or "O-be-joyful," celebrating the clever strategem employed by one of the company's experienced foragers. Pop skull and rifle knock-knee were other euphemisms applied to alcohol by soldiers of both armies.

On June 6 General Robert S. Garnett was ordered to take command of Rebel forces in western Virginia. The West Point graduate expressed dismay at the "miserable condition" of the "arms, clothing, equipment, and discipline" of his new troops but began to fortify his lines in order to thwart further advances by McClellan.

General Garnett was relieved by our coming, and we were pleased at the prospect of a rest from our long march. We found there a line of breastworks already prepared that we thought entirely useless, for was not the Glade Spring Rifle Company on the ground? We were located in camp along and behind the breastworks, and soon we were snugly settled, we supposed, for the summer. We (my mess) supplied ourselves while at Richmond with a colored gentlemen from Farmville to do our cooking, washing, and foraging. He was to act the Samaritan in case any or all of us became sick or wounded. He was of African descent and in color resembled a coal bin—Samuel by name. We were well pleased with him on the trip, for he kept us supplied with chickens, butter, and milk; but we frequently suspected that the money we gave him to buy chickens failed of its purpose. It was only a short time after our advent to Laurel Hill that, through Sam's manipulations, we appeared spick and span, clothes washed, boots shined, uniforms and hats brushed up, and so little of our wearisome march left visible that we might have easily been mistaken for country gentlemen. The boys all through the command regained their equanimity. There was life in the camp, and soon the surrounding neighborhood began to realize their presence. Spring houses unsecured failed to retain their milk and butter, and poultry began mysteriously to disappear, even the ducks and geese. On one occasion a member of the Glade Spring Rifle Company, a descendant of a King's Mountain ancestor and the owner of two one-gallon jugs, decided to go foraging. He was successful in his get-away, but on his return encountered the officer of the day, who accosted him with inquiry as to the contents of his jugs. There being a strick embargo on the introduction of "O-be-joyful" into the camp, the officer thought he had a case to report. But our member with honored ancestors was no fledgling. He handed the officer one of the jugs to examine, which he found to contain buttermilk. The other jug was then presented to him, but had previously been well smeared around the bung with milk; and, on seeing its condition, he let our strategist pass on.

LIEUTENANT CHARLES LEIB
11TH U.S. INFANTRY

Leib, who refers to himself in the third person and gives himself a promotion in the account below, was besieged by civilians seeking financial redress for depredations, real and imagined, caused by the "Rebles." Although such claimants may have irritated Leib, he reserved a special loathing for the region's dangerous "bushwackers." Such men, he claimed, were "noted for their ignorance, indolence, duplicity and dishonesty," and killed merely "for the sake of killing, . . . and for the love of gain."

On the arrival of troops at Buckhannon, they found that nearly all the Seccessionists had fled, fearing they would be arrested. Their houses were taken possession of, and converted into barracks. Nearly every man who was there, had a claim against the Government. One had lost his rails, another had had his horse taken by the army, others had been robbed of their cattle or poultry. It seemed as if every man was making an effort "to make all he could out of the war," as some of them declared they would, and to compel the Government to pay them for sending troops to Western Virginia, to protect their homes and firesides, while they remained quietly at home, waiting to see which party would triumph, before taking a decided stand; such is the position of many persons in that country. The Acting Quartermaster at Buckhannon had no funds, and referred their claims to Captain Leib. Down they came like so many hungry wolves, and with a pertinacity that knew no bounds, urged their payment. In many cases, they had no evidence to support their statements as to the damage they professed to have sustained.

MAJOR GENERAL GEORGE B. MCCLELLAN
COMMANDER, DEPARTMENT OF THE OHIO

McClellan arrived in Grafton to take personal command of his troops on June 23. The 34-year-old general, already hailed by some as the North's Little Napoleon, began to position his 12,000 troops between Philippi and Buckhannon for another blow at the 1,300 men Garnett had posted to oppose him. In this statement he admonished his men to act in a conciliatory fashion toward the local citizens, so as to help preserve their fragile loyalty to the United States government.

Headquarters Department of the Ohio, Grafton, Va., June 25, 1861. To the Soldiers of the Army of the West: You are here to support the Government of your country, and to protect the lives and liberties of your brethren, threatened by a rebellious and traitorous foe. No higher and nobler quality could devolve upon you, and I expect you to bring to its performance the highest and noblest qualities of soldiers—discipline, courage, and mercy. I call upon the officers of every grade to enforce the strictest discipline, and I know that those of all grades, privates and officers, will display in battle cool, heroic courage, and will know how to show mercy to a disarmed enemy.

Bear in mind that you are in the country of friends, not of enemies; that you are here to protect, not to destroy. Take nothing, destroy nothing, unless you are ordered to do so by your general officers. Remember that I have pledged my word to the people of Western Virginia that their rights in person and property shall be respected. I ask every one of you to make good this promise in its broadest sense. We come here to save, not to upturn. I do not appeal to the fear of punishment, but to your appreciation of the sacredness of the cause in which we are engaged. Carry with you into battle the conviction that you are right, and that God is on your side.

Your enemies have violated every moral law; neither God nor man can sustain them. They have, without cause, rebelled against a mild and paternal Government; they have seized upon public and private property; they have outraged the persons of Northern men merely because they came from the North, and of Southern Union men merely because they loved the Union; they have placed themselves beneath contempt, unless they can retrieve some honor on the field of battle. You will pursue a different course. You will be honest, brave, and merciful; you will respect the right of private opinion; you will punish no man for opinion's sake. Show to the world that you differ from our enemies in the points of honor, honesty, and respect for private opinion, and that we inaugurate no reign of terror where we go.

Soldiers! I have heard that there was danger here. I have come to place myself at your head and to share it with you. I fear now but one thing—that you will not find foemen worthy of your steel. I know that I can rely upon you.

LIEUTENANT ORLANDO M. POE

STAFF, MAJOR GENERAL GEORGE B. McCLELLAN

Poe's strong and capable bearing, evidenced in the steady gaze he exhibits in this photograph, led McClellan to select him as his topographical officer. The Navarre, Ohio, resident finished this letter to his wife moments before participating in an assault up Rich Mountain on the Rebel stronghold known as Camp Garnett.

This day the battle is to be fought. The enemy is in position less than two miles in advance. They have thrown up breastworks on the spur of the mountain, and are awaiting us. The order has been given to storm them, and one column has marched to the attack. This column is composed of four thousand men under command of Genl. Rosecrans—Genl. McClellan commands the reserve—which is to attack the enemy in front as soon as Genl. R—— opens fire upon their rear which he had almost gained when the last courier came in a few minutes ago. The reconnoissance was made yesterday—*and I made it.* The reconnoitering party was a strong one under command of Col. McCook of the 9th Ohio Vols. . . . We had one man killed and several wounded. But we forced our way right to their works. . . . We moved forward driving the enemy's pickets before us, until we arrived within 400 yards of the works. I carried a spy-glass, and a compass, and made a complete survey as we went along though the crashing of rifle

& cannon balls through the brush around me rather tended to disconcert me. I have often wondered how I would feel when I saw men fall, shot down like sheep, but the very slight experience of yesterday seems to indicate all want of emotion of any kind. I have the field book and notes in pencil of my observations, and I am going to send it to you some day, or rather *bring* it to show you that it is possible to write under fire. We all wanted to go ahead and storm the works. Our men were eager for it, and were so close that they were picking off the Enemy's gunners with their rifles, but our orders were positive not to bring on an engagement —but simply to find exactly where the enemy was, and how to attack him.

Good bye. I'm suddenly ordered to the front. Deepest warmest love to you all.

BRIGADIER GENERAL WILLIAM S. ROSECRANS

BRIGADE COMMANDER, DEPARTMENT OF THE OHIO

"Old Rosy" was well liked by his men, who habitually misspelled his name as Rosecrantz or Rosecranz in their letters. The general planned and successfully executed the flank attack that avoided the earthworks of Lieutenant Colonel John Pegram's Confederate forces on Rich Mountain.

Colonel Lander, accompanied by the guide, led the way through a pathless forest, over rocks and ravines, keeping far down on the southeastern declivities of the mountain spurs, and using no ax, to avoid discovery by the enemy, whom we supposed would be on the alert, by reason of the appearance of unusual stir in our camp, and the lateness of the hour. A rain set in about 6 a.m. and lasted until about 11 o'clock a.m. with intermissions, during which the column pushed cautiously and steadily forward, and arrived at last and halted in rear of the crest on the

THE BATTLE OF RICH MOUNTAIN, VIRGINIA, JULY 13, 1861.

In this incorrectly dated engraving, Hoosier and Buckeye soldiers emerge from the woods covering Rich Mountain's slopes to fall upon the Confederate rear guard commanded by Julius A. de Lagnel. Three of the 46 casualties incurred by the Yankees lie sprawled between the attacking battle lines.

top of Rich Mountain. Hungry, and weary with an eight hours' march over a most unkindly road, they laid down to rest, while Colonel Lander and the general examined the country. It was found that the guide was too much scared to be with us longer, and we had another valley to cross, another hill to climb, another descent beyond that to make, before we could reach the Beverly road at the top of the mountain. On this road we started at 2 o'clock, and reached the top of the mountain, after the loss of an hour's time by mistake in the direction of the head of the column, in rectifying which the Tenth Indiana took the advance.

Shortly after passing over the crest of the hill, the head of the column, ordered to be covered by a company deployed as skirmishers, was fired on by the enemy's pickets, killing Sergeant James A. Taggart and dangerously wounding Capt. Christopher Miller, of the Tenth.

The column then advanced through dense brushwood, emerging into rather more open brush-wood and trees, when the rebels opened a fire of both musketry and 6-pounders, firing some case shot and a few shells.

Troops of the 13th Indiana (left), sporting the "light colored, . . . felt wool hats" distinctive of the early war garb of many soldiers from that state, rush upon a Rebel fieldpiece forsaken by gunners of the Lee Battery. Union columns quickly severed the road to Beverly, forcing the Confederates to retreat on narrow, rugged paths, abandoning much of their ordnance. The 13th Indiana, a three-year outfit that would reenlist in December 1863, served throughout the war in the eastern theater, losing 255 men to battle wounds and disease.

Thomas A. Brander, a lieutenant in the 20th Virginia, earned a citation in Pegram's report of the battle for his efforts to slow Rosecrans' brigade. In 1862 he joined the Letcher Artillery, and by 1863 he commanded this unit. Brander survived a close call at Fredericksburg, when a solid shot "just graz[ed] his ribs," to return to his hometown of Richmond at war's end.

"We there understood that the entire command of Cols. Heck and Pegram was either killed or taken prisoner."

CORPORAL JAMES E. HALL
31ST VIRGINIA INFANTRY

A Philippi native, Hall had an interest in the engagements being fought practically at his doorstep. Garnett posted several regiments, including Hall's, near his headquarters on Laurel Hill, north of Rich Mountain. As the main battle raged to the south, Hall's regiment skirmished with the enemy and wondered about the fate of their comrades. Later wounded and captured at Gettysburg, Hall was able to return to the Philippi region in 1865, residing there until he died in 1915.

We accompanied Col. Taliaferro's Regt. which went to relieve the skirmishers. We stopped a few hundred yards from the enemy's outpost. The Regt. went on and engaged the enemy. We were sheltered from the balls by a huge log. We remained on our post until morning, when the enemy's fire became so hot, we retired nearer our camp, but not out of range of their guns. They endeavored to drive the whole guard back to camp, and to accomplish it, shot cannon balls, case shot and canister at us for near ten hours. We were sheltered from them however, by the large trees of the woods. Several of us came very near being struck by their balls nevertheless. A few having the mud and dirt thrown over them by the explosion of shells. We picked up a few of their balls. A six pounder was sent down the road and fired some six shots at a house which was occupied by the Yankees. The house was utterly demolished. The enemy ceased firing when they heard the discharge of our gun. We were shortly relieved, and on the following evening went with our Regt. out as skirmishers. We engaged the enemy and had a brisk fire for a few minutes.

Next morning we began cooking provisions for 4 days. We were not yet done when the command "fall in" was heard all around. We immediately formed lines and commenced our line of march,—a retreat. Our intention was to go by way of Beverly, but finding the road blockaded, the entire command changed directions to go through the counties of Preston, Tucker, Hardy, etc. We there understood that the entire command of Cols. Heck and Pegram was either killed or taken prisoner. We marched all that day, and at night encamped on the opposite bank of Shavers Fork of Cheat River, without anything to eat and much fatigued by the march.

LIEUTENANT CHARLES W. STATHAM
LEE BATTERY, VIRGINIA

Statham and his men did good service at Rich Mountain, rapidly turning about their cannon to fire at the Union lines attacking their rear. Through a combination of a rapid fire and fuses cut for quick detonation, the crew repulsed two attacks before excessive casualties forced the survivors to retire without their gun. Statham fell, "shot through the right hand," and was taken captive by the Yankees.

I moved with one gun and a detachment of twenty-one men to occupy this pass in Rich Mountain. We took our position about 1 o'clock p.m. In less than two hours the enemy made their appearance in large column, six regiments strong, immediately on the hill south of the pass. We reversed our gun, which was pointed down the pass, and prepared to receive the enemy in the direction in which he was approaching. In a few minutes the sharpshooters of the enemy commenced a fire upon us from behind trees and rocks at a distance ranging from two to three hundred yards, the body of the enemy being still farther. We opened upon the main body with spherical shot, which I cut at first one second and a quarter, and could distinctly see them burst in their midst. I knew we did good execution, as I could distinctly hear their officers give vehement commands to close up ranks. After firing this way some little time at the rate of near four shots per minute we forced the enemy to retire.

LIEUTENANT COLONEL JOHN PEGRAM
COMMANDER, CONFEDERATE FORCES AT CAMP GARNETT

Cut off from the main Rebel force, Pegram had the ignominious duty of surrendering the 555 men left in his shattered command. Later exchanged, he attained a promotion to brigadier general and died in the 1865 Battle of Hatcher's Run, Virginia, just three weeks after getting married.

Headquarters at Mr. Kittle's House, Near Tygart's Valley River, 6 Miles from Beverly, July 12, 1861. Commanding Officer of Northern Forces, Beverly, Va.:

Sir: I write to state to you that I have, in consequence of the retreat of General Garnett, and the jaded and reduced condition of my command, most of them having been without food for two days, concluded, with the concurrence of a majority of my captains and field officers, to surrender my command to you to-morrow as prisoners of war. I have only to add, I trust they will only receive at your hands such treatment as has been invariably shown to the Northern prisoners by the South.

I am, sir, your obedient servant,

John Pegram

Buckhannon resident John C. Higginbotham left Lynchburg College to raise and lead Company B of the 25th Virginia. The 18-year-old returned early from a furlough to help defend the mountain that overlooked his home, and received the first of seven wounds he sustained in battle. He died at Spotsylvania in 1864.

LIEUTENANT ORLANDO M. POE
STAFF, GENERAL GEORGE B. McCLELLAN

Poe felt his sensibilities assailed by the brutal sights of the battle's aftermath, little imagining that such gore would soon become commonplace. He also overlooked the fact that the battle plan had called for McClellan to assault the front of the Rebel lines after the flank attack had begun. Displaying the "hesitancy to throw in his whole force" that became his hallmark, McClellan left Rosecrans to fight alone.

The battle of "Rich Mountain" has been fought and we have won it. We succeeded in cutting a road over the mountain and throwing Genl. Rosecrans with his brigade in rear of the enemy. Genl. R—— stormed their defenses at the summit of the mountain, and carried them with a loss of only 8 men killed and 20 or 30 wounded, while the enemy had at least 60 killed (I saw 56 dead bodies) and 100 to 150 wounded. It was a bloody affair when we consider the number engaged. The main work was in front of Genl. McClellan and we expected to storm it this morning but the rebels ran, leaving all their wounded, Camp Equipage, provisions horses, wagons, swords, cannon &c. It is impossible to conceive of a more complete rout. I got from the tent of their engineer officer a plan of the works which he had left behind in his haste to get away. His hurry was so great, that his supper was left half cooked on the fire. Their stampede was caused by a reconnoissance which I made yesterday evening during the time that Rosecrans was fighting—the object of which was to place a battery so as to enfilade their works. I found the point I wanted, and at once cut a road to it, which was finished about dark. Just before we had completed it they gave us several rounds of grape shot, which rattled all around us but hurt no one. We were completely hidden by the woods and they fired at random. It was to do this work that I was so suddenly ordered to the front, yesterday, and had to stop my letter. The chopping and the falling of the trees alarmed them, and they didn't stop upon the order of their going, but went at once. And who do you think was in command of the rebels?—No one else than Johnny Pegram—late of the U.S. Dragoons. Dr. Archibald Taylor, late of the Army was there & we have him a prisoner. Genl. Garnett is still at Laurel Hill with the main body of the force, and we expect to have another fight when we get there. I rather hope not, for it is dreadful to see the killed and wounded. To see human beings as I saw 28 this morning—thrown into a ditch and covered with earth, only sufficient to enable others to say they *buried* them, is horrible.

CORPORAL JAMES E. HALL

31st Virginia Infantry

Hall's eloquently triumphant description of the July 13 rearguard action and his wildly exaggerated report of the ratio of Yankee to Rebel casualties was written in the context of a sorrowful, plodding Confederate retreat toward Monterey, hampered by rainfall that turned mountain paths into quagmires. When Garnett was shot dead, the Rebel column fled in disorder, leaving behind its supply train.

Next morning we started early, crossing this same stream as many as three times in as many miles. About noon that day we first became aware of the presence of the enemy. They overtook our rear guard at Cheat River. A terrible fire ensued. Our artillery firing into their ranks of four deep, at the distance of 200 yards. The cries of the wounded could be heard, and the flying of their guns into the air when struck by our shells, could be distinctly seen by our men. Nobly did our men repel the advancing foe. Cheat River ran red with their blood as they attempted to charge our columns. After 2 hours of hard

fighting, our forces retired from so unequal a contest, but not until our brave commander Gen. Garnett, had fallen. The enemy then ceased their pursuit. They having lost about 700 men and we only 16.

It is said authentically that the Northern Commander Gen. McClellan shed tears of sympathy over the body of our brave but fallen hero. They having fought together, side by side on the plains of Buena Vista, were reared together, and were warm personal friends until the present war. Truly from the dawn of man's existence he is a creature of change. Mutation is surely a cardinal principle of his being.

After advancing a few miles further we were informed that our retreat would soon be intercepted by forces from West Union. Two pieces of artillery were brought up to the advance. We had no engagement however. It was over two days since we had eaten anything, and had been marching continually through the rain and mud, often crossing streams when three or four would have to lock hand to maintain their equilibrium. We now passed several wagons of ammunition and ordnance, the teams being unable to carry them farther. We also trampled over the finest clothing, linens, stacks of knapsacks and haversacks lying in heaps, together with everything necessary for a well fitted army. That night, I with some others, could proceed no further. We laid down by the side of the road with no protection, but not withstanding we slept soundly, not knowing it had rained upon us till morning when we awoke.

Die Schlacht bei Corricks Ford, West-Virginien, am 14. Juli 1861. Das siebente Indiana-Regiment, Oberst Dumont, watet durch den Cheat River, um einen Bayonett-Angriff auf die feindliche Batterie zu machen.

Sodden Union troops, wearing overcoats discarded by their Confederate foes, struggle across the Cheat River at Corrick's Ford. They were slowed by a drenching rainstorm, rapidly rising water, and desperate Rebel resistance from the 30-foot-high far bank. This small but nasty battle cost the Confederacy some 80 men killed, wounded, or captured, while the Federals reported 53 casualties. Contrary to what is portrayed here and stated in many contemporary images and accounts, Garnett actually suffered his fatal wound at another crossing point on the Cheat.

"The whole campaign has been a grand mistake, bad in its inception, bad in its conduct, really only good in the retreat."

Infantrymen of the 7th Indiana, hidden by the dripping boughs of a sycamore tree, fire a deadly volley at Garnett and an aide, who are inaccurately depicted on foot by the artist. In actuality, the general was mounted, frantically trying to organize a meager delaying action of 10 soldiers when he fell with a bullet in his back. On being assigned to western Virginia, Garnett had prophetically stated, "They have not given me an adequate force. I can do nothing. They have sent me to my death."

PRIVATE HENRY C. WHEELER
7TH INDIANA INFANTRY

A former farmer from Dearborn, Indiana, Wheeler survived two wounds during the war: At Gettysburg, on July 2, 1863, "a minie ball . . . glanc[ed] off . . . his cartridge box," severely bruising him, and he was shot in the ankle while along the North Anna River in May 1864. The intrepid Hoosier mustered out in October 1864 and returned home. In an act of reconciliation, and perhaps personal catharsis, Wheeler sent this letter to a member of the Garnett family in 1903.

My Regt the 7 Ind was the first regt to ford the stream while the conflict still raged & when we reached the opposite shore the road out of the river & up the bank was jamed with disabled traines Wagons Horses & I remember one old antiquated Iron Cannon & Cason so ower Colonel attempted to get his regt. up through the lawrel thicket which grew as thick as hair on the precipitous piece of ground to the right of the road & he got hopelessly entangled & when my co. E, color co. emerged from the river & saw no chance of a forward movement about a dozen of us worked ower way through & past the wagons for about 100 yds & found the road entirely open for travel. firing by this time had entirely ceased & ower little band of not over a dozen men pushed forward for say 1/3 or 1/2 mile when we came to another ford & a portion of the enemy posted behind an old drift on the opisite side of the river Suppose they wer acting as a rear guard (my Brother who was afterwards killed by a sharpshooter at minerun) was first to discover the enemy he being in the lead took to a tree & fired & then their whol party opened on us as we were running single file for the ford my brother called to me to take a tree & fire at the officer & I placed my gun alongside the tree for a sid rest & at the same time shealding my body from the scatering fire that came from the drift just at that moment orderly Sergt R F Burlingame & another party came up & told me to wate & we would give him a voley & he gave the word of command ready aim fire & Garnet fell & there was no more firing from the direction of the drift wood but a general stampead occured & ower little band rushed acrost the river & found the general in the throws of death he was a verry fine looking man of I would Judge 30 years or more he was in the full dress of a brigadier General Regulation Blue I think was the color his opera glass lay by his side I think he had a Gauntlet glove in one hand there was a heavy gold watch chain acrost his brest which was partialy exposed.

COLONEL WILLIAM B. TALIAFERRO
23D VIRGINIA INFANTRY

For the North, the western Virginia campaign had been a grand success—for the South, disaster. The disgusted sentiments Taliaferro expressed in this missive to Confederate congressman James Lyons were widely shared throughout the Confederacy, as the infant nation coped with the loss of prestige, vital territory, some 700 men, and the death of "Poor Garnett."

The whole campaign has been a grand mistake, bad in its inception, bad in its conduct, really only good in the retreat from a position unfortunately taken. Genl Garnett was led into the error of advancing his forces to Laurel Mountain, which with the force he had was utterly untenable (his rear being open to attack and liable to be turned not only at Rich Mountain but at [Roaring Creek] Gap on the other flank.) chiefly I think from what he said to me that he had the full assurance of the government that at least ten thousand native troops would join his standard in a week. In this he was very disappointed only eight men coming into his ranks in ten days. And the small command he had with him, and which had been worked to death almost, in marches, in felling trees for abattis in guard duty, and for any kind of fatigue duty, badly fed, in the eternal rain & cold, racked by sickness (epidemic diseases) under the physical depression produced by a constant anticipation day and night for five days of skirmishing and cannonading found itself menaced by fifteen thousand of the enemy on both flanks and in front.

Of the retreat. The night was pitch dark, the roads as slippery as glass, the rain falling in torrents. The men started without provision except a few crackers in their haversacks to last them two days and to add to the gloom orders were given that perfect silence was to be observed and that not the crack of a whip would be permitted. We marched on in the gloom and silence until sunrise caught us with[in] three miles of Beverly when we were suddenly halted and ordered to march back and file off.

Face to Face at Bull Run

Washington was still busy celebrating McClellan's triumph in western Virginia when on July 16 a new wave of excitement raced through the city. The 35,000-man army that had been gathering in and around Washington for three months was marching at last, heading westward under General Irvin McDowell to attack the main Confederate army, which was guarding the vital Confederate rail crossing at Manassas Junction.

To most Northerners, the success of Federal arms in the impending contest seemed certain. In western Virginia a Union force of 18,000 men under General Robert Patterson had crossed the Potomac at Williamsport, Maryland, to engage the 11,000 Confederate troops in the Shenandoah Valley under General Joseph E. Johnston and keep them from slipping east to reinforce the Confederates at Manassas.

On July 2 Patterson's advance guard, con-

sisting of Colonel John J. Abercrombie's brigade, Wisconsin and Pennsylvania troops, and a small cadre of regulars, collided with Colonel Thomas J. Jackson's Rebel infantry at Hoke's Run, just beyond the village of Falling Waters on the road to Martinsburg. After a sharp exchange of musketry and artillery fire, Jackson broke off the action, following orders to avoid a major engagement if the Federals were in strength. That evening Jackson withdrew past Martinsburg to join Johnston's main force at Darkesville, near Winchester.

On the following day the Federals entered Martinsburg. Patterson's dispatches promised an imminent move against Johnston and assured the Union high command that he had the Rebel force pinned down at Bunker Hill, a few miles north of Winchester.

Thus the Yankee army at Washington, with numbers well in its favor and certain of the justice of its cause, marched confidently out to chastise and vanquish the Rebels around Manassas. Caught up in the martial fervor, crowds of Washingtonians—congressmen, businessmen, merchants and their wives—came jaunting along behind the army, the women armed with picnic baskets, all eager to watch the great show.

General Joseph Johnston exhorts a Georgia color party to stand fast while rallying the scattered survivors of Colonel Francis Bartow's brigade on Henry House Hill. The intervention of Johnston and Beauregard returned parts of several Rebel brigades to the fight.

The army's own progress had something of a picnic atmosphere as well. On the frequent occasions when the long, ill-disciplined columns bunched up on the road and stumbled to a halt, the troops would fall out helter-skelter to loot houses, pick blackberries, or forage for pigs and chickens. It took a full day for the lead brigades to move a mere six miles to the nearby villages of Vienna and Annandale and another day and a half for them to advance less than a dozen miles more past Fairfax to the area of Centreville, the staging point for the planned attack.

The delays gave Beauregard, commanding the Confederates since June, yet more time to get ready. Now certain that McDowell was on the move, he had Richmond order General Johnston to hurry his army eastward from the Shenandoah Valley. If Johnston's four brigades could get to Manassas in time, Beauregard would have about 32,000 men, almost as many as McDowell.

But Johnston was convinced that he faced imminent attack by a vastly larger enemy force, and he sent urgent dispatches to Richmond stating his intention to fight to the last around Winchester. In fact, Johnston's opponent was equally worried. Patterson believed that his 18,000 men faced a Rebel army of more than 26,000. With the enlistments of many of his volunteer regiments about to expire, and plagued by problems with his lines of supply, Patterson grew increasingly reluctant to move forward.

While awaiting the expected arrival of Johnston's troops, Beauregard was also busy deploying his forces. The best defensive line, he had decided, was along the southern bank of Bull Run, which flowed on a roughly northwest-southeast line, cutting between Centreville and Manassas. The stream's brush-cloaked,

five-foot-high banks made for a formidable barrier against enemy attack, and there was only one solid bridge, a stone span carrying the Centreville-Warrenton Turnpike.

Bull Run had numerous other crossing points, however, notably Mitchell's and Blackburn's Fords a few miles downstream from the Stone Bridge. Beauregard had convinced himself that Mitchell's Ford was where McDowell would strike, and he deployed half his army in the area, with two more brigades on the right, still farther south. On his far left, to guard the bridge, Beauregard stationed only a half brigade commanded by a gruff, profane South Carolina West Pointer, Colonel Nathan G. "Shanks" Evans. The fords north of the bridge he left unprotected, dismissing any idea that McDowell might attack there.

But Beauregard's defensive dispositions were not his primary concern. The aggressive-minded general had offensive plans. Once the enemy was engaged with the Confederate forces around Mitchell's Ford, Beauregard would order an attack by his heavily reinforced right flank, across Bull Run into the Federal left and rear. By doing so he could then roll up the Federal line and strike to cut off any reinforcements and line of retreat at Centreville.

Beauregard's defensive line got a first test on July 18 when Union brigadier general Daniel Tyler, reaching Centreville with his division, sent Colonel Israel B. Richardson and parts of his brigade to stage a reconnaissance in force toward Blackburn's Ford. Probing down a slope toward Bull Run, troops of Richardson's lead regiment, the 1st Massachusetts, quickly found themselves dodging bullets from Confederate skirmishers hidden in trees and brush on the stream's north

bank. Advancing farther, the Union troops were caught in a heavy cross fire from more Rebels on the south bank. "We were in the thick of it full fifteen minutes, the balls humming like a bee-hive," noted the 1st Massachusetts commander, Lieutenant Colonel George D. Wells. "I am sure I shall see nothing so close hereafter."

Wells' troops had in fact run into Brigadier General James Longstreet's brigade and its supporting artillery, the Rebel guns soon firing shells hot and fast into the Union line. Despite the heavy fire, General Tyler, who had been instructed by McDowell not to bring on a fight, ordered up the rest of Richardson's brigade along with more Federal cannon, which furiously traded shots with the Confederate gunners. Longstreet responded by sending parts of two Virginia regiments charging across Bull Run, hitting the 1st Massachusetts and 2d Michigan and routing the 12th New York.

Finally, in midafternoon, Tyler decided to disengage—and was angrily reprimanded by McDowell for having provoked the bloody little Battle of Blackburn's Ford. The fracas was nonetheless useful to McDowell. He had in fact initially intended to attack across the downstream fords, just as Beauregard had expected. Now he was sure they were heavily guarded and their approaches too rough for movement by a large army. Some other route would have to be found.

As McDowell pondered a new plan of attack at Manassas, General Johnston in the Shenandoah Valley was coming to the realization that Patterson did not have the will to take the offense against the Confederates. Thus, he was in a position to respond rapidly when, on the morning of July 18, he received an order from Richmond to move east. On the following morning Johnston and his brigades boarded trains for a rendezvous with Beauregard at Manassas.

It took McDowell two days, July 19 and 20, to draw up a new battle plan, but it was a bold one. Two entire divisions led by a pair of grim-faced old West Pointers, Brigadier General David Hunter and Colonel Samuel P. Heintzelman, would head off well to the north, in effect turning their backs on the enemy, and cross Bull Run by way of distant Sudley Ford. Once across, the divisions would wheel to the south and descend on Beauregard's open left flank and rear before he could move troops to meet the threat.

Success depended on speed, and the Federal army lurched into motion promptly at 2:30 a.m. on July 21—only to be slowed to a snail's pace. Tyler's division, ordered to make a diversionary demonstration at the Stone Bridge, took hours to get down the Warrenton Pike, stalling Hunter's and Heintzelman's divisions, which had been placed in line behind it despite their much longer march. When these divisions finally turned north off the pike, they were slowed again by the roads leading to Sudley Ford, which turned out to be barely passable cart paths.

At last, about 9:00 a.m. Colonel Ambrose E. Burnside's brigade, leading Hunter's division, struggled across the ford and started south, followed by the brigade of Colonel Andrew Porter. For all the delays, McDowell still had the jump on Beauregard. Rebel pickets were scarce; the way into the Confederate rear was open.

But not for long. Acting fast when lookouts reported danger on the left, Shanks Evans sent most of his small 1,100-man force speeding north toward a rise called Matthews Hill. There, only a mile south of Sudley Ford, he quickly deployed his troops, six companies

of the 4th South Carolina on the left, Major Roberdeau Wheat's Louisiana battalion of tough New Orleans dockwallopers called the Tigers on the right. Behind the infantry were a pair of cannon.

Once in place, Evans' troops began pouring a furious fire into Burnside's skirmishers.

Then, amazingly, the vastly outnumbered Confederates launched an attack, with Wheat's 500 Tigers ramming head-on into the Union line. Not until Wheat himself was wounded and a third of his men put out of action did the Rebels fall back.

Recovering from the enemy assault, Burn-

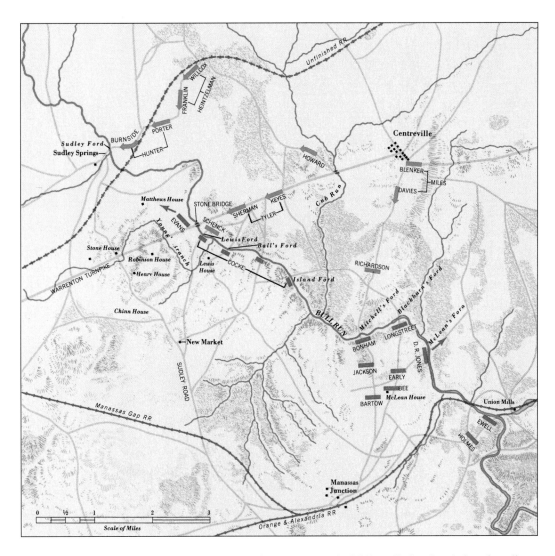

When his probe at Blackburn's Ford was repulsed, Federal commander McDowell abandoned plans for a direct advance on Manassas Junction. Instead he sent two divisions across Bull Run upstream at Sudley Ford to flank the Rebel left while other brigades threatened the Stone Bridge and the fords farther east to create a diversion. Confederate commander Beauregard had only the brigade of Nathan Evans available to meet the threat.

side managed to deploy his and Porter's men in battle lines that, overlapping the Confederate position, threatened to engulf Evans' survivors. But then, about 11:00, reinforcements suddenly arrived—Brigadier General Barnard E. Bee's brigade from Johnston's army followed by the 7th and 8th Georgia under Colonel Francis S. Bartow.

Taking position on Evans' right, the newcomers joined in the firing against Burnside's troops, the battle exploding all across a quarter-mile front. "Seemingly a thousand rifles were flashing and the air was alive with whistling bullets," recalled one of Bartow's Georgians. "It is only surprising that any of us escaped."

Finally Burnside lurched forward again, while Porter, joined by two batteries of Federal guns, managed to deploy on a hill to the west, beyond Evans' left flank. At the same time a brigade from Tyler's division, ordered across a ford just north of the Stone Bridge by an impatient colonel named William Tecumseh Sherman, began moving straight at Bartow's right rear.

Now hammered on all sides, the Confederates were forced to fall back. Evans' men and Bartow's retreated first, followed by Bee's, all scrambling south across the Warrenton Turnpike, then climbing the north slope of a hill named for a dwelling that stood there, Henry house.

Seeing the Rebels in full flight, McDowell rode to the front of the Federal line and shouted, "Victory! Victory! The day is ours!" The outburst would prove a trifle premature. Evans' stand had stalled the Federal advance for more than two hours, and Beauregard was taking advantage of the respite to feverishly shift some of his distant brigades to Henry House Hill to meet the attack. There the fight would take on a violence heretofore unimagined.

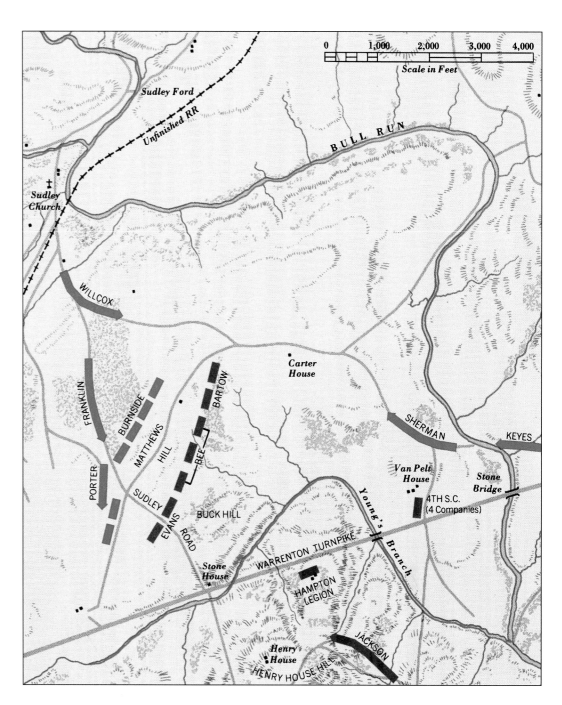

Shortly after the Federals crossed Sudley Ford, Evans deployed his brigade on Matthews Hill to block them. As Federal pressure mounted, Evans was reinforced by the brigades of Bee and Bartow. By late afternoon, with the Federal brigades of Burnside and Porter threatening their left, and those of Sherman and General Erasmus D. Keyes crossing at the Stone Bridge behind them, the Confederates fell back in disorder toward Henry House Hill.

ORDER OF BATTLE

CONFEDERATE FORCES

Johnston

ARMY OF THE POTOMAC

Beauregard 21,800 men

1st Brigade Bonham	2d Brigade Ewell	3d Brigade D. R. Jones	4th Brigade Longstreet
5th Brigade Cocke	6th Brigade Early	7th Brigade Evans	Reserve Brigade Holmes

ARMY OF THE SHENANDOAH

Johnston 9,500 men

1st Brigade Jackson	2d Brigade Bartow	3d Brigade Bee	4th Brigade Kirby Smith

UNION ARMY

McDowell 35,700 men

1st Division Tyler	2d Division Hunter	3d Division Heintzelman	4th Division Runyon	5th Division Miles
Keyes' Brigade	*Porter's Brigade*	*Franklin's Brigade*	*Eight Unbrigaded Regiments*	*Blenker's Brigade*
Schenck's Brigade	*Burnside's Brigade*	*Willcox's Brigade*		*Davies' Brigade*
Sherman's Brigade		*Howard's Brigade*		
Richardson's Brigade				

SERGEANT JAMES B. THOMAS
20TH PENNSYLVANIA INFANTRY

On July 2 Union major general Robert Patterson pushed a brigade across the Potomac River from Maryland into Virginia, entering at Falling Waters. The 27-year-old Thomas was dismayed by the fact his company had to remain behind and guard supply wagons during the ensuing skirmish.

We laid about during the day and at dark wrapped up for short nap. At midnight the order was given but as usual we did not get off untill 9 o.c. and then what do you think, Compy I was detached to guard the train. You had better believe there was some tall growling done and to make it worse just at that moment the reports of cannon & musketry were heard from the Va. side. Our brigade, except Co. I, were ordered off at Hardee time. We pushed up the drivers and reached the fording nearly as soon as they, but on they went while we had to stop.

I have frequently read of and seen pictures of military armies & trains crossing a river and I have now witnessed it and such a scene is well worth a journey to see, especially when the artillery & infantry few in number are fighting with a much superior force within hearing. Our brigade went through the river on double quick, full compy abreast. Sometimes the water was not more than knee deep, again it would reach the arm pits, but they let nothing stop them. Next came the wagons and Compy I. At one time we had 50 wagons in the river at once and the excitement was equal to that of the men crossing. The body guard to each team (3) mounted a horse, the driver used the whip and they done the yelling. Now & then one would stall, then in we would go to push it out, and so it went untill we had the train across, altogether 223 wagons without the ambulances for the sick and wounded which had crossed with the main army which numbers about 20,000 men.

I will give you the particulars of the fight as I received them from several of the Wisconsin boys. Our advance, consisting of one regmt of Wisconsin Infantry, the 11th Penna and 5 compys of Regulars (cavalry), the First City Troop & McMullins Rangers, commenced crossing at midnight but the night being very dark it was near daylight before they all reached the opposite shore. They marched ahead supported by 4 peices of Perkins Flying Battery. They discovered nothing untill winding around the hill upon which the village of Falling Waters is built, where 3 horsemen made their appearance and, after takeing a survey of the force, galloped up the road. General Abercombie, in command of the Wisconsin regmt supposeing they were only the advance pickets, paid but little attention to them, but before proceeding a mile near a town called Hainsville they were suddenly surprised at receiveing a volley from behind a house & barn, one on each side of the road

Captain Robert S. Foster of the 11th Indiana Zouaves leans against the pole of his tent and relaxes with comrades while on picket duty in western Virginia. Though Foster resigned on July 3, 1861, many members of this regiment, including its colonel, Lew Wallace, reenlisted for three years and saw hard fighting at the Battle of Shiloh.

Frenetic activity animates the Baltimore & Ohio Railroad's Martinsburg, Virginia, yard in this Alfred Wordsworth Thompson sketch as excited Rebels cheer and proudly wave a Stars and Bars flag while boarding cars bound for Harpers Ferry. Nearby an artillery driver smartly applies his whip to maintain the pace of his galloping team. Harpers Ferry had been abandoned by the Yankees on April 18, and when the Confederates occupied the town the next day they were able to salvage valuable arms-making equipment for their cause. The Union high command hoped that Patterson's movement across the Potomac would force the Rebels to abandon the town.

which was very narrow at this point. He immediately ordered a halt and placed his right wing in battle order. There not being room enough for the left to take part, the 11th Penna was then ordered to go through the fields and attack them in the rear while the cavalry did execution at every available point. The Wisconsin boys did not fire a shot untill the 11th had started for their rear, then the order was "give it to them boys," and they did, it doing fearful execution among them. There still was a regmt behind & in the barn which could not be reached untill the artillery sent several balls into it setting it a fire. When that was done, the enemy fled in every direction leaveing 3 dead on the field & 11 wounded. They made another stand about one mile further on but the 23rd, haveing come up to the assistance of the Wisconsin & 11th, they were again routed and chased 3 miles leaveing behind knapsacks, haversacks, canteens, blankets, revolvers, knives, &c, which were picked up and what was worth carrying was taken care of by the boys. But there is one thing certain, if they can't fight they can *run*.

Sergeant Warren M. Graham, of Company B, 1st Wisconsin Infantry, was wearing this frock coat when he was killed by a bullet piercing his left lung during the action at Falling Waters. Graham was the first soldier from the Badger State to fall in battle during the war. Many local militia units outfitted their troops in gray, the traditional uniform color of U.S. militia.

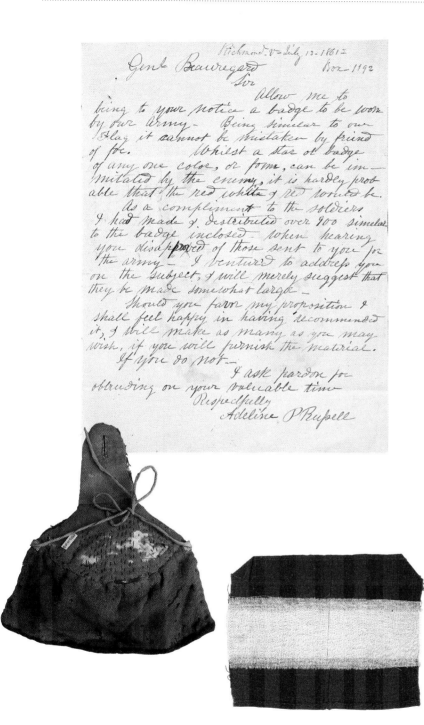

PRIVATE GILBERT D. WILKINSON

4TH ALABAMA INFANTRY, BEE'S BRIGADE

Although Wilkinson did not have the opportunity to come to grips with the Union force commanded by Patterson, his regiment did fight at First Manassas. There the Alabamian fell when a bullet ripped through his hips. Wilkinson survived, but his left leg healed three inches shorter than his right, disabling him and requiring him to wear special shoes to walk normally.

Because Rebel uniforms also came in many hues, the Confederacy tried several different types of identifying "badges." General Beauregard received this note from a Mrs. Adeline P. Russell touting collar badges she had designed (above, right). Also shown is a two-color, reversible epaulet-style "wing badge."

Teusday the 2d July 1861 This day at one o clock precisely we received orders to be ready to march in ten minutes time. Gen Johnston having received a dispatch from Col. Jackson that his command was then ingaged in furious combat with the enemy in overwhelming odds under the command of General Patterson at Martinsburg some 22 miles distant from this place. Col. Jackson's command is the advance guard of the army of the Shenandoah. At the tap of the drum our regiment fell into line and amidst the most vociferous cheering rapidly took up the line of march followed by the other regiments of our brigade & also two others in all about eight thousand strong, we left our tents standing taking nothing but our knapsacks and guns, reached the little town of Bunkers Hill at dark camped and some of our companies got their suppers whilst others having no cooking utensils lay down on the hard ground to seek rest and repose, probably the last this side of the cold grave. The clouds looked lowering but luckily we were spared this the most unpleasant mishap of a soldier's career a cold rain at night without tents. Gradually towards ten the clouds cleared away and full in the North a blazing comet met our gaze, it was truly sublime. Its tail almost spanned the heavens its head in the direction we are marching. What this may portend I cannot tell if anything at all probably some heavenly visitant sent to mark the fratricidal strife now forced upon us. It is said that a comet appeared in the time of the great

Napolean at three of the most interesting periods of his eventful career, The rise, the zenith of his fame, and his fall.

July 3d 1861 precisely at three o clock our troops were wakened at the tap of the drum and immediately and in good order fell into line of march. noiselessly and rapidly we moved onward untill we reached the little town of Darksville to which the Virginia regiments had fallen back to after the fight. We reached this place just as the first gray streaks of dawn were gilding the east and at once prepared for refreshing the inner man, some went to cooking, some strayed off to the village to hunt something to eat whilst others too tired for either streched their wearied limbs beneath the shade of the tall trees which grow around. Here another one of those painful episodes in the careless handling of firearms occurred. A soldier, a fine young in the prime of manhood lay reclining in profound sleep upon the ground, a companion of his more wakeful was sitting beside him arranging his pistols after reloading them, through some mishap the pistol exploded the ball taking effect in his sleeping friend's back severing the spinal column producing a frightful if not mortal wound. What must have been the feelings of him who unintentionaly had ruined if not killed his best friend, I will not attempt to describe them. After breakfast and a careful reconnaisance Gen. Johnston moved his columns forward and took up his position in battle array one mile beyond this town fully expecting that Gen Patterson the commander of the Lincoln forces now reinforced to 20 thousand strong would immediately attack us. Our position is a splendid one and well chosen. The ground had a gentle rise commanding the country for a mile or so whilst a line of stone fence ran completely across our position with here and there a grove of tall timber with heavy under growth a splendid place for positioning sharp shooters and skirmishers a branch of war in which our troops far excel the Yankees the regiment to which I belong had for their position the center of the field protected by a strong stone wall with a beautiful grove in rear where in to camp or fall back upon, here we found many springs of excellent water a thing appreciated by our soldiers after their furious marching through the heat and dust. Our men stacked their arms in front of their position and took to the shade prepared to fall in whenever the enemy should make their appearance once which he declined to do and again this night we lay down to rest quietly again.

BRIGADIER GENERAL PIERRE G. T. BEAUREGARD

COMMANDER, ARMY OF THE POTOMAC

Described as being "jaunty in gait and dashing in manner," Beauregard loved the trappings of military life and high command, but he had little respect for his Northern foes, whom he considered an "armed rabble." This fact is reflected in the wildly unrealistic optimism of this note he wrote to General Joseph Johnston.

Manassas Junction, Va.
July 13th 1861
Dear General,

I write in haste. What a pity we cannot carry into effect the following plan of operations! That you should leave four or five thousand men to guard the passes of the Blue Ridge, and unite the mass of your troops with mine; we will probably have in a few days about forty thousand men to operate with. This number would enable us to destroy the forces of Genls Scott and McDowell in my front; then we could go back with as many men as necessary to attack and disperse General Patterson's Army before he could know positively what had become of you; we could then proceed to General McClelland's theatre of war, and treat him likewise; after which we could pass over into Maryland, to operate in the war of Washington. I think this whole campaign could be completed brilliantly in from fifteen to twenty five days. Oh! that we had but one good head to conduct all our operations; we are laboring unfortunately under the disadvantage of having about seven Armies in the field under as many independent Commanders, which is contrary to the first principles of the Art of War.

Wishing you, however, ample success in your operations, I remain
Yours Very Truly
G. T. Beauregard

"Huge pillars of smoke at times showed the Virginians that the invaders had wantonly commenced burning country houses—the first sign of hostilities."

PRIVATE FREDERICK S. DANIEL
RICHMOND HOWITZERS, BONHAM'S BRIGADE

Since late June the Richmond Howitzers had been comfortably quartered at Fairfax Court House. This idyll ended when more than 30,000 Federal troops finally moved westward on the roads that led toward Centreville, Manassas, and Bull Run. The presence of the enemy in such numbers signaled to Daniel and his comrades the end to what had until then been a "shadow war."

The glittering bayonets of the winding columns and the white-topped wagons in the early morning sunshine could be distinctly and closely seen right across the field where the Howitzers had put up their earthworks, and where they at once took position, without breakfast for the first time in their warlike life, ready to open fire at command. On came the enemy's columns, without opening fire and leisurely, as if they intended to go on to Richmond without so much as noticing the presence of the "rebels," squatted by the wayside, and who, from the very outset of the long campaigning, were standing strictly on the defensive, with fire reserved against attack. After a brief spell of hurry-skurry in getting ready for a dignified departure, the battery and supporting brigade headed back towards Centreville and Bull Run, the enemy marching quietly in the rear, though huge pillars of smoke at times showed the Virginians that the invaders had wantonly commenced burning country houses—the first sign of hostilities. The roads were dusty and hot and the battery slowly made its way back, stopping for drinks at the roadside wells, for feeding and resting the horses and men; the march was continued during the night, under strict orders not to light a pipe, not to strike a match, or speak above whispers, as a concealment against any spies that might be lurking in the forest on either side of the way.

The pastoral setting of Wilmer McLean's farm, near Bull Run, was forever changed when Beauregard chose this location for his headquarters. During the skirmish at Blackburn's Ford, Federal artillery shells bounded across the yard, and one shot smashed through McLean's kitchen. McLean soon moved to be out of the path of war. His new residence was in a sleepy, southwestern Virginia town—Appomattox Court House.

PRIVATE MARTIN A. HAYNES
2D NEW HAMPSHIRE INFANTRY, BURNSIDE'S BRIGADE

A resident of Portsmouth, Haynes was 19 years old when he enlisted for a three-year term on May 9, 1861. He remained a private throughout his service, though he did become the regiment's postmaster in March 1864. In 1865 Haynes wrote the unit's regimental history, from which the account below, describing the Federal advance toward Beauregard's line, is extracted.

Our camp that night was at Bailey's Cross Roads, and the march was resumed early the next morning. Evidences of the recent occupation of the country by the rebels soon began to appear, for at various points the road had been obstructed by felled trees, the removal of which cost the pioneers much hard labor. At about eleven o'clock in the forenoon the word was passed down the line that the advance had come upon a rebel earthwork, and that the chances for a fight were promising. The column was halted and formed in sections. For a minute, the ring of rammers driving home the charges in thousands of guns was heard, and then the column pressed rapidly on. We soon came in sight of the work, a heavy battery of sandbags, but it was deserted. No cannon belched defiance from its embrasures, no bristling line of rifles rattled death into the advancing column. All was quiet as the grave, until we entered the deserted work, when shout after shout arose over our "bloodless victory." Immediately to the rear was a camp of bough huts, which had been deserted in such haste that many valuable articles were left scattered around. About a mile beyond was the little village of Fairfax Court House, which we entered as was becoming great conquerors, with flaunting banners and serried columns, while the bands played patriotic airs for the edification of the few secesh who remained. The brigade marched into the village green and stacked their arms, while the flag of the Second was flung out from the most conspicuous point in the vicinity—the cupola of the Court House. No sooner were the ranks broken than the entire brigade resolved itself into an army of foragers. The deserted rebel camps in the vicinity were thoroughly ransacked for hard-tack, bacon, &c.; the squeals and shrieks of suffering porkers filled the air, and little clouds of smoke in various quarters indicated where hives of bees were suffering "martyrdom at the stake," their stores of sweets proving their ruin. But sometimes the bees had their minute of revenge, for we saw more than one fellow with honey dripping from his hands, making across the fields with strides more vigorous than elegant, and leaping five-rail fences with

apparently no more trouble than if they had been so many straws, followed by clouds of the vicious little insects, who not being thoroughly smothered, had revived and attacked their enemy with a vigor which admitted of nothing but an inglorious retreat.

Not the least interesting of the captures was a rebel mail bag. The contents were most decidedly Southern, the letters being filled with those inordinate boastings and conceits with which the rebels plumed themselvs until Yankee steel had taught them to respect Yankee valor. The recent dashing charges which Lieut. TOMPKINS and his dragoons had made into the village, over and through their whole force, was often spoken of, and they always found much consolation in the idea that their thousands gave the few Yankee squadrons "as much as they could handle." Well, those were days when each party misjudged the other: while they looked upon us as arrant cowards, we were equally confident that the campaign which we had inaugurated was to end in the defeat of the rebel armies, the capture of Richmond, and the complete overthrow of the Confederate Government.

LIEUTENANT PETER C. HAINS
BATTERY E, 2D U.S. ARTILLERY, SCHENCK'S BRIGADE

Hains' boyish features belie his martial pose in this graduation photo from the West Point class of 1861. Nor was his 30-pounder Parrott rifle all it seemed. Aside from signaling the Union advance, the gun saw little action. The largest piece of ordnance on the field, it was designed as a siege weapon.

I well remember how the men loved that huge gun. It was amazing. The piece weighed six thousand pounds; a huge casting reënforced by a breech band to stand the strain of the discharge. The shot was more than four inches in diameter and over a foot in length, weighing about thirty-three pounds. Upon the rear of the projectile was shrunk a soft metal band with a hollow opening about a sixteenth of an inch wide all round the base. The gas from the discharge was expected to fill this opening and swell the band to make it take the rifling of the gun. It generally did so, and when one remembers the crudeness of artillery at that time it is wonderful how accurately we could shoot with such a gun at a range of a mile or more. The men had great confidence in it. I have seen them come to it and pat its breech affectionately. "Good old boy, you'll make 'em sit up—just wait a bit," they would say. They had an idea that that great gun would win the cause of the Union. And how they would struggle with it on the hard places! It was all very human, very touching, and after all these years the memory of it almost brings tears.

We sallied forth. The roads promised much, and at first the gun behaved very well indeed. But we soon came to a hill. The ten horses threw themselves into their collars. The gun started up a bit, then the pace slowed, paused, and—then the giant gun began slowly to drift backward down the grade. We quickly blocked the wheels, as there were no brakes. I rode up and down the line of march.

"Get out the prolonges," I ordered, and these lines of about three-inch rope and knotted together to about a hundred feet in length, were quickly hooked to the axle of the gun. Two hundred men instantly trailed onto them. With wild yells and cheers they started that gun forward, the ten horses and two hundred men soon dragging it upward to the crest. It was great. And most of us were very young indeed.

But arriving upon the crest of the hill was not the climax at all. There was the other side of the question—to go down that hill. Without resting, away they went. At first the gun followed gently. Then it began to gain headway. After a hundred feet it began to push my good wheelers a bit, and they crowded upon the forward horses. Six thousand pounds on wheels had started down the grade. Away the line went, and before they arrived at the foot the wheel-horses were galloping frantically for their very lives, with that monstrous engine of destruction thundering after them with a rumbling roar and a cloud of dust. But no one even grinned. It was as it should be, and my gallant team kept up the desperate pace until the leveling roadway slowed down the wild chase. Covered with dust and foam, the horses recovered themselves a mile farther on, while the two hundred men, myself among them, came panting in the rear.

CAPTAIN FRANCIS F. MEAGHER

69TH NEW YORK INFANTRY, SHERMAN'S BRIGADE

At the war's outbreak, Meagher, a colorful Irish revolutionary living in America after he had been banished from his homeland, recruited a company of soldiers from New York City's large Irish population that was incorporated into the 69th. The regiment later became part of the famed "Irish Brigade," under the command of Meagher, then a brigadier general.

I have already spoken of this village as a dingy, aged, miserable little handful of houses. It is the coldest picture conceivable of municipal smallness and decripitude. Set down on certain military maps in flaming capitals as CENTREVILLE, one is astounded on entering it, to find that a mole hill has been magnified into a mountain. Southerners may sneer at New England—toss off their inspiring cocktails, and contemptuously air the tips of their sensitive noses as they give vent to their disdain, repudiation, and defiance of the North—I wager there is not a village of shabbier aspect and such reduced resources, as that of Centreville. It looks, for all the world, as though it had done its business, whatever it was, if it ever had any, full eight years ago, and since then had bolted its doors, put out its fires and gone to sleep. . . . Most of the houses in Centreville are built with stone—rugged, grayish, gloomily speckled and mottled stone—and you follow them up and down two or three little hills and hollows, over a road or through a street which has ruts and rocks, boulders and pit-falls in it, enough to shake the shoes from off a thousand horses, and more than enough to rattle to pieces and disable a thousand waggons. Some of these houses retreat a little from the road or street, behind a dingy fence and two or three leafless and colorless and dwarfed old trees. Others break in with an uncouth and bold protuberance upon the road or street; and thus with a violent intrusion destroy the symetrical effect of their more modest sisterhood.

"It is the coldest picture conceivable of municipal smallness and decripitude."

The dusty hamlet of Centreville stands bleakly before the camera's lens under a harsh, cloudless sky in this wartime photograph. Small, agriculturally based towns like this were common in the South, and many were devastated by the conflict. The repeated movements of both armies through such places, even when they did not become scenes of actual combat, could quickly deplete and destroy the lifetime efforts of the local farmers and merchants and their families.

PRIVATE ALEXANDER HUNTER
17TH VIRGINIA INFANTRY, LONGSTREET'S BRIGADE

Only 17 years old when he enlisted, Hunter came through the fray at Blackburn's Ford unscathed, although he found later battles much more eventful for himself. By war's end Hunter, who eventually transferred to the 4th Virginia Cavalry, had been captured three times and wounded at Todd's Tavern in 1864.

Eleven Oclock came, and the men were scattered into an irregular line, some sleeping, and others engaged in their various diversions. Our scouts detailed from the Company, had first returned from a scary reconnoisance and reported everything quiet, and nothing was heard but the drowsy hum of the big blue bottles, and the cawing of the crows, who sailed lazily in circles high in the bright clouds. I recollect that I was leaning against a tree, my musket between my knees, wondering if war was really so terrible as represented, and looking around at my various comrades in arms, most of them boys, not out of their teens, and wondering too whether such boys were fitted to engage in grim visiged war, and whether all of us youngsters would not incontinintly take to our heels at the first volley in spite of ourselves. Most of them seemed much more in their element in a large school ground; playing bundy at foot ball. I had yet to learn that mere boys could do more fighting, and go through more hardships with less grumbling than any of their older companions. I had just put out my pipe and had lain down intending to try and go to sleep, when suddenly bang, bang two guns went off on the opposite side, and our two pickets (Col Terry & another Texan) rushed for our side of the river, immediately every man was on his feet gun in hand and the order Fall in right dress was rapidly given as the men were forming, all in disorder, a stunning and rattling volley beginning far below us, and running above us came from the opposite bank and the running flash of the guns showed at once that we were attached in force, and with a suddeness that showed that they were bent on a storming, the deadly hiss of the minie was now heard by us for the first time, as they went hurtling over us fortunately too high, cutting of twigs from the trees, which whin sh-sh, sh, bang-bang, the shells came right and left over our heads they burst sending a shower of sticks and branches down on us, it was useless to attempt any order now, every man acted for themselves, most stood and gallantly delivered their fire in return, though we couldnt see a thing, but away we fired as fast as we could load, blazing away in every direction. Others ran at the first fire to the edge of the timbers and got behind the trees fired at the gun that was now in the meridian in a most valorous manner, the firing from the opposite bank, close pistol range increased in intensity. It was no longer volleys battling up and down the bank but a roar, not a dull sound, but precisely like the cracklin of the woods, when a forest was on fire, and every now and then a cheer

During the artillery duel at Blackburn's Ford, a ball from a Federal 20-pounder shell wedged itself just above the sole of this brogan worn by Private George H. Lyles, a comrade of Hunter's in the 17th Virginia, leaving him unhurt. Ironically, the lucky Virginian practiced the vocation of shoemaking both before and after the conflict.

would run along their lines. The shells came whiring among the trees, bursting with a loud report that added to terrors at the scene, and men began to fall every second, some dead, others choking as the cruel ball would tear through them. Our front line fighting without order was borne back to the edge of the trees, some twenty yards from the run. Some of the men were running in every direction, Officers urging them on, the cries of the wounded men, with the shrill whing of the bullet, and the thud of the ball as it hit the trunk of the trees, the shrieking sound of the shrapnell shot, and the wild yells of the enemy increased the uproar and everything seemed going against us.

The Washington Artillery fired many projectiles like this one, known as Archer bolts, at Blackburn's Ford. They were widely considered to be "utterly useless," as they tumbled and whirled when fired and had "neither range nor accuracy."

PRIVATE HENRY H. BAKER
WASHINGTON ARTILLERY OF NEW ORLEANS, LONGSTREET'S BRIGADE

Although many in Baker's unit were from prominent families, he had worked as a clerk before the war. At Blackburn's Ford, several guns of his battery returned fire against their blue-clad counterparts. While Baker was rushing ammunition to his gun, a shell fragment smashed into his leg, crumpling him to the ground. The injury was sufficient to keep him out of the ranks until the following March.

Our commissary wagon had gone astray and I was hungry and fatigued, but nevertheless I slept the sleep of the blessed. Just before the break of day I was disturbed by some one shaking me to wake me up. I was startled for an instant, but I saw my captain, who had come to keep his promise. "Now, Baker," he said "if you are in earnest you have the opportunity this morning. Get up and go over to the First Company and ask for Sergeant Payne. I have arranged with him to take you with his detachment." The First Company was to engage the enemy at Blackburn's Ford. I was soon with Sergeant Payne and the company was off in a jiffy to meet the enemy. We halted for a few minutes on the roadside, and as we were without rations, we filled our caps with blackberries, which grew in great profusion. Our battery had not long to tarry, however, for a courier dashed up and ordered the guns forward at a gallop. Cannons were booming from the opposite side of Blackburn's Ford, warning us "to be quick," for there was serious work for us to do there. Excited horses with wagonloads of supplies were dashing pell-mell over the fields, ambulances scurrying hither and thither, picking up the wounded. All the animated confusion, and the dead lying on the roadside as we passed to the front, presented a very exciting and harrowing scene, particularly to the mind of a young and inexperienced boy like myself. Just across the field, well up in the front, stood General Beauregard, holding a small riding whip, switching his trousers, as unconcerned as if he were merely a looker-on, when in reality he was directing the placing of the troops. Our battery was halted for an instant behind a neck of woods, so that we might select a commanding position; then we unlimbered and the battle commenced in earnest. The enemy having gotten our range, we were literally pelted with shot and shell. We hastened to advance our position, so as to get out of their range, and while their shot screeched over our heads our guns were having telling effect and doing great execution. I was acting as a supernumerary on Sergeant Payne's detachment, and my duty was to carry ammunition from the caisson to the guns. George Muse, whom I was assisting, would dive down in the caisson chest and hand me the cartridge. Taking it quickly, I would dash up to the front with it. On one of these trips I missed Muse. I looked around and saw him lying on his back with a crucifix to his lips and the blood gushing from his shoulder. I quickly bent over him and asked him what had happened. He replied, "Baker, I am done for; I am going to die." I tried to assure him that he would be all right soon, and binding a handkerchief about the wound to try to stop the flow of blood, I left him to resume the carrying of cartridges alone. Poor Muse died that night. In one of these runs I was suddenly brought to a halt by a stinging lick, which carried me to the ground. I was lifted by two infantrymen, and little dreaming that I had been seriously wounded, I waved my hand to the boys and assured them that I would be back in a minute.

Though attired in a new uniform in this early war photo, Brigadier General James Longstreet wore mufti on July 18. Longstreet handled his brigade well, rebuffing several Yankee attacks, and inspired his raw soldiers with his bravery. An aide recalled that the general rode "amid a perfect shower of balls, . . . with his cigar in his mouth, rallying . . . [and] encouraging" his troops.

ADAMS S. HILL
REPORTER, NEW YORK TRIBUNE

A native of Boston and a graduate of Harvard University, Hill accompanied the 1st Massachusetts during its initial campaign. As the Bay Staters cautiously approached the banks of Bull Run, Hill watched from a nearby prominence, waiting hopefully for a quick Union victory. Instead, the reporter saw the sad spectacle of green troops blundering about in the heavy woods that lined the stream. William H. B. Smith was the "second lieutenant" whose death Hill describes below.

While they worked forward, the 1st Massachusetts regiment, which led the line, was sent down into the valley, and formed close to the thickets. The 2d and 3d Michigan regiments followed them, but were almost immediately afterward sent over to a distant field on the right, from which they were never called excepting to retire. Before these troops were fully formed, a series of tremendous musketry or rifle volleys was heard among the trees. These were directed against the skirmishers, who had encountered a large body at the skirt of the woods. From this time little attention was given to the right of the road, where the Michigan men were stationed, the left being the region of the conflict. For a time the skirmishers received the entire attention of the enemy; but a few minutes after their disappearance the right company of the Massachusetts regiment was instructed to occupy the house and barn before mentioned as having been held by the rebels. They reached it under a sharp and regular fire, found that it was now vacant, and so reported. They were immediately afterward ordered to enter the wood as skirmishers—a duty which cost them their second lieutenant and several men. The circumstances of the lieutenant's death were peculiar. He first discovered the enemy, but doubting, from their gray uniforms, that they were hostile, he ran forward, shouting, "Who are you?" The answer came, "Who are you?" to which he answered, "Massachusetts men." The enemy then cheered violently, and sent a volley, by which the lieutenant was killed.

A West Point graduate from Connecticut, Daniel Tyler had long since resigned from the Regular Army and was the successful president of Georgia's Macon & Western Railroad before the shelling of Fort Sumter caused him to rejoin the National forces. Tyler, commissioned a brigadier general, drew censure from Irvin McDowell for exceeding his orders at Blackburn's Ford and bringing on an engagement that cost the Union 83 casualties.

"Colonel Richardson's remarks to the Major, when he discovered our position, and proceeded to unravel us, were not of a character to be repeated, even at this late date."

ASSISTANT SURGEON HENRY F. LYSTER
2D MICHIGAN INFANTRY, RICHARDSON'S BRIGADE

Posted in reserve during the engagement, the 2d suffered few casualties but did bear witness to Colonel Israel Richardson's harsh manner of exhorting and organizing his brigade. Lyster's perceptive grasp of soldier psychology proved a boon to the wounded lieutenant. The surgeon served until his enlistment ran out in 1863, despite bouts of typhoid fever that frequently sent him to the hospital.

The bellicose personality that earned Israel Richardson the nickname Fighting Dick is apparent in this photograph taken after the battle. At times, Richardson's mettle could approach the irrational. At Blackburn's Ford, he wanted to lead a final bayonet charge to "clean out" the Rebel forces. Tyler, though, wisely denied this request. Later promoted to major general, Richardson suffered a fatal wound at Antietam.

Colonel Richardson shortly after came over from the front, and in a scornful sort of manner, suggested to the regiment, that we had better be getting back or the enemy's cavalry would cut us off. Upon this we moved back into the woods. Loss in the 3d Brigade, 19 killed; 38 wounded; 26 missing. Rebel loss, 15 killed; 53 wounded. It was upon this occasion that Major Williams, after having moved the regiment well into the woods, formed them into a hollow square to resist an expected charge of cavalry. How well I can remember the beautiful appearance the regiment presented in the timber, with fixed bayonets. In the movement I was left on the outside, and tried in vain, to get into the place where the Adjutant and Major seemed so safely protected. Colonel Richardson's remarks to the Major, when he discovered our position, and proceeded to unravel us, were not of a character to be repeated, even at this late date.

It was on our way in from the place where Wollenweber had been wounded, and at the edge of the woods, that I found one of our lieutenants lying at the foot of a large oak tree, quite white and limp. He had been in the Mexican war and we regarded him as an experienced soldier. I stopped an army wagon and tried to load him in, supposing he had been taken seriously ill. Colonel Richardson, who seemed to be ubiquitous, ordered him out, and spoke very harshly to him, and took quite an unprofessional view of the case. After the Colonel had gone on, I ordered the Lieutenant loaded in again, and as the last order is usually the one obeyed, we carried him back in safety.

"As the men were so intensely anxious to meet the enemy, they preferred going on at the earliest possible moment."

FLORENCE
RESIDENT OF MANASSAS

For the civilians of the region, the approach of so many Federal troops meant that the patriotic fervor and righteous outrage in which many had indulged would give way to the uncertainties of genuine war. Groveton, just west of the intersection of the Warrenton Turnpike and the Manassas–Sudley road, was thrown into panic by the cannonading of July 18. The boom of guns was an alien sound to ears accustomed to the noises of meadow and barnyard.

All day the 18th the distant roar of cannon saluted our ears, but so secure did we feel that in the evening I determined to ride over to Groveton to see if I could hear anything reliable from the scene of conflict. My horse was at the door, and I lingering, whip in hand, to exchange a few last words with Aunt Lizzie, when the door was burst open by an old negro woman from an adjoining plantation, her dark face ashy and her gray hair seeming actually to stand on end from the excess of terror. "Oh! Miss Lizabeth," she exclaimed, as soon as her eyes fell upon my aunt, "run for your lives—de Yankees is right up here in de big woods back of our place. Mars Jeemes seed em hisself and sent me to tell you dey was comin! Then ensued a scene that beggars description. Aunt Anne flew into her room and slammed the door, Uncle William started running to the stables, Aunt Lizzie burst into tears, and the children screamed in concert.

As soon as I could disencumber myself of my hat and riding-skirt I ran out to find Aunt Lizzie, who had disappeared. When I reached the porch, alarmed as I was I could not help laughing as I recognised her tall form almost flying over the high weeds in an adjacent field to secrete a tin box containing her valuable papers in a stone pile.

SERGEANT MAJOR ROBERT T. COLES
4TH ALABAMA INFANTRY, BEE'S BRIGADE

Coles left his class at Alabama's Old LaGrange Military Academy to enlist in the 4th and was appointed sergeant major of the regiment on May 1. The Huntsville native was promoted to adjutant of the hard-fighting unit in 1862 and served until the regiment surrendered with Robert E. Lee at Appomattox.

The regiment moved out from camp in light marching order on the evening of the 18th. Every one was in a jolly mood, in anticipation of meeting the enemy, until the town was reached and the head of the column turned in the opposite direction from the enemy. The street, as the regiment passed down it at a long swinging gait, was thronged with ladies, old men and children wringing their hands and crying out in distress: "Oh, you will certainly not leave us to the mercy of the Yankees." It was whispered among the men that the move resembled very much a retreat. Both the citizens and the troops became very much depressed as it appeared that General Johnston purported evacuating Winchester and retreating from in front of General Patterson. . . .

After getting a few hours rest, the march was resumed before daylight, and we soon reached the Shenandoah, which was fordable. Had we been veterans, no time would have been lost in wading the stream, but at least five hours of valuable time was lost before the brigade reached the opposite bank.

To have a column of infantry blocked, moving up a few feet at a time for hours, as all soldiers know, is the most trying and disagreeable position in which an already exhausted soldier can be placed. From the Shenandoah we hurriedly marched through Ashby's Gap across the Blue Ridge Mountains to Piedmont, a station on the Manassas Gap Railway, reaching there about an hour after dark. As this was our first long march and a forced one, the men were very much exhausted.

While awaiting cars to transport us to Manassas, the men procured a few hours sleep in the rain. Having consumed their two days rations issued before leaving Winchester, it was discretionary with the regiment whether we would proceed that night or wait until the next morning for rations. As the men were so intensely anxious to meet the enemy, they preferred going on at the earliest possible moment; the 4th Alabama, two companies of the 11th and the 2nd Mississippi (Generals Johnston and Bee accompanying us) reached the Junction about noon on the 20th.

General Joseph Johnston (above), concerned about the forces of General Robert Patterson in the Shenandoah, found that the Yankee commander had no will to engage him. Johnston was able to rush his army to Manassas, making what was called "the first use of a railroad to achieve strategic mobility."

PRIVATE GEORGE S. BARNSLEY
8TH GEORGIA INFANTRY, BARTOW'S BRIGADE

The urgency of moving Johnston's forces from the Shenandoah to reinforce Beauregard at Manassas necessitated a pace that exhausted the new soldiers of the Confederacy. Soon Barnsley and his fellow Georgians would become accustomed to the rigors of hard marching on low rations—and learn to take their rest well away from dangerous roadways. Assigned to be a hospital steward in 1862, Barnsley was eventually transferred to Richmond, serving in the medical department there. His efforts earned him a promotion to assistant surgeon in March 1865.

All of a sudden we were hurried off from the Valley to Manassas Junction. The hurry was so pressing that we broke camp, without cooking any food, or necessary rations. Then the serious business and affairs arose—We broke camp without dinner, although it was ready, and marched steadily in the dust along a long narrow country road; at dark we came to a river, which had to be forded, and as it was warm, we were wet with perspiration—In Co A of the 8th Ga, which was at the head of the Brigade, my place was in the fourth file in the front marching four abreast. When we reached the river there was great procession behind; some troops had already crossed. Those in front of me refused or hesitated to enter into the water, so I put some sugar in a handerchief and my gold watch on the point of my bayonet and plunged in. The water was cold, the river quite wide, up to my armpits. I could see by the ripples in the water where the ford lay, and there were pine torches on the other side. I got through all, only once or twice slipping. Then the Regmt followed, but as many men did like to take to the water it took quite a time to get across. During this time our officers did not have the practical sense to have stacked arms so that we could wring out some of our clothing, but kept us on parade—how I shivered! In a hour or more we were hurried along the road. There was a steep bluff to get up—Blue Blazes! how I suffered! Then farther on we formed along the side of the road—I was so cold, so stiff, so prostrated that when we stacked arms, I dropped by the side of my stack in the dust. I must have slept several hours. What awoke me was the wheel of an artillery wagon, driven by a careless soldier, which scraped my . . . head. This was a close shave. Then more miles of marching, and fortunately I perspired, in a hurry to catch a train at a station of a railroad. Here some rations were issued of fat bacon and flour. We had to collect sticks to make fires, and then try to cook the flour mixed with water to a paste frying in bacon grease. Some fellows seemed apt and got a crust on the dough poured into the pan. I could not get hold of the frying pan until late and the "thing" I tried to cook would not go down to my stomach—and I really thought . . . an ostrich might have called for help to swallow. So Lucien and I had nothing to eat, except some sugar and pieces of raw flesh of a small piece of bacon which Lucien had got hold of. As the train stopped a few minutes at a station a kind woman gave me a drink of clabber.

CAPTAIN ROBERT GRANT
8TH GEORGIA INFANTRY, BARTOW'S BRIGADE

Although Grant had enlisted as a private on May 21, he had been promoted to acting assistant adjutant general by the time of Manassas, functioning as a private secretary to Colonel Francis S. Bartow. Grant wrote his mother on July 24, telling her of his adventures and thanking "Almighty God for his watchful care and providence" in seeing him through the battle. In the excerpt below he recounts his brigade's march to reach the eastbound train at Piedmont Station.

During the eight-hour trip to Manassas Junction, the overloaded trains had to stop often for fuel and water. This sketch shows a typical scene en route, a young lady bidding farewell to her beau as an older woman looks on sadly. The locomotive's whistle would soon part their clutched hands, and the train would continue on its way with its cargo of soldiers toward the rolling plains of Manassas.

About 11 o'clock at night our regiment reached the river, we being the advance of our brigade. Gaining the brink, the order was given to prepare for fording, in other words shuck, take your clothes off and go it au naturel. "What a" picture "was there, my countrymen," as company after company struck the cold, icy water, after a long hot march, with clothing and accoutrements hung to their guns, and that high over the shoulder. We struck in water waist deep, and made for the other shore, over the stoniest bottom ever heard of, guided by a light which had been built for the purpose. Many were the jokes and laughs we had crossing that river. Some tall fellows, being waggishly inclined, and seeing short ones behind, would walk in a stooping position, making the water appear very deep, and then enjoy immensely the disconsolate looks of the little fellows, who were manfully stemming the tide. . . .

The fording was successful and successively accomplished, clothing readjusted, and we commenced the ascent of the Blue Ridge, crossing which we halted in the valley on the other side, at a little place called Paris, about 4 a.m., having come twenty-one miles, where we laid down and slept. Such sleep! We never did as much sleeping in the same time. In an hour and a half we were again on the march, and before —— o'clock had accomplished seven miles—half a day's march—arriving at Piedmont Station, where, stacking arms, we awaited our turn on the trains which were to convey us to Manassas Junction. Here we met every kindness and attention, wagons of cooked provisions, barrels of milk, water, etc., were there, and served by fair hands to brave hearts. Along this whole line, at every village, the ladies were out handing edibles and water to the boys.

ELIHU B. WASHBURNE

U.S. Congressman, Illinois

Washburne, a friend of Lincoln's, was an influential force in Washington throughout the war. He is credited with having brought to Lincoln's attention the abilities of another Illinois resident—Ulysses S. Grant. On the eve of July 20, Washburne visited General Irvin McDowell's headquarters. His assessment of McDowell's state of mind left him shaken and doubting the Union's chances for victory.

I went to the tent of Genl. McDowell and had quite a conversation with him. I never had much of an opinion of him as a General, and I left his tent with a feeling of great sadness and a sort of a prescience of coming disaster. He seemed discouraged and in low spirits, and appeared very doubtful of the result of the approaching conflict. That was a bad symptom. As night came on I went into the miserable, straggling old village of Centreville and found a place to stay with a decayed Virginia gentlemen. All we could get to eat was some poor bread and poor ham. The troops were under marching orders for two o'clock the next morning to advance to the field of battle. I laid down to rest with feelings such as I had never before conceived. The thought of the inevitable contest of the next day and of the untold results to follow it, oppressed me heavily. I slept a few hours and before daylight I was up to see the march of the troops. They poured along in one continued stream for many hours, and the earth fairly shook beneath the heavy tread of nearly thirty thousand troops, as they poured down on what is called the "Gainesville road," toward the battle ground. About 5,000 went on another road, in the direction of Manassas Junction, and a reserve of 4,000 was left at Centreville, commanded by Col. Blenker, a dashing and brilliant German officer, reminding one of Eugene Beauharnais or Poniatowski. By eight or nine o'clock the whole army, except the reserve, had passed thro' Centreville and was out of sight. From an eminence in the village the whole country round about could be seen, but it was so broken and there was so much timber, no movements of the army could be seen except by the clouds of dust which it raised wherever it went. About nine o'clock, Mr. Daily, Delegate from Nebraska, and myself took our horse and buggy and went to the head of the left column, which was the small column of 5000 men.

General Irvin McDowell stands surrounded by his staff on the steps of Robert E. Lee's confiscated home in Arlington, Virginia, a few weeks before Manassas. McDowell was often chided for gluttony—he could eat an entire watermelon at one sitting—and the peculiar cap he wore. One soldier likened the headgear to an "esqimaux canoe . . . wrong side up." Unlike his counterparts in the Confederate high command, McDowell approached the battle wracked with doubts about the fighting qualities of his inexperienced soldiers and not overly sanguine about his ability to carry off his own weighty responsibilities.

CHAPLAIN AUGUSTUS WOODBURY

2D RHODE ISLAND INFANTRY, BURNSIDE'S BRIGADE

Woodbury offers details of the Union flanking movement begun early on July 21 by the 13,000 Union troops under division commanders David Hunter and Samuel Heintzelman. The march was not easy; the "road" the Federals took was in reality a dark, narrow, and twisting path through heavy woods. The Confederates, taking no chances, had made the journey more difficult by hastily felling large trees across the trace, slowing the column even more.

What a toilsome march it was through the woods! What wearisome work in clearing away the fallen trees, which now and then obstructed the path! The Second Regiment led the van, with skirmishers well thrown out on either side. The artillery could be moved but with difficulty. Colonel Hunter, who was lame, proceeded in a carriage. Other vehicles were along, with civilians, who wished to see the battle. The march was necessarily slow, and it was not till 9 o'clock, that the head of the column emerged from the woods, and came out upon a comparatively good farm road, along which were scattered a few comfortable-looking houses, about a mile from Sudley Ford. The inhabitants of the neighborhood were out, dressed in their Sunday clothes, apparently preparing to go to church. But the little building, which has become historical as Sudley Church, was to witness no worship on that day. By the time usually assigned for the beginning

Sudley Church, on a prominence just west of the Manassas–Sudley road, overlooked Sudley Ford on Catharpin Run, a branch of Bull Run. This was a vital crossing for the Federal troops on their flank march. Around 9:30 a.m., shocked churchgoers witnessed the beginning of the war's first major land battle when the head of the Federal column splashed across the stream. The churchyard soon rang with oaths and threats as officers struggled to realign their troops for the drive on the Rebel flank.

of the service, it had become a hospital, and was filled with wounded and dying men.

The division passed the ford slowly, for the day had become very warm, and the horses and men were thirsty. General McDowell and his staff came riding up in haste, saying, as he passed Colonel Burnside, "The enemy is moving heavy columns from Manassas." The men at once quickened their steps. Colonel Hunter, with Slocum and the Second Regiment, hurried forward, rounded a small piece of forest that concealed the crest of the hill above the Warrenton turnpike, and came out upon an open field beyond. Upon the left of this open space was a small house, with outbuildings, belonging to a man named Mathews. Sloping down to a piece of woods in front was a large corn-field. The plateau upon which the column emerged was an admirable position, and commanded a wide and pleasant prospect.

CAPTAIN GEORGE M. FINCH
2D OHIO INFANTRY, SCHENCK'S BRIGADE

Finch was among the troops of Tyler's division, which McDowell ordered down the Warrenton Turnpike to a position in front of the Stone Bridge. There the appearance of the division distracted the Confederates so much that they overlooked the flanking column's approach. Finch mustered out on August 9 but served again in 1864, as a lieutenant colonel in the 137th Ohio, a 100-days regiment.

Tyler's division marched at about 3 A.M. We advanced on the pike crossing Bull Run at the Stone Bridge. My company was deployed as skirmishers on the left of the road. We scrambled along through the dense woods and thickets, the darkness so intense that, literally, you could not see your hand before your face. We had to *feel* our way, keeping up our alignment at right angles with the road, as best we could, by the voice of the next man on the right. We never knew where a fence or a tree was located in front of us, until we ran slap against it. Many of the skirmishers had bloody noses and bruised limbs from such collisions. That I might be able to receive and transmit orders, I walked in the road on the right of my company, with the captain in command of the skirmishers to the right. When we reached Cub Run, a branch of Bull Run, which the pike at this point crossed at right angles by a bridge, we halted. It was apparently a deep ditch of still water, too wide to jump across, too deep to ford, and the perpendicular

banks too high to climb in or out. So it appeared in the early gray of dawn, and I passed the order for the skirmish line to march by the right flank and cross on the bridge. Just at this time, Colonel McCook rode up, and, seeing the men crossing, he said, with some contempt in his usual kindly voice: "Who taught you fellows the skirmish drill?" Calling his attention to his own men, crossing in the same way, I replied: "The same man that taught you'ns." As he had been our instructor, no further remarks seemed necessary.

As we approached a little wayside log school-house, two Confederate videttes hustled out from behind and fired their carbines, the bullets knocking up the dust around us, and then galloped down the pike toward the Stone Bridge in hot haste. Reaching the edge of the woods at the crest of the gentle incline leading to the bridge, we at once engaged the enemy's skirmish line on the north bank of Bull Run, and pushed them across. Carlisle's battery unlimbered for action in a meadow adjoining the road. At 6 A.M. they fired the first shot of the battle, to indicate that the division was in the position directed by the commanding general.

LIEUTENANT DOUGLAS S. FORREST
17TH VIRGINIA INFANTRY, LONGSTREET'S BRIGADE

Forrest, a 23-year-old lawyer from Alexandria, was the son of the Confederate naval officer French Forrest, who commanded the James River Squadron in 1863 and 1864. Douglas never advanced beyond the rank of lieutenant, although he later served as an aide to General Isaac Trimble. On July 21 advancing Union troops nearly captured Forrest as he daydreamed while on picket duty.

The next morning, partly refreshed, we were ordered over the ford as scouts in that direction. I was creeping over the field when the enemy threw a shell at my party which exploded just in advance of us. Here we passed a body, one of the Massachusetts slain, blackened and ghastly.

After a few hours we were ordered to our reserve and, without breakfast, to deploy as skirmishers. The first reserve had been left in charge of Willie Fowle. I led the second further on, while the captain placed himself in the skirt of the wood, having established a line of sentries. Here he watched the enemy's batteries, and would report their movements to the general.

Becoming anxious about him I left my reserve under Lieutenant

Zimmerman and advanced to the spot. The captain said, "Doug, I am awfully sleepy and will just take a nap if you will watch those fellows there." I cheerfully acquiesced and relieved Jordan, one of our men, who was the actual lookout at the fence. Here I lay on my face, my time pleasantly occupied with the proceedings at the batteries, the ceaseless explosions of the guns and the rattle of musketry from the great fight below being in strong contrast with the quiet scenery of mountain and valleys.

I unclasped my sword belt and yielded myself to the seductions of the scene, and was startled from my almost reverie by the cry of Lovelace, one of my men posted on the right:

"Look out, Lieutenant! Here they are!"

Looking around I saw their skirmishers within about thirty yards, with their pieces at a ready and advancing just as sportsmen approach a covey of partridges.

Edward S. Gregory of the 11th Virginia typified the look of many Southern soldiers in 1861, as he stood for the photographer fully accoutered and wearing his "battle shirt"—basically an oversize shirt decorated to produce a martial effect.

CAPTAIN E. PORTER ALEXANDER

CHIEF SIGNAL OFFICER, STAFF, GENERAL P. G. T. BEAUREGARD

After narrowly missing being the victim of a shell from Peter Hains' immense Parrott rifle, Alexander mounted his signal platform to keep a watch on his foes. His sharp eyes detected the Union flanking march, and he alertly signaled to Colonel Nathan G. Evans, posted at the Stone Bridge, that his left was in danger.

The Federals had brought one very heavy gun, for field service, a 30 lb. Parrot rifle they called "Long Tom." Long Tom was on the pike opposite Stone Bridge & opened the day with a shot at my little signal station near the Stone Bridge, & the shot went through the tent but hurt nobody. Every where else things were quiet. I exchanged messages with all the stations when I got on Wilcoxen's Hill & then fixed my glass on the Stone Bridge station looking for the earliest developments there.

And while looking at them, as well as I remember about 8:30 A.M., suddenly a little flash of light in the same field of view but far beyond them caught my eye. I was looking to the west & the sun was low in the east, & this flash was the reflection of the sun from a brass cannon in McDowell's flanking column approaching Sudley Ford. It was about 8 miles from me in an air line & was but a faint gleam, indescribably quick, but I had a fine glass & well trained eyes, & I knew at once what it was. And careful observation also detected the glitter of bayonets all along a road crossing the valley, & I felt sure that I was "on to" McDowell's plan & saw what was the best part of his army.

But I had heard stories about reconnoitering officers seeing a little & reporting a great deal so I determined to be very exact in my reports. First I signalled to Evans as of most immediate consequence, "Look out for your left. You are flanked," & then wrote a note for Gen. Beauregard by courier as he was not near a station.

When photographed in 1862, the area around Sudley Ford was quiet enough for children, some wearing military-style kepis, to play without risk in the presence of a Union cavalry squad picketing the crossing. The morning of the previous July 21 was far different, as the fields beyond the ford swarmed with thirsty Yankee soldiers. To their dismay, the Federal troops were unable to fill their canteens here, for thousands of tramping feet had churned the stream into a muddy ooze.

Colonel Ambrose Burnside, in the center, relaxes with his staff after the battle. Many soldiers under Burnside's command at Manassas commented on his bravery during the action on Matthews Hill. His brigade, which consisted of the 1st and 2d Rhode Island, the 2d New Hampshire, the 71st New York Militia, and Reynolds' battery, suffered an aggregate of 369 casualties in this, their first fight. Later, as commander of the Army of the Potomac, Burnside was excoriated for his role in the disastrous Union defeat at Fredericksburg in December 1862.

LIEUTENANT J. ALBERT MONROE

REYNOLDS' BATTERY, RHODE ISLAND ARTILLERY, BURNSIDE'S BRIGADE

Monroe, second in command to Captain William Reynolds, had helped raise this battery of six 13-pounder James rifles. Monroe would become a lieutenant colonel and command the artillery brigades of the Army of the Potomac's II and IX Corps before mustering out in 1864. Here he describes his battery's rush to gain the critical heights of Matthews Hill, east of the Manassas-Sudley road.

General Hunter's column, to which Colonel Burnside's brigade was attached, was the right of the advancing line, and soon after sunrise the report of heavy guns to the left told us that the work of the day had commenced. Steadily, however, the column pushed on, but with frequent halts, until Sudley Church was reached, where a short stop was made in the shade of the thick foliage of the trees in the vicinity of the church. The battery was following the Second Rhode Island, a portion of which were deployed as skirmishers, and contrary to the custom of throwing them, the skirmishers, well in advance, they moved directly on the flanks of the column. Suddenly the outposts of the enemy opened fire, which, to our inexperienced ears, sounded like the explosion of several bunches of fire crackers. Immediately after came the order, "FORWARD YOUR BATTERY!" Although the order was distinctly heard by both officers and men of the battery, I have never believed that it was definitely known whether it was given by General McDowell or General Hunter. With most commendable promptness, but without that caution which a battery commander learns to observe only by experience, Captain Reynolds rushed his battery forward at once at a sharp gallop. The road at this point was skirted by woods, but a short distance beyond, the battery emerged upon an open field, and at once went into position and opened fire.

The battery was now considerably in advance of the infantry and could easily have been captured and taken from the field by the enemy, before the supporting infantry were formed in line of battle; and two years later under the same circumstances, the entire battery would have been lost; but neither side hardly understood the rudiments of the art of war. When we reached the open field the air seemed to be filled with myriads of serpents, such was the sound of the bullets passing through it. Above us and around us on every side, they seemed to be hissing, writhing and twisting. I have been under many a hot fire, but I don't think that, in nearly four years experience, I ever heard so many bullets in such a short space of time.

Lynchburg, Virginia, resident Captain John D. Alexander led the Campbell Rangers cavalry company at Manassas and helped direct reinforcements to Matthews Hill to bolster Colonel Evans' beleaguered South Carolinians. Campbell, 42 years old at the time of the battle, suffered a "slight wound" in his leg for his efforts. Later in the day, his Rangers harassed the retreating Union columns.

John D. Alexander

PRIVATE MARTIN A. HAYNES
2D NEW HAMPSHIRE INFANTRY, BURNSIDE'S BRIGADE

The men of the 2d reacted like many troops exposed to enemy fire that day for the first time—they threw themselves upon the ground in shock and gaped at the awful scenes unfolding before them. To the officers leading these green warriors fell the responsibility of rallying their men to their duty. In their efforts to do so they often made handsome targets. As Haynes relates, it was not long before the regimental commander, Colonel Gilman Marston, fell wounded.

We filed into the field upon the right of the road, fired a few scattering shots at a line of skirmishers which opened on us, and then threw ourselves upon the ground to escape the fire of a rebel battery upon the opposite slope which had begun to pay its attention to us. By this time the Rhode Island battery was in position and opened fire. Its first shot was directed against the battery which was annoying us, and with splendid accuracy. The shell struck right upon the little work behind which the gunners were protected, and the demoralized artillerists streamed to the rear like ants from an ant hill,

COMMENCEMENT OF THE BATTLE AT BULL'S RUN.—SKETCHED BY OUR SPECIAL ARTIST.—[SEE PAGE 491.]

This drawing shows Captain Reynolds, atop Matthews Hill, scanning with his telescope the ground west of the Manassas–Sudley road, which can be seen to the right as it crosses the lower, gentle crest of Buck Hill. His gunners, however, remain focused to their front, delivering a heavy fire upon the 4th South Carolina. Reynolds would have been better off looking to his left, from which direction approached the 1st Special Louisiana Infantry Battalion, bent on helping their fellow Confederates.

"The sounds of their missiles, running through the whole scale of warlike music, from the savage rush of twelve pound shells to the spiteful 'pish' of the minie bullet, was ruinous to weak nerves."

but they were rallied by the officers and led back to their work.

They soon got a good range upon us, and many a poor fellow was carried gasping and bleeding to the rear. For half an hour we suffered this merciless pelting, when the enemy showed themselves in great numbers in front of the Rhode Islanders, evidently intending to charge the battery, and we were ordered to the left of the road to assist in repelling the threatened attack. Col. MARSTON was at this moment consulting with Col. BURNSIDE. "Attention! left face—double-quick—march!" shouted Colonel FISKE, who, in his shirt sleeves, and with perspiration pouring from his face, had been striding up and down the line.

As we rushed past the battery we were exposed to the concentrated fire of the entire rebel force then in action, and the sounds of their missiles, running through the whole scale of warlike music, from the savage rush of twelve pound shells to the spiteful "pish" of the minie bullet, was ruinous to weak nerves.

We reached our position amidst this galling fire, and threw ourselves upon the ground to await any demonstration. It soon came. Along the edge of the woods some three hundred yards in front of the battery, the rebels appeared in strong force. The two howitzers of the Seventy-First opened with grape and shrapnell, while we rose from the ground and rushing with the Seventy-First over an intervening fence and through a cornfield, engaged in a sharp fight with the rebels. It was hot work for a

short time. They were under cover of the woods,—we fully exposed to their aim. They soon fell back, but not until the green leaves of the growing corn had been dyed red with Northern blood and the ground strewn with corpses. Col. MARSTON was wounded at this point. He had hardly given the word "Attention!"—for us to rise from the ground, when he fell with a rifle ball in his shoulder and was carried to the rear.

Edward N. Whittier of the 1st Rhode Island wore this state-issue dark blue blouse and kepi during the battle. Rhode Islanders contended that such practical clothing made them "look ready for business," in contrast to more natty regiments. Later in the war Whittier rose to command of the 5th Maine Light Artillery.

PRIVATE EBEN GORDON
2D RHODE ISLAND INFANTRY, BURNSIDE'S BRIGADE

Though born in Farmington, Maine, Gordon was residing and working as a printer in Providence, Rhode Island, when the Civil War began. He enlisted in the 2d Rhode Island on June 5 for a period of three years, but like countless soldiers on both sides he became seriously ill in the army. His "incipient tuberculosis" forced the 34-year-old to take a medical discharge in September 1863.

Soon the order was given—
"Forward, 2d R.I.!"
The order was obeyed with alacrity, our men shouting like so many fiends, and we rushed wildly and impetuously through the woods, over a fence, and then found we were rather mixed up. But we did not mind it, and immediately commenced firing without the order to fire, and so briskly was it kept up that the enemy soon ceased their fire, leaving the cornfield between us, and started for their batteries and their companions in the woods.

About this time our gallant Colonel received his death wound. This, however, did not stop the almost mad career of our men. They continued the firing until the enemy started from the woods which sheltered them, with hardly a moment's cessation. At one time the order was given to cease firing. I was ordered by Capt. Viall to assist in picking up our wounded comrades. The first I came to was one of my own mess, James McCabe, wounded in the right leg just below the hip, the ball passing entirely through his leg. The brave fellow, after I got assistance to take him from the field, fairly begged us to leave him and go back and fight. Finally we left him in the Surgeon's care, he bidding me good-by, telling me to remember him, but not to come to him until we had whipped the rebels. Poor, brave fellow! He was loved by all his messmates, and we often speak of him.

As Colonel John S. Slocum, pictured here, and his infantrymen of the 2d Rhode Island raced to the top of Matthews Hill, they were exposed to "a perfect hail storm of bullets," delivered by the soldiers of Colonel Nathan Evans' command. Slocum lost his life to this terrible fire when a Rebel bullet slammed into his head as he was climbing over a rail fence on the hill's summit.

SERGEANT ABNER R. SMALL
3D MAINE INFANTRY, HOWARD'S BRIGADE

One of the last Federal units deployed, Colonel Oliver O. Howard's brigade raced at a fatiguing pace in the afternoon heat through fields and woods, pausing only for a quick drink at Sudley Ford. Small survived the battle and re-enlisted in the 16th Maine, then was appointed to Howard's staff in late 1862. Promoted to captain, Small was captured near Richmond in August 1864 and spent six months as a prisoner of war.

Shortly after noon a mounted officer came dashing out of the woods and drew rein where Colonel Howard was fidgeting. There was a sudden stir, a shouting of orders, and we started up the forest track. We marched through the woods and came to an open flat, where Lieutenant Burt met us and told our commander that we were to hurry. We went on at the double quick, but a mile of this was all that we could do; the heat and the fretting of our long wait had weakened us; men dropped, exhausted and fainting, by the wayside. Another mile, and another, we hurried on at quick time; this meant double quick at the rear, and we lost other stragglers. Men still on their feet and pressing forward threw away their blankets, their haversacks, their coats, even their canteens. When we got to Bull Run at Sudley's Ford, many stopped to drink; scooped up muddy water in their hands, their hats, their shoes; drank too much; were lost to service for that day. Not half the brigade, nor half the regiment, crossed the run.

Beyond the stream, we went up through a scattering of trees and came out into cleared lands. We passed an improvised hospital near Sudley Church. I can see today, as I saw then, the dead and hurt men lying limp on the ground. Up the road from ahead of us came ambulances filled with wounded. Farther away there were rattles of musketry and the quick and heavy thuddings of artillery. Puffs of white smoke and straggling clouds of dust rose wavering into the still air. There was the battle, and we were coming to it late; it must have been three o'clock, by then.

We hurried on, down the road and off obliquely to our right through the fields. When at last we neared the scene of battle, broken regiments and scattering stragglers were drifting back. We pushed on across the Warrenton turnpike, splashed through the muddy shallows of Young's Branch, and turned to our left in a ravine; and there, under cover of the trees and bushes that screened its farther slope, we caught our breath and wondered for the last time, confusedly, what it was going to be like to face fire.

Confederate general Barnard Bee had resigned from the U.S. Army in March but still wore his National uniform at Manassas. Bee had posted his brigade, consisting of units from Alabama, Mississippi, and North Carolina, and four guns of Virginia's Staunton Artillery, on Henry House Hill. At about 11:00 a.m. he ordered three of his regiments to Matthews Hill to reinforce Evans.

SERGEANT MAJOR ROBERT T. COLES
4TH ALABAMA INFANTRY, BEE'S BRIGADE

Throughout most of the morning, while Evans' two regiments fought for their lives on Matthews Hill, two of Bee's regiments, including the 4th Alabama, remained outside the fight on adjacent Henry House Hill. Along with two regiments under Bartow, they were, however, subjected to a heavy bombardment from Reynolds' Rhode Island Battery. Just before 11:00 a.m., an excited General Bee rode up to the 4th Alabama's line and ordered them into the fray.

In the meantime the 4th Alabama had been marched from its original position on the Henry House Hill across an intervening valley, through which flows Young's Branch, and halted. From this position we were moved up the hill to a low fence surrounding a piece of growing corn. General Bee, who had been reconnoitering on our left, and finding Evans about to be repulsed, came riding down from that direction and upon reaching the centre of the regiment, with a wave of his hand, in a loud commanding tone called out: "Up Alabamians."

The men were rushed over the fence and advanced at a double quick to the crest of the hill; before reaching there we met Colonel Wheat and his Tigers falling back. Our position was on the right and somewhat in advance of General Evans' line. The right and part of the left centre of the 4th Alabama was in the cultivated field and the ex-

The 4th Alabama led the way as Bee's brigade surged up the slopes of Matthews Hill. In command of the regiment's Company K was a farmer from Larkinsville, Captain Lewis Lindsay, pictured at left. As the Alabamians came into range, Burnside's troops loosed a deadly fire upon them, and the 41-year-old Lindsay fell dead.

treme left was in the pine woods. The part in the open did the most execution. The extreme left, being in such dense cover, did very little effective work. By the time we reached the crest of the hill, the turning column of the enemy, which had been attacking General Evans, had moved farther to our left, continuing their flanking movement. General Heintzelman's division now appearing in our front, the men firing at will, opened a terrific fire on his leading regiment. Our battery posted on the Henry House plateau lent its aid and did splendid execution.

good nature, whom we all called "Coon Mitchell." I had got one of my legs over the upper rail, when Coon climbed up besides me. The rail broke. I went backwards, wrenched myself fierce, and in a few minutes was getting over again, when what should I see but Coon's red head slowly arise out the green leafy blackberry bushes; he must have fallen on his head as he was dazed. He stared around, shook himself and then cried out "Boys where was I hit." It was so ludicrous that I could not help laughing so that I lost a few more minutes. I rushed on at a run to my position in the ranks, which was drawn up at the edge of the thicket . . . and also already had commenced firing at the Yankee infantry across a field, with a fence just in front of them. I could not get into my place as the field was closed, and then I asked the Lieutenant could I go to the extreme front. He agreed. When I got there, some fifty yards, I had gone too far, so I concluded to go shooting on my own private account; and as I had been trained in the Zouave drill, I decided that this would the best to begin with. In this drill you shoot from the knee, turn over on your back and load the gun. I did not take any especial aim except at the line of "blue coats" which I could see well. . . . Before my last shot and was loading on my back a bullet passed close to my head. I happened to be just loaded, and as swinging to position, I saw a large man, who had thrown down the fence and had advanced. I took him to be the fellow who came so close to killing me, and I took good aim at a bright brass button on his bluecoat. He fell. There were others shooting, but I think I killed him. At least I did then, and turned over to load again, taking off my hat and shouting "Boys I got one anyway." I looked around and I was all alone.

LIEUTENANT JOHN C. REID
8TH GEORGIA INFANTRY, BARTOW'S BRIGADE

Reid and his comrades formed the far right of the Confederate line of battle on Matthews Hill. The 8th stood on the edge of a thicket at right angles to the main line, enfilading the advancing enemy with musket fire. Their situation grew critical, however, as fresh Federal units were fed into the battle. Reid recalled the wounding of James T. Lewis and the death of August H. Daniel of his company.

From the fence came a volley that roared more loudly than any I ever heard afterwards, but it seemed to do no hurt. Huddled up in some places seven or eight deep, and even more, our firing commenced. I observed three colors at regular intervals, just on the other side of the long fence. A dwelling was a little beyond it, and four out-houses were on its line, and some grain stacks besides. The

Private William A. Favor joined the 7th Georgia in May 1861 and fought with his regiment on Matthews Hill. He survived the battle but was wounded two years later at Funkstown, Maryland, during the Confederate withdrawal after the Battle of Gettysburg. Captured, Favor was paroled at City Point, Virginia, in September 1863 but was unable to return to active duty because of his wound.

dwelling and out-houses were opposite the left and right center of the regiment. The . . . out-houses and stacks were lined with federals. An ice-house was a few yards nearer on our side of the fence, . . . and more federals were around it; and they extended in rather desultory order, in front, to a point not far to its right. To the left of the ice-house, in an oblique line towards the fence, by which the 4th. Alabama were lying, another regiment took position, just after our fighting commenced, and its musketry was very destructive to companies K and I, as it approached somewhat to an enfilade and many of the men of these companies were pushed out into the open. This last mentioned regiment fired buck and ball, as I discovered from the marks on the trees the next day, the other regiments fired Minie balls. Now, were we not in a pickle? The houses, the stacks, the fence, the line of the regiment on our left,—all seemed a continually playing flash. The trees were becoming white all around us, from having the bark cut away, though I noted that numerous bullets were going too high and bringing down leaves. Many of our men were wounded, and there were frequent cries of pain, "O,! Lord!" becoming from that time on the ejaculation that I usually heard a man make when struck in battle. But the loading and firing kept up with eagerness. Jim Lewis, one of the company, came to me and told me goodbye. The brains and blood seemed to be running out of his forehead. I never expected to see him again, but the next day it appeared that the ball had gone around and not through the skull. I shall never forget how pale, stiff and thoroughly dead Gus Daniel, another one of the company, looked as I glanced down when I had stumbled over him. This was the first dead man I saw.

Colonel Ambrose Burnside, astride a restive horse, directs his brigade up the slope of Matthews Hill in this sketch by artist-correspondent Alfred Waud. In the rear of the battle line musicians, detailed as stretcher-bearers, carry off the wounded. Burnside's brigade suffered 189 casualties, including 40 fatalities, in the assault on Matthews Hill. Waud portrayed the Rhode Island regiments wearing their distinctive hats, blouses, and red blanket rolls.

LIEUTENANT DAINGERFIELD PARKER
3D U.S. INFANTRY, HUNTER'S BRIGADE

The well-drilled battalion of U.S. regulars assigned to General David Hunter's brigade was seen as representing steadiness and martial prowess. In fact, however, most of these "regulars" were new recruits, including the 29-year-old Parker, who had only received his commission in April. Badly wounded at Gettysburg, Parker returned to service toward the war's end. He retired in 1896 as a colonel.

The remainder of the battalion advanced across an open plain, the right skirting a belt of heavy timber. Having arrived at the apex of the angle formed by the southern limit of this wood with its eastern side, we changed direction to the right, and wheeling into line took up position to support the Rhode Island Battery. This battery was served and handled with much gallantry. As an illustration however of the general, and inevitable inexperience of some of the officers taking part in this action, I will mention this incident: The captain of the battery totally unaware, seemingly, that troops supporting a battery lie down as a matter of course unless it is threatened with assault, and further, that the support would take orders only from their own officers, called upon some of the men "to get up and help serve the battery" to which no attention was paid. "Cowards," he exclaimed, "Cowards! What are you lying down there for?" I overheard an old sergeant mutter: "We'll come out there directly and show you how to serve that battery!" This was accordingly done, for Sykes coming out of the wood a few minutes thereafter and observing that they were short-handed on account of casualties in battle said: "get up there, some of you men, and help serve the battery." There being many old artillerymen in our command the battery captain speedily found himself *embarras des richesses.*

"Gentlemen, you have got me, but a hundred thousand more await you!"

LIEUTENANT EUGENE CARTER
3D U.S. INFANTRY, HUNTER'S BRIGADE

Carter graduated from West Point in 1857 and was commissioned a second lieutenant in June 1861. He fought with Major George Sykes' battalion of regulars at Manassas and ended the war as a captain. Carter received two brevets for gallantry during the war—one for the Peninsula campaign and a second for Fredericksburg.

W e could see the Rhode Island Battery firing and see the return shots from the rebel battery. We marched in this direction by fours, and came behind the two Rhode Island regiments. We met Burnside and he ran toward us, saying, "Good God! Major Sykes, you regulars are just what we want: form on my left and give aid to my men who are being cut to pieces!" We formed "on the right by file into line!" on the run, the Rhode Islanders cheering and exciting our men.

As soon as we were formed, we commenced firing, and the rebels did not like the taste of our long range rifles. Our men fired badly; they were excited, and some of the recruits fired at the stars. There was some confusion, but we immediately formed line of battle and marched across the field in splendid order for about forty rods. We were then wheeled by company to the right, to gain a wood on our right, but immediately took our men out of column of companies by the command, "Right flank, by file left!" As we got to the edge of the wood we observed a white flag upon a sword, held by someone lying down. We went to the spot and found Colonel Jones of one of the Alabama regiments mortally wounded. He asked for a drink of water, which we gave him. He asked what we intended to do, and we told him to whip them. He said, "Gentlemen, you have got me, but a hundred thousand more await you!

LIEUTENANT JOHN C. REID
8TH GEORGIA INFANTRY, BARTOW'S BRIGADE

Threatened by Federal pressure on both flanks and with no reinforcements in sight, the Confederates fighting on Matthews Hill began to waver. Reid recounted the withdrawal of the 8th Georgia toward the Warrenton Turnpike and Henry House Hill. Reid served through several major campaigns and was wounded at Gettysburg in 1863. He surrendered at Appomattox as a captain.

B artow vociferated to the captain of the Atlanta Grays, "We must get these men out of here." Several times he ordered us to fall back, but I was among those who did not hear. Nothing could be understood in the din to which our ears were so new. But some of the men at last, misunderstanding the order to fall back, begun a disorderly retreat. On the right of the first platoon, close behind it, I was encouraging some of the men of our company to fire with more coolness, and reminded them that the enemy's fire was slackening. The regiment furtherest to the left had disappeared—its smooth-bores probably being no match for the Mississippi rifles of company K—and the line before us looked thinner along the fence; and there was nobody standing on our side of it. Ransome, one of my men, lying on the ground, was keeping his musket quiet. He seemed very cool, and with much warmth I asked him why he had ceased to fire. He fired at once, begun to load, and shouted to me that he had been obeying orders; and he rolled his eyes in such a manner that I glanced to the left and then to the right. Nearly everybody was going back at about quick time. Of course I could not stay. I carried off my squad very doggedly. Their sulleness increased mine. At every step they seemed on the point of rushing back, and some would turn and fire.

This solid shot, from Matthews Hill, was fired by one of the bronze six-pounder guns of the Lynchburg Artillery of Virginia. By 1863 the six-pound ball was judged to be too light, and most of the guns were phased out of the Virginia theater.

A Savage Bloodletting on Henry House Hill

The events of Sunday morning, July 21, plunged General Beauregard, sitting in his headquarters at the McLean house, into a fit of despair. His own long-planned attack across Bull Run by the Confederate brigades massed near the downstream fords had misfired completely. The plan called for the brigade of Brigadier General Richard S. Ewell, posted on the Confederate far right, to kick off the attack in the early morning. But Ewell somehow never received his orders, and he made no advance. The neighboring commands of Generals David R. Jones and James Longstreet were directed to time their attacks to the sound of Ewell's guns. They obediently crossed Bull Run but then halted, under Federal artillery fire, to await Ewell's advance.

Far more alarming, Beauregard could now hear musket and artillery fire echoing from the north, many miles from where his main forces were stationed. The battle was clearly careering out of control. "My heart for a moment failed me!" the Creole general later wrote. "I felt as though all was lost."

Beauregard was finally roused from his funk by General Johnston, who had arrived the day before with his army from the Shenandoah and was acting as second in command. The Confederate left, he told Beauregard, had to be reinforced, and fast. "The battle is there," he announced. "I am going." Quickly Beauregard ordered several brigades to start north from their distant bivouacks. Then he rode off, following Johnston to Henry House Hill to see in person what was going on.

What the generals saw was a scene of chaos. Only one small unit, the 600 South Carolinians of Colonel Wade Hampton's "Legion,"

had marched to reinforce the troops of Colonels Bartow and Evans and General Bee that for two hours had struggled to stem the Federal advance. But Hampton's men had come up just as the Confederate line broke and, after a desperate stand near the Warrenton Turnpike, had joined the mob of men streaming to the shelter of the reverse slope of Henry House Hill.

Mercifully for the Confederates, the Federals, with the exception of an unsupported attack by two regiments of Brigadier General Erasmus D. Keyes' brigade, did not pursue their fleeing enemy. General McDowell, thinking the battle already won, proceeded to spend nearly two hours organizing his line, even though, with fresh units coming up, he soon had a force of nearly 18,000 men on the field.

Given this gift of time, the Confederate officers feverishly patched together a sketchy defense. General Jackson, marching without waiting for orders toward the sound of gunfire, placed his five Virginia regiments in line just behind the crest of Henry House Hill. At the same time Evans, Bartow, and Bee desperately tried to untangle their weary, confused troops and, with the help of Johnston and Beauregard, get them back into the line now forming. While the line was being stabilized, Bee rode to confer with Jackson. "General, they are driving us," Bee exclaimed. "Sir, we will give them the bayonet," sternly replied Jackson.

The fighting exploded at last when at about 2:00 McDowell ordered his line forward, the regiments of Heintzelman's division now in the lead, charging up the grassy, open slope of Henry House Hill. To spearhead the attack, McDowell also ordered up two batteries of

guns commanded by a pair of tough regulars, Captains Charles Griffin and James B. Ricketts.

The artillerymen unlimbered within 300 yards of the enemy line. Behind came their infantry support, the 11th New York—the colorful Fire Zouaves—and following them the 14th Brooklyn, the 1st Minnesota, and a battalion of marines. The guns were hardly in place when they were hit by vicious counterfire from enemy cannon, then by furious volleys from Jackson's troops that toppled gunners and raked the front ranks of the Federal infantry. Many of the Zouaves broke and ran—and kept running when Rebel cavalry under Colonel James E. B. Stuart, the soon to be famous Jeb, charged into their flank and rear.

With the Union guns now largely stripped of supporting infantry, Colonel Arthur Cummings advanced down the slope with his 33d Virginia—the men dressed in blue uniforms, which some Confederate units still wore. Captain Griffin was set to fire on them when he was stopped by the army's head of artillery, Major William F. Barry, who insisted, "Those are your battery support." Allowed to advance within 70 yards, Cummings' men suddenly loosed a ferocious volley, killing a score of gunners and wounding Ricketts. The Rebels then swarmed over the guns, driving the remaining Zouaves and the marines down the hill.

Cummings' Virginians were hit in turn by men of the 14th Brooklyn. But immediately the rest of Jackson's troops opened fire, riddling the Brooklynites, then on Jackson's orders surged forward in a wild yelling charge that sent the last Zouaves along with other Union troops rushing in terror for the rear.

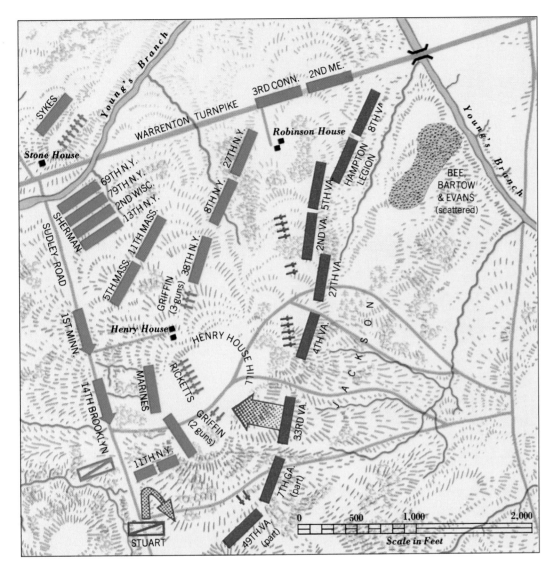

By late morning, having driven the Confederates off Matthews Hill, Federal forces massed to continue their attack. Despite his early success, McDowell permitted a lull of nearly two hours, a break in his advance that gave the Confederates valuable time to rally their forces behind Brigadier General Thomas J. Jackson's Virginia Brigade on Henry House Hill. When the Federal assault resumed, it was led by the batteries of Captains Charles Griffin and James B. Ricketts, who deployed near the crest of the hill and opened on the Confederate line. Massed musketry from Jackson's left decimated the Federal gunners, and a daring attack by the 33d Virginia Infantry overran the guns.

Henry House Hill, the air choked with gunsmoke, the ground littered with the bodies of the dead and dying. Finally, about 3:30, the last Federal unit to go up the hill, Colonel Oliver O. Howard's brigade of Maine and Vermont troops, moved to the attack. But the troops were so exhausted from long marching in the July heat they could barely stagger and were sent reeling back by heavy Confederate fire.

Through it all McDowell had ridden along his line, encouraging the men but, under the pressure of the moment, committing only one regiment at a time instead of harder-hitting brigades—and forgetting to order up his reserves. By midafternoon fresh Confederates were being funneled toward Henry House Hill from the rear by Johnston. Their attacks would be devastating, turning what had seemed a sure Federal triumph into a nightmare.

Despite this success, the Confederate left flank was still threatened by an advancing enemy with superior numbers. Johnston worked feverishly to hurry reinforcements to the front, while other officers struggled to reorganize the hundreds of men milling around on the reverse slope of the hill. Riding among his own troops, Bee was heard to say, "Look men, there is Jackson standing like a stone wall! Let us determine to die here and we will conquer!" The courageous Bee, who would be killed charging the enemy in the fighting to come, had given Jackson his famous nickname, Stonewall.

On the hill, the Rebel assault that had captured Ricketts' guns was driven back by sheets of Union bullets, as was another that followed. Shortly, fresh Federal units, including Orlando Willcox's 1st Michigan and two Massachusetts regiments led by Colonel William B. Franklin, staged their own attacks, only to be raked back by fearful enemy fire. For the next hour more charges and counterthrusts seesawed across

CAPTAIN JAMES CONNER

HAMPTON LEGION,
SOUTH CAROLINA,
HOLMES' BRIGADE

Deploying in the Warrenton Pike at the foot of the Robinson Farm lane, 600 soldiers of Wade Hampton's legion attempted to cover the retreat of Bartow's Georgians. Conner, a former Charleston attorney who would eventually attain the rank of general, described this action in a letter to his mother.

We marched about 5 miles and were halted by the Colonel just under the brow of a hill. I was sent forward to view the position or rather the Colonel permitted me to go standing on the hill. I could see the battle going on in the valley below. A battery of Artillery moved up at a gallop on our left and commenced firing on the U.S. troops. This drew their fire in our direction and as we lay down behind the hill the grape shot and round shot came singing over our heads, sometimes so close you could feel the air as they passed. The fight at this point was altogether an artillery one and finding that we were exposed without doing any good, the Colonel ordered us back to the shelter of some woods. We then moved forward some distance, when we received orders to advance to the support of some Georgia regiments. They had been forced back, and we met them and formed in front of them, we laying down behind a fence and commencing to fire on the Yankees. At this moment a body of Yankees were seen moving around and endeavouring to turn the flank of the army and get in our rear. The order was given to us to outflank them and we moved down a lane running at right angles to that in which we were. It was a hard lane or country road, with deep gullies on either side. The troops opposed to us were Infantry supported by Artillery. I could see their numbers but could not estimate them. Gen'l Beauregard told Hampton today that they were at least 4000. As we commenced the movement, they opened a terrible fire upon us of grape-canister and musketry. The

balls flew like hail and knocked the flying rocks whirling all around us. I was in advance—my Company heading the Legion. We faced to the right and ordered the men into the gully and under the cover of that and the fence on top of the bank, returned the fire. It was here we had the hardest fighting and met the heaviest loss. At the very commencement of it poor Col Johnson was killed, shot through the head. He was in line with the 1st platoon of my Company. He threw his sword up, and fell back lifeless. Hot and heavy the fire fell all around us. By this time, I had gotten the rest of the men—the companies—down into the gully and at work, but for the first four or five minutes[,] may be only of half of this time, the Light Infantry were *alone* in the lane, and receiving the whole fire. Hampton was in the centre, and I on the right, the men in the gully and he and I on the top of the bank looking out at the enemy and cautioning the men to keep cool and aim deliberately . . . and above all to deploy out and not crowd.

This frock coat was worn by Corporal Robert A. Bomar of the Hampton Legion, who was wounded three times at Manassas. Colonel Hampton, a wealthy planter, personally covered the cost of outfitting his unit, including its uniforms.

"As I was in the act of reloading, a rifle ball struck me in the head, a little above the forehead; and the violence of the concussion felled me to the earth immediately."

PRIVATE CHARLES W. HUTSON
HAMPTON LEGION, SOUTH CAROLINA, HOLMES' BRIGADE

Unable to stem the Yankee onslaught, Hampton's soldiers abandoned their position in the Warrenton Pike and fell back through the yard of the Robinson house. Although he was wounded in the head, Hutson was able to make his way to the rear and recounted his experience in a letter to his parents the day after the battle. The following year he was captured at the Battle of Fair Oaks but was exchanged after two months.

The artillery having then withdrawn from one side, we marched down the hill, unfortunately in disorder. We were halted half way down in a hollow place, where we had the protection of a few trees and bushes. Here, seeing that our men hesitated to fire upon the force below, because doubtful whether they were not friends, I entreated the Captain to let me advance alone near enough to the ranks of those who were firing upon us to ascertain whether they were Federals or Confederates. But the Captain would not consent, and wished to go himself: this, however, Col. Hampton would not permit. Seeing I could do nothing there, I attempted to persuade our men not to dodge, satisfied that we could never keep orderly ranks as long as the men persisted in dodging. But all my efforts in this line were unavailing: the men were fearless and advanced undauntedly enough; but I suppose they thought dodging was a "help" anyhow to escape from the balls. Iredell Jones and the officers kept erect, and neither they nor I were any the worse for it. Our next advance was to a fence in the valley at the bottom of the hill. Here we made a stand, and here our company fought absolutely alone, the other legionary companies having retreated to a yard at the top of the hill where houses gave them shelter. Here they re-formed.

Meanwhile our men were subjected to a raking fire. I was the first who fell. I had put on my spectacles, taken good aim, and fired my first

Aristocratic Wade Hampton was a skilled horseman and powerful athlete who inspired the devotion of his men. Wounded in the fight at Manassas, he finished the war a lieutenant general and later served as governor of South Carolina.

shot. As I was in the act of reloading, a rifle ball struck me in the head, a little above the forehead; and the violence of the concussion felled me to the earth immediately. I drew off my spectacles and flung them aside; and, not believing my wound a bad one, as it was not painful, I attempted to reload. But the blood was gushing over my face and blinding my eyes, and I found it impossible to do so. I knew pretty well the extent of my wound, as I had probed it with my finger as I fell; and, as the gash seemed to be a deep one, I feared faintness would ensue from loss of blood, especially as there was a large puddle of it where I first lay. So, I put aside my gun for awhile, and put my white handkerchief inside my hat upon the wound, and tied my silk one around the hat.

they shook out the Rebel flag and opened a terrific fire of musketry on us. That settled it, and gallantly and coolly directed by Colonel Slocum, Lieutenant-Colonel Chambers, and Major Bartlett, we gave them the best we had. Their batteries and reserves on our right rear across the Warrenton Pike joined in the fight, and when one company seemed somewhat nervous, Lieutenant-Colonel Chambers encouraged them by saying, "Ne-ne-ne-never mind a f-f-few shells, boys G-G-G-God Almighty is m-m-merciful." One lieutenant, with the large whites of his eyes showing like saucers, manfully stood his post and fired his revolver in the air. Riding up and down the rear of the regiment, the lieutenant-colonel continued his Scriptural injunctions, and noticing my company doing the most telling execution, said, "G-g-g-give it to 'em b-b-boys; God l-l-loves a cheerful g-g-giver." The troops that engaged us soon passed over Young's Branch and across the Warrenton Turnpike out of sight near the Robinson house with their main line and batteries, and as our regiment was without support, Colonel Slocum withdrew it up the hill into the grove from which the troops we had encountered came receiving a bullet through the leg while directing the movement.

LIEUTENANT H. SEYMOUR HALL
27TH NEW YORK INFANTRY, PORTER'S BRIGADE

Forging ahead of the rest of their brigade, Hall's regiment gained the Warrenton Pike near its intersection with the road to Sudley Church. Hall described the unit's confusion as to the identity of the troops in their front. A farmer from upstate New York, Hall later received the Medal of Honor for gallantry in the Peninsula campaign and was awarded the brevet rank of brigadier general following the July 1864 Battle of the Crater, where he lost his right arm.

At this moment the enemy, finding their left turned by us retired by their right, and we saw them moving out of the grove parallel to our front, deliberately making signs as if they were friends. Their colors were furled, and their gray uniforms did not sufficiently designate them, as many of our own troops wore the same color. We were yet lacking in discipline, so while some of us shouted, "Fire!" others yelled "Don't shoot; it is a Massachusetts regiment, or the Eighth New York." Tall Bob Frazee at my elbow on the right of my company, with a voice like a fog-horn, shouted to them, "Show your colors," when

Shown here as a major general, a rank he attained in 1862, Henry W. Slocum was struck in the thigh while leading the 27th New York at Manassas. An 1852 graduate of West Point, Slocum left the Regular Army and was practicing law in Syracuse when the war began. He later commanded the XII and XX Corps.

PRIVATE RICHARD H. HABERSHAM
Hampton Legion, South Carolina, Holmes' Brigade

From their position near the Robinson house, Hampton's South Carolinians were able briefly to check the Federal advance but then had to give way when Sherman's and Keyes' Federal brigades appeared and threatened their flank. A 17-year-old volunteer in Company C of the legion, Habersham was among 120 casualties in the unit's fight at Manassas. After recuperating in a Richmond hospital, he returned to the front and in June 1862 was transferred to the artillery.

*I*t was in a little kind of hollow just in a situation well calculated to be cut to pieces in. While there I happened to look over towards the Battery and saw the puff of a Cannon in our direction. I kept my Eye in that direction, and in a few seconds saw the ball coming exactly where I was standing; by stepping aside to the left, the ball missed me, killing three of my company and cut off my 3rd Lieut's. right foot. By order of Col. H. we then filed to the right and took up our positions in a Road about fifty yards from there. By that time the Enemy had got near enough for us to open fire. We were ordered to do so, and at the same time the Enemy opened on us with their Muskets. So we were exposed to a heavy fire from both Artillery & Musketry. Well! According to orders, we opened on them—every man firing & loading as fast as he could. My first shot fell about 200 yds. too short, my second I aimed a little higher and got about a hundred yds. nearer, my third I aimed still higher and got within a few yds. of them; my fourth and fifth were aimed a little above their heads and I saw neither of them strike the ground, so I took it for granted that they went into the Enemy ranks. They then retreated into some woods that was near, and an increasing Column of Regulars advanced on us in beautiful style at "double-quick" & passed in a heavy fire on us. We were ordered to lie down in the ditch instantly. Every man dropped down, and the bullets of Cannon and Muskets whistled over us by thousands. As soon as they had passed I asked the Captain if we might commence firing again. He told us to pitch in, and we all jumped up and commenced on them again. This made my sixth shot, and just as my gun exploded, the rebound threw me back a little, and . . . a rifle bullet crushed the bridge of my nose knocking me down and stunning me for a few seconds. As soon as I recovered, I jumped up, and began loading again—the blood all the time flowing from my nose. It so completely exausted me that I had not strength left to draw my ram-rod. I gave it up and sunk down on the [ground] almost ready to faint. . . . While in that condition I concluded that the best place for me was the Hospital, so I started for and finally reached it, and tried to get the flow of blood stopped, but the Surgeon hadn't time to attend to me, and told me to retire to some woods. I did so in company with David Dubose—who was wounded in the shoulder but had lost no blood and was able to get on faster than I could.

Second in command of the Hampton Legion, Lieutenant Colonel Benjamin J. Johnson was killed near the Robinson house. A graduate of William and Mary College, Johnson had served in the South Carolina Legislature but lost his bid for governor in 1860. A subordinate recalled him as "brave, large and awkward."

SERGEANT HORATIO STAPLES
2d Maine Infantry, Keyes' Brigade

After fording Bull Run and coming into action alongside Sherman's troops, the 2d Maine and 3d Connecticut regiments of Keyes' brigade routed the wavering Rebel line at the Robinson house. The Yankees continued up the slope of Henry House Hill, where the Confederates prepared to make a last-ditch stand. Staples emerged from his first battle unscathed and later became an officer.

I can't conscientiously say that our alignment would have suited a West Point drill cadet, but we got to the top, helped and heartened by the lusty cheering of a Connecticut regiment then deploying a few hundred yards to our right. Coming to the top of the rise we saw just the other side of a dilapidated Virginia fence, a line or two of rebel infantry, and just back of them—or mingled with them—some field-pieces. The instant we made our appearance on their premises

"Down went twenty, thirty, forty, brave fellows."

they gave us a hearty "how'd 'doo" in the shape of a volley of musketry slap in our faces. To this very day I confidently believe the rascals did it on purpose. We gave them five hundred of the same kind of pills. 'Twas the first time we had shot and been shot at in earnest. It was our first gunpowder christening—a species of battle confirmation so to speak. Were we scared?

Well, honestly, I never knew; there wasn't time for first sensations; if I had sat right down then and there in the most comfortable rocking-chair on that hill, and tried to analyze our feelings, I doubt if I could have made a logical job of it.

There were guns to be fired, and guns to load and fire again; there was a nasty line of grizzly gray scoundrels on the other side of that fence to practice real shooting on. Moreover we were in search of that rebel Johnston, but the dickens of it was, there wasn't either time or quietness to inquire across the fence which *was* Johnston, the man we had come to smash. Down went our splendid California flag. Down went the bearer of it, Sergeant William A. Deane, shot fatally through the throat, and the flag was on the ground, only for a fraction of a minute however, for Corporal Moore caught it and held it aloft. Down it went once more, and the brave corporal never spoke again. Down went another of our three flags, the bearer of that killed. Down went Captain Skinner, commander of Company C, close to the colors. Down went twenty, thirty, forty, brave fellows.

I said a moment ago that I didn't know what our sensations were. I can tell you what they were getting to be about this part of the fight. It was mad, clear, stark, swearing mad (some of us were church members, too,) a burning desire to get at the gray rats beyond that fence. Somebody caught up one of the fallen flags. Gus Farnham—I beg his pardon—I mean Adjutant-General Farnham, caught up the other. I am quite sure he did—at any rate I saw the flag in his hands somewhere about this time. Meanwhile we moved slowly forward, loading and firing, while the thin barrels of our ancient muskets got so hot and swollen that it was impossible for ramrods to force the cartridge into them. The rebel infantry sneaked behind their guns. Some of our men were half over the fence, when along came a staff officer with orders for us to retire to the shelter of some rising ground, a little to the left.

Sergeant William A. Deane of the 2d Maine Infantry was shot through the neck while carrying the regimental colors—a rich silk banner commissioned by Maine women living in California and bearing the coats of arms of both states.

Rallying his men to retake his unit's fallen colors, 2d Maine captain Elisha N. Jones was shot in the back. A fellow officer helped him to a field hospital, where he was taken prisoner. He died of his wound while in prison in Richmond.

Photographers George N. Barnard and James F. Gibson recorded this view of the Stone house in March 1862, when Federal forces returned to the battlefield at Manassas. Constructed in 1805 at the intersection of the Sudley road and the Warrenton Turnpike, the structure had served at various times as a tavern and a private residence. In August 1862 the Stone house was again caught in the cross fire during the Battle of Second Manassas.

PRIVATE
JOHN T. COXE
HAMPTON LEGION,
SOUTH CAROLINA,
HOLMES' BRIGADE

Having bought time by their stand at the Warrenton Pike and Robinson house, the legion's survivors withdrew to the woods on the east flank of Henry House Hill. Coxe was 16 when he ran away from the home of his guardian in Greenville, South Carolina, and enlisted.

By this time we didn't care much as to what happened. Our rifle fire sounded like the popping of caps, our throats were choked with powder, and we were burning up with thirst. At length, becoming alarmed at our isolated position, Conner shouted and said: "Fall back in good order men!" And after we got back of the Robinson house there was a lull in the noise of battle. We got mixed up with many strange troops, apparently in panic and whom it was said that our fighting at the Warrenton Turnpike had saved, but just how we didn't know. After this the Legion fought in squads, sometimes under company officers, but more often alone.

Filtering down to the lower rim of the plateau, we found many mounted officers re-forming tangled lines and receiving fresh troops, now constantly arriving from Lower Bull Run. I saw many men and horses charging about the Henry house, and soon one of our batteries,

"It was not from any bravery or foolhardiness on my part that I walked through this cross-fire of musket balls and cannon balls."

a little to the right on the plateau, opened fire in that direction. Then a big, fine regiment arrived from below and in line of battle was sent through the edge of the pine woods on the left toward the Henry house. Then a big crowd of us went down into the pines and drank from a muddy pool and saw a squadron of our cavalry in line of battle with drawn sabers. As we returned to the plateau we heard a great volley of musketry about the Henry house and some cheering. By this time there were many Confederates on the plateau, and lines of battle were forming. I looked down the Run and saw many regiments hastening up to us with banners streaming.

PRIVATE GEORGE S. BARNSLEY
8TH GEORGIA INFANTRY, BARTOW'S BRIGADE

Bloodied in the morning's fight on Matthews Hill, Colonel Bartow's brigade made a disorderly retreat to Henry House Hill, where officers struggled to rally the exhausted survivors. Barnsley's regiment sustained 200 casualties—the greatest loss of any Confederate regiment in the battle—but eventually managed to re-form under cover of the woods. Later in the day Bartow, mislabeled a general in this account, was killed while personally carrying the regimental flag.

This box knapsack—so called because its canvas cover was stretched over a wooden frame—belonged to Private George T. Stovall of Company A of the 8th Georgia Infantry, the Rome Light Guards. Stovall was killed on Matthews Hill.

At the fence in the hollow we had passed through were quite a body of men. One of the gallant boys of Oglethorpe Light Infantry, of Sav. had got hold of our colors, and was sitting on the fence—I stopped a few minutes to gather the half ripe blackberries, for my lips were cracked and bleeding from the powder of the cartridges and my tongue and mouth dry as a chip of pine lying in the sun. I did not feel hungry, but tired to almost indifference. What stopped the men was a young man, an aide-de-camp of several Virginia Regmts. named Washington—some of us recollected him, not agreeably, at Winchester. He was harraunging the colorbearer, and calling him and us cowards. This was of course for only a few moments or so, and then some one ordered or said that we should rally at the house on the hill, and the whole went down the gully to get to a wood,

and under cover reach the house. I was too tired and proposed to Jett, for we were behind, that in place of going around that we should go through the field straight up to the house. We started and got to a fence in the middle. Getting over Jett got a ball and fell backwards. He would not let me stay with him, so I continued to walk on. It was not from any bravery or foolhardiness on my part that I walked through this cross-fire of musket balls and cannon balls. The fact was I had lost all consciousness of danger, I suppose from physical fatigue. Before I reached the house I met Genl. Bartow, and stopped with him looking down across the big field at some New Orleans Zouaves trying to take a battery. The men ran up and down the hill, and it seemed to me wanted help. I asked the General if I could go to them. He told me that I had better go on to my colors.

DRILLMASTER CHARLES C. WIGHT
27TH VIRGINIA INFANTRY, JACKSON'S BRIGADE

For nearly four hours Jackson's men held their ground on Henry House Hill, supporting Confederate artillery and subjected to a deadly barrage from Yankee batteries. Wight, a 19-year-old cadet from VMI on temporary duty with the 27th Virginia, recalled the terror of his first battle and then the odd relief he felt when his unit was finally ordered forward to engage the enemy. During the charge Wight was briefly knocked unconscious by a bullet that grazed his scalp.

As soon as our battery commences to fire, a perfect storm of shot passes over us. It seems as if the enemy had just found out where we are. A caisson standing near us is blow up and startles us so that good many spring for their feet, but Major Grigsby of the 27th Regt. draws his sword and orders all to lie down. We lie here a long while flat on our faces in the broiling hot sun, the firing seeming to approach rather than recede. Many men were killed and wounded while we are here.

The wounded cry out . . . every moment, and are borne to the rear by their friends. Some are killed so instantly that those who were nearest to them would not know it. We begin to think that a battle is not so nice as some had imagined. We have plenty of time to think, and the constant scream of the shell & the occasional whistle of a bullet impress upon us the danger of our situation. At last guns in front of us are moved back. The fire of the enemy's batteries slackens; but the musketry increases in volume. At this moment we are ordered to rise and though we feel that our part is not done; still it is a relief to stand up. As we rise we leave many bodies of our comrades lying, as if asleep, and so hard is it to realize that they are no longer of us that we fell like calling on them to take their places in ranks. We are ordered forward, and as the long line moves toward the crest of the hill that conceals the enemy, the sight rekindles our enthusiasm. I can never forget the sight that bursts upon us as we reach the summit of the slope. Opposite to us was a hill partly wooded, partly cleared. The open portion of this was black with men and along the edge of the wood we can see the glistening of muskets.

This March 1862 photograph by George N. Barnard was taken from a viewpoint looking northward across the Warrenton Turnpike (middle distance) to the slope of Henry House Hill. After driving the shattered brigades of Bee, Bartow, and Evans across the pike, McDowell's Federals discontinued their advance to re-form their ranks before resuming. This fateful pause enabled arriving Confederate units to rush into place and rally alongside Jackson's brigade on the crest of the hill.

blood on the face, and some borne by friends. A few were utterly demoralized and declared that the battle was lost. Up a lane, then to the right in the open field a little below the crest, and we dismounted and unlimbered. And there was a battlefield—lines of blue, with volleys and wreaths of smoke, batteries belching flames—before us. Right and left of us were our own people of the First Brigade. Back of us rode Beauregard and his staff. To and fro passed Jackson, holding up a bandaged hand. Our guns were shotted and fired, and it seemed the greatest noise we had ever heard. As I ran from caisson to gun carrying shot, a minie ball flattened itself on the tire of the gun wheel and then struck my right arm, making a bruise like the flow of a stone.

PRIVATE JAMES P. SMITH
ROCKBRIDGE ARTILLERY, VIRGINIA, JACKSON'S BRIGADE

Shortly before noon Colonel William N. Pendleton bolstered Jackson's line on Henry House Hill with four guns from the Rockbridge Artillery. Along with several other Confederate batteries the Virginians kept up a heavy fire that checked the advancing enemy. A native of Ohio, Smith was promoted to lieutenant in September of the following year and assigned to Stonewall Jackson's staff.

At once we were in motion. Have you ever seen a battery move into action? It is a spirited sight. Cannoneers swing to their seats on the limber chests, horses are spurred and lashed into a gallop, officers draw their sabers and shout their orders in ringing tones. Soon we met the wounded, limping, or bearing bleeding arms, or with

Lieutenant Alexander S. "Sandie" Pendleton, the 20-year-old son of General Joseph E. Johnston's chief of artillery, left the University of Virginia to serve on Jackson's staff. Pendleton's horse was killed beneath him as the lieutenant led a counterattack on Henry House Hill.

PRIVATE CLEMENT D. FISHBURNE
ROCKBRIDGE ARTILLERY, VIRGINIA, JACKSON'S BRIGADE

By 3:00 p.m. Jackson had more than a dozen pieces of artillery supporting his five regiments on Henry House Hill. Their firepower held the Federal formations at bay and allowed the battered Confederate units to rally. But the gunners' ammunition was running low, and at 3:30 Jackson decided to launch the first in a series of counterattacks. Fishburne's concern about whether dodging bullets might be less than manly was shared by countless soldiers on both sides.

Then we began to see men straggling back who said the battle was going on hotly, and many intimated that all was lost. Presently we met wounded men who called to us to hurry on, some badly wounded were less despondent than the sound men we met. Some of the sufferers called out words of encouragement. Our rapid motion and the frequent running conversations with these men whom we met, kept us from any grave reflections on the danger into which we were running. We reached the top of the hill and turned to our right in an old field and unlimbered our guns and commenced firing to the left of the direction in which we entered the field. Just in the rear of the Battery, we found the Infantry lying on the ground, the Colonels and field officers at the head of each and Gen. Jackson riding backwards in front of them. All the horses heads were turned to the front. Some anxiety had been expressed lest we would have difficulty in holding the horses, which we assumed would be scared and give us trouble. Men were assigned to aid the drivers if necessary. To our surprise the horses seemed to be perfectly indifferent to the danger and the only trouble was to keep them from getting tangled in the harness in their efforts to eat the scanty grass at their feet. I was chief of caisson and had to give out ammunition to the men who were detailed to carry it to the gun. Our caisson chests were mounted on the running gear of common country wagons so that I sat on the edge and in this position I reached out the ammunition and handed it to the men who carried it. Whilst occupying this perch I remember distinctly woundering if it would be unsoldier-like in me to dodge these minie balls, which were flitting by my ears or bow when those horrid shells passed over me. I saw Capt. Pendleton who had just been commissioned Colonel, make a motion like dodging and thought there could be no harm in it, but I saw Gen. Jackson, who in riding along his beat, was often not fifty steps in rear of me, sitting on horse which had been shot in the thigh, with his chin cocked up as if he was expecting a rain and was not averse to having a drop of it on his face. He had his hand raised, wrapped in a handkerchief, and was evidently wounded, but he refused to dodge. I do not know whether I tried to imitate him or not, but I dare say I bowed involuntarily more than once. I learned, by the way afterwards, that dodging was not inconsistent with the highest courage.

SERGEANT MAJOR ROBERT T. COLES
4TH ALABAMA INFANTRY, BEE'S BRIGADE

With nearly 200 of their number dead or wounded, the soldiers of Coles' regiment rallied around their brigade commander, General Bee, who led them back into the fight on Henry Hill. It was Bee's rallying cry that gave the sobriquet Stonewall to Jackson, whose stalwart Virginians formed the linchpin of the new Confederate line. While supporting Jackson's counterattack Bee was shot in the abdomen and carried to the rear. He succumbed to his wound the following day.

It was now about two o'clock. The enemy were preparing to advance with fresh troops over our line of retreat. . . . General Bee, very much depressed at the unfortunate turn of affairs, then proceeded to collect his scattered forces. Riding up to the 4th Alabama, he inquired, "What regiment is this?" Captain Richard Clarke, or Captain Porter King, quickly replied: "Why General, don't you know your own men—this is what is left of the 4th Alabama." After stating that this was the only part of his command he had been fortunate enough to find, he then said: "Come with me and go yonder where Jackson stands like a stonewall."

As soon as the water detail which had been sent out returned and the men had satisfied their thirst, the regiment fell into line and followed General Bee to the support of General Jackson. While getting into position with his battery, Lieutenant John Pelham commanding Alburtis' battery, cut the regiment at the centre to pass through. When the two battalions joined, it was learned that our beloved and gallant leader, General Bee, had fallen severely wounded.

"At that moment some of our men who, evidently, had the 'buck fever,' commenced, without orders, firing some scattering shots."

Jackson, a 33-year-old professor at VMI when this ambrotype was taken, wore the blue frock coat at right in action at Manassas. Beauregard praised the puritanical Virginian as "an able, fearless soldier and sagacious commander," and Jackson was hailed throughout the South for his stand on Henry House Hill. Characteristically, Jackson attributed his success to divine intervention, writing, "God made my brigade more instrumental than any other in repulsing the main attack."

PRIVATE JOHN O. CASLER
33D VIRGINIA INFANTRY, JACKSON'S BRIGADE

A farmer from Hampshire County, Casler served in the Potomac Guards—Company A of the 33d Virginia—which anchored Jackson's left flank on the hill. Deploying forward from the Sudley road, the advancing Federal units were unaware of Jackson's presence on the reverse slope until the Virginians rose up and opened fire. The Yankee troops Casler describes were members of either the 11th New York Fire Zouaves or the 1st Minnesota Infantry; both regiments wore red shirts.

They passed through our brigade and formed in the rear. I knew they were South Carolinians by the "Palmetto tree" on their caps. General Bee and Colonel Bartow fell, mortally wounded. The enemy, flushed with victory, pushed on, never dreaming what was lying just behind the brow of the hill in the pines. There seemed to be a lull in the firing just at this time, and Sergeant James P. Daily, of my company, walked up to the brow of the hill, but soon returned with the exclamation: "Boys, there is the prettiest sight from the top of the hill you ever saw; they are coming up on the other side in four ranks, and all dressed in red."

When we heard that, I, with several others, jumped up and started to see, but Colonel Cummings ordered us to "stay in ranks," and Daily remarked: "We will see them soon enough." Sure enough, in a few seconds the head of the column made its appearance, with three officers on horseback in front, and marching by the flank, with the intention of flanking one of our batteries—the Rockbridge Artillery, Captain W. N. Pendleton. In a few minutes they spied us lying there, and I heard one of the officers say: "Hello! what men are these?" At that moment some of our men who, evidently, had the "buck fever," commenced, without orders, firing some scattering shots. The enemy then poured a volley into us, but as we were lying down the balls went over our heads, harmless.

COLONEL WILLIS A. GORMAN
1ST MINNESOTA INFANTRY, FRANKLIN'S BRIGADE

With his army on the brink of victory, McDowell ordered the U.S. Artillery batteries of Captains Charles Griffin and James Ricketts to pave the way for a climactic assault. Griffin unlimbered his guns north of the Henry house, and Ricketts came into position just south of the building. The Fire Zouaves and Gorman's regiment deployed as support for the Union cannon but met with disaster when division commander Samuel Heintzelman mistook Jackson's troops for Federals.

After remaining in this position for some ten minutes I received orders from both your aides and those of Colonel Heintzelman to pass the whole front of the enemy's line, in support of Ricketts' battery, and proceed to the extreme right of our line and the left of the enemy, a distance of about a mile or more. The movement was effected at "quick" and "double-quick" time, both by the infantry and

"Instantly a blaze of fire was poured into the faces of the combatants, each producing terrible destruction owing to the close proximity of the forces, which was followed by volley after volley."

artillery, during which march the men threw from their shoulders their haversacks, blankets, and most of their canteens, to facilitate their eagerness to engage the enemy. On arriving at the point indicated . . . in advance of all other of our troops, and where I was informed officially that two other regiments had declined to charge, we formed a line of battle, our right resting within a few feet of the woods and the left at and around Ricketts' battery and upon the crest of the hill, within fifty or sixty feet of the enemy's line of infantry, with whom we could have conversed in an ordinary tone of voice. Immediately upon Ricketts' battery coming into position, and we in "line of battle," Colonel Heintzelman rode up between our lines and that of the enemy, within pistol shot of each, which circumstance staggered my judgment whether those in front were friends or enemies, it being equally manifest that the enemy were in the same dilemma as to our identity. But a few seconds, however, undeceived both, they displaying the rebel and we the Union flag. Instantly a blaze of fire was poured into the faces of the combatants, each producing terrible destruction owing to the close proximity of the forces, which was followed by volley after volley, in regular and irregular order as to time, until Ricketts' battery was disabled, and cut to pieces and a large portion of its officers and men had fallen, and until Companies H, I, K, C, G, and those immediately surrounding my regimental flag were so desperately cut to pieces as to make it more of a slaughter than an equal combat, the enemy manifestly numbering five guns to our one, besides being intrenched in the woods and behind ditches and pits, plainly perceptible, and with batteries on the enemy's right enfilading my left flank and within 350 yards direct range.

A former instructor of artillery tactics at West Point, Captain Charles Griffin effectively countered the Rebel batteries facing him on Henry House Hill. But Griffin doubted the ability of the New York Fire Zouaves to defend his guns. "Mark my words," he told artillery chief William Barry, "they will not support us."

PRIVATE ORVILLE D. THATCHER

1st Minnesota Infantry, Franklin's Brigade

Hurrying past the Fire Zouaves, who had already suffered many casualties, Thatcher's regiment filed into woods east of the Sudley road and formed a line of battle. Griffin shifted two of his cannon south of Ricketts' guns to support the Minnesotans' advance. Thatcher recalled the sudden confrontation with a Confederate force and the ensuing chaos. He survived but was wounded at Gettysburg.

Suddenly we were ordered to change positions at quick and double quick time as we reached the field, marching by the flank across the open space—which was a sort of grain stubble— past some straw stacks to the extreme right of the line; in the transit dodging the shells from the enemy's batteries, to which ours were replying. Reaching the vicinity of the Henry House, we descended the ravine toward the run and ascended the opposite slope, passing a small body of Regular cavalry which had halted in the ravine for protection from flying missiles, and who gave us a word of warning *en passant,* something to this effect: "Lookout boys, you're going into a hot place now!" It was on this slope that I saw the first dead soldier lying on his back, head down hill, with a ghastly wound, apparently from a piece of shell, which had torn away a portion of his upturned features. We

formed in line of battle among or near some pine bushes at the summit, with a thick grove of trees near our right flank, supporting Ricketts's battery. One of his or Griffin's guns subsequently broke into our line and fired with stunning effect to me personally, as the charge seemed to pass uncomfortably close to my right ear.

As I have previously stated, the Fire Zouaves (11th N.Y.) were on our left and the 14th (Brooklyn) N.Y. on our right rear. We had but just formed this line when, as if by magic, an opposing force confronted us within seemingly pistol range. Gen. Heintzelman's command, given with his peculiar nasal twang, "Fire once, boys, then charge, and you've got 'em," I shall never forget. I plainly saw this body of men facing us and distinctly recollect their white cross-belts and gray uniforms. At that moment some officer shouted "Don't fire men, those are our friends," or words to that effect; but in an instant all was confusion. The whole rebel line opened fire upon us, and we—nearly every man of my regiment, I believe—went down flat upon the ground to avoid the deadly shower of lead they sent among us.

A native of St. Anthony, William D. Mitchell enlisted in Company E of the 1st Minnesota. He emerged unscathed from Manassas, although 48 of his comrades were killed or died of their wounds. Taken prisoner at the Battle of Antietam, Mitchell was at first reported killed but was exchanged in October 1862. He finished his service in the ranks of the Veteran Reserve Corps.

SERGEANT MAJOR RANDOLPH J. BARTON

33d Virginia Infantry, Jackson's Brigade

The tide of battle on Henry House Hill turned in favor of the Confederates when Barton's regiment charged the Yankee batteries. The teenage Barton—who eventually became a captain—was among a cadre of VMI cadets who joined their former professor, Jackson, in the Stonewall Brigade.

After taking our position on the left of the brigade, we laid upon the ground listening to the musketry and cannonading going on to our right, or, rather, somewhat in front of our right, from the Confederate force, which was being vigorously responded to by the Yankees. The "Henry house" was in front of our brigade, over the hill—

the upper part of the house visible—and the Robinson house was to the right of that a few hundred yards. Occasional shells would explode over our regiment, and the solemn wonderment written on the faces of the men as they would crane their heads around to look for falling branches was almost amusing. I was near the left flank of the regiment, a few steps in rear, where, upon the formation of the regiment in line of battle, I belonged. Doubtless I wished I was home, but I had to stick. I remember an elderly man riding leisurely by towards the left, in rear of us, apparently giving orders. Some one, possibly myself, asked him who he was. He turned his horse and said: "I am Colonel Smith, otherwise Governor Smith, otherwise Extra Billy Smith." It was, in fact, Colonel Smith, a game old fellow, who, I suppose, was looking over the ground for a position for his regiment, the 49th Virginia, as it subsequently took position on our left, and finally united in one of the charges upon Griffin's Battery.

Colonel Cummings and Lieutenant Colonel Lee were in front of our regiment, perhaps a hundred yards, stooping down, and occasionally standing to get a view over the crest of the hill that rose gently before us for a little over a hundred yards. The musketry kept up on our right, and then Colonels Cummings and Lee were seen to rise and, bending down, to come back with somewhat quickened steps to the regiment. I remember, as Colonel Cummings drew near, he called out: "Boys, they are coming, now wait until they get close before you fire."

Almost immediately several pieces of artillery, their horses in front, made their appearance on the hill in front of us, curving as if going into battery, and at the same time I descried the spear-point and upper portion of a United States flag, as it rose in the hands of its bearer over the hill; then I saw the bearer, and the heads of the men composing the line of battle to the right and left of him. At the sight several of our men rose from the ranks, leveled their muskets at the line, and, although I called out, "Do not fire yet," it was of no use; they fired and then the shrill cry of Colonel Cummings was heard, "Charge!" and away the regiment went, firing as they ran, into the ranks of the enemy, and particularly at the battery towards which our line rapidly approached.

Although bearing a non-commissioned officer's sword, I had obtained a cartridge box, belted it on, and had in some way secured a flintlock musket, with which one of our companies was armed. This gun, after two futile efforts, I fired at a man on horseback in the battery, one of the drivers, I think. I got near enough to the battery to see that it was thoroughly disabled, horses and men falling, and our line driving ahead, when I felt the sting of a bullet tearing a piece from my side, just under my cartridge box, which I had pulled well around on the right and front of my waist. I called out that I was wounded to my uncle, Frank Jones, who helped me up on his horse, and carried me to the rear.

Corporal Clarence A. Fonerdon of the 27th Virginia was wearing this leather cartridge box in the charge on Ricketts' battery. Fonerdon was spared a wound when the box, with its load of paper-wrapped musket rounds, stopped a Yankee bullet.

This sword belonged to Ricketts, who, wounded four times, fell from his saddle and lay unconscious amid the wreck of his battery until he was taken prisoner. A Federal trooper picked up the sword to prevent it from falling into Rebel hands.

PRIVATE JOHN G. SONDERMAN

1ST MINNESOTA INFANTRY, FRANKLIN'S BRIGADE

Though Sonderman castigated both Captain Griffin and Major Barry for failing to open fire on the advancing Confederate ranks, in fact Barry was the guilty party. Griffin was convinced that the soldiers were Rebels, rather than his "battery support," as the major assured him. The dispirited Alabama and Mississippi soldiers encountered by Sonderman's regiment were survivors of Barnard Bee's brigade who had come back into the fight alongside Jackson's Virginians.

Their advance from the woods was deliberate and quiet, and, though perceived from the batteries, they were senselessly held by Griffin and Maj. Barry, the Chief of Artillery, as friends; and so, coming close up, our regiment withholding its fire on account of the Griffin-Barry statement, delivered the first volley, which took effect in the center of our regiment, as well as the batteries, killing our Color Sergeant and wounding three Corporals of the color guard, also killing and wounding 30 men of the color company. Capt. Lewis McKune, of Co. G, was killed, other companies suffering severely, and the colors were riddled with bullets. The men of our regiment at the center and on the left dropped on the slope and returned the fire, and we on the right, engaged in the front, now for the first time discovering the enemy, turned our fire on his left rear at close range.

But they pushed over the batteries, pretty well jammed up, and finally faced about toward us, and we expected their volley. Instead came a frantic waving of arms and fearful yells, of which we could not distinguish the words because of our fire, which was kept up till the enemy faced to the rear, and after awhile gained distance enough to step out and then to run, when we broke through the fence to follow alongside.

We found the roads full of fleeing Alabamians, and picked up half a dozen too badly demoralized to run. I should have stated that before we crossed the fence, and at the hight of our fire, we captured a mounted officer of the 2d Miss., who had come around to us by the woods and the Sudley road to "remonstrate against firing on our friends." He was astonished on learning who we were.

The Alabamians wore home-made clothing, mostly red shirts; and our red shirts, dim through the smoke, and in the supposed direction of the Alabamians, had misled the enemy's charging column, and they got a taste of their own medicine.

Colonel Samuel P. Heintzelman was a 35-year veteran of the Regular Army whose seniority earned him command of a division in McDowell's force. Wounded on Henry House Hill, Heintzelman blamed the defeat on his volunteers' "want of discipline," reporting, "Such a rout I never witnessed before."

PRIVATE HARRISON H. COMINGS
11TH NEW YORK INFANTRY, WILLCOX'S BRIGADE

While screening Jackson's left flank with 150 troopers of the 1st Virginia Cavalry, Colonel J. E. B. Stuart emerged from a patch of timber to find the red-shirted Fire Zouaves of the 11th New York directly in his front. Stuart shouted, "Charge" and led his horsemen pounding through the ranks of the startled New Yorkers, throwing them into disorder. Officers managed to rally and re-form the line of battle, but a number of soldiers, Comings among them, took to their heels.

Among the Confederate fatalities on Henry House Hill was Private James W. Crowell of the 4th Virginia Infantry. Crowell, a carpenter by trade, had enlisted in his home county of Pulaski in southwestern Virginia. In the fighting for the hilltop, his regiment suffered heavy casualties—31 dead and 100 wounded.

Our march was over a dusty road, and before we went into a piece of woods orders came for knapsacks to be left on the side of the road, to be taken up on our return from the battle. Now I know of one who either forgot where he left his knapsack or did not deem it wise to spend a great amount of time looking for the same. Previous to being ordered into action, as we came into an open space by column of companies, marching across the field, the first Minnesota on our right, a shell or shot struck the ground about 50 feet from the left of the company. It scooped out about a cart load of dirt, and making a bound passed over our heads and landed about 200 feet on the other side of us. I was somewhat stirred up, as that was my first experience. Presently the order came "By companies, left wheel," and then "Double quick." Rickett's battery was in the advance, and as soon as the top of the hill was reached the cannon were prepared for action. We were held as the support. The rebels made two distinct charges, each time being driven back. The first Minnesota regiment, which should have been close to us, was about 200 feet away, the space being left open. That which was called the Black Horse cavalry made the charge. It was at first supposed that they were of the Union army, but we soon found out our mistake, and as soon as our flank was well covered we received a volley at short range. Col. Farnham was mortally wounded, the major and adjutant unhorsed, and many of our regiment were either killed or wounded. Our first sergeant was badly wounded and taken prisoner along with a great many others. Our regiment was in a confused state, having no head to direct it, and every man was for himself. In going back I was stopped by a cavalryman, who made a strike at me with his sabre, but thanks to my musket and the position in which I held it at the time, I was spared to be here with you to tell my little story. I was ridden down by this same cavalryman, who seemed to be bent upon my extinction, but fate decreed otherwise. As he turned to leave I noticed the 14th regiment of New York coming towards us. I hardly knew what to do, as if I stood up I would be liable to be hit either from one side or the other. How I got off of that field I am at loss to tell; but I did get away and made for the woods, the same I supposed that we came from. Presently I met our color bearer who was in the act of taking our flag from its staff. I asked him what he intended to do, and suiting the action to the word he placed the flag in his bosom and threw the staff away.

Picked up by a Rebel soldier following the fight on Henry House Hill, this fez most likely belonged to one of the Fire Zouaves. Though widely condemned for poor discipline, the 11th New York lost 173 men defending Ricketts' and Griffin's guns.

LIEUTENANT WILLIAM W. BLACKFORD
1ST VIRGINIA CAVALRY

One of five brothers in Confederate service, at Manassas Blackford served as adjutant of the 1st Virginia and galloped his horse in the forefront of the charge on the Fire Zouaves. Blackford's antagonist may actually have been a member of the red-legged 14th Brooklyn, as the Zouaves wore blue trousers.

William L. Clark, a graduate of Yale University, left his law practice in Winchester to command Company F of the 2d Virginia in Jackson's brigade. Wounded on Henry House Hill, he resigned in 1862 and was invalided home. He returned to service late in the war.

Colonel Stuart and myself were riding at the head of the column as the grand panorama opened before us, and there right in front, about seventy yards distant, and in strong relief against the smoke beyond, stretched a brilliant line of scarlet—a regiment of New York Zouaves in column of fours, marching out of the Sudley road to attack the flank of our line of battle. Dressed in scarlet caps and trousers, blue jackets with quantities of gilt buttons, and white gaiters, with a fringe of bayonets swaying above them as they moved, their appearance was indeed magnificent. The Sudley road was here in deep depression and the rear of the column was still hid from view—there were about five hundred men in sight—they were all looking toward the battlefield and did not see us. Waving his sabre, Stuart ordered a charge, but instantly pulled up and called a halt and turning to me said, "Blackford, are those our men or the enemy?" I said I could not tell, but I had heard that Beauregard had a regiment of Zouaves from New Orleans, dressed, I had been told, like these men. Just then, however, all doubt was removed by the appearance of their colors, emerging from the road—the Stars and Stripes. I shall never forget the feelings with which I regarded this emblem of our country so long beloved, and now seen for the first time in the hands of a mortal foe. But there was no time for sentiment then. The instant the flag appeared, Stuart ordered the charge, and at them we went like an arrow from a bow.

As we were in column of fours it was necessary to deploy, and our gallant Colonel waved his sabre for the rear to oblique to the left, "on right into line," so as to strike the enemy in "echelon" and this they did. While a Lieutenant in my company, I had carried a Sharp's carbine slung to my shoulder and this I still wore; I also had my sabre and a large sized five-shooter. In the occupation of the moment I had not thought which of my weapons to draw until I had started, and as it does not take long for a horse at full speed to pass over seventy yards, I had little time to make the selection. I found in fact that it would be impossible to get either my sabre or pistol in time, and as the carbine hung conveniently under my right hand I seized and cocked that, holding it in my right hand with my thumb on the hammer and finger on the trigger. I thought I would fire it and then use it for a crushing blow, in which it would be almost as effective against a man standing on the ground as a sabre.

Half the distance was passed before they saw the avalanche coming upon them, but then they came to a "front face"—a long line of bright muskets was leveled—a sheet of red flame gleamed, and we could see no more. Capt. Welby Carter's horse sprang forward and rolled over dead, almost in front of Comet, so that a less active animal would have been thrown down, but Comet recovered himself and cleared the struggling horse and his rider. The smoke which wrapped them from our sight also hid us from them, and thinking perhaps that we had been swept away by the volley, they, instead of coming to a "charge bayo-

net," lowered their pieces to load, and in this position we struck them. The tremendous impetus of horses at full speed broke through and scattered their line like chaff before the wind. As the scarlet line appeared through the smoke, when within a couple of horse's lengths of them, I leaned down, with my carbine cocked, thumb on hammer and forefinger on trigger, and fixed my eye on a tall fellow I saw would be the one my course would place in the right position for the carbine, while the man next to him, in front of the horse, I would have to leave to Comet. I then plunged the spurs into Comet's flanks and he evidently thought I wanted him to jump over this strange looking wall I was riding him at, for he rose to make the leap; but he was too close and going too fast to rise higher than the breast of the man, and he struck him full on the chest, rolling him over and over under his hoofs and knocking him about ten feet backwards, depriving him of all further interest in the subsequent proceedings, and knocking the rear rank man to one side. As Comet rose to make the leap, I leaned down from the saddle, rammed the muzzle of the carbine into the stomach of my man and pulled the trigger. I could not help feeling a little sorry for the fellow as he lifted his handsome face to mine while he tried to get his bayonet up to meet me; but he was too slow, for the carbine blew a hole as big as my arm clear through him.

Joined by surviving Fire Zouaves, the 14th Brooklyn desperately tried to retake the batteries of Ricketts and Griffin. Three times they charged, and once managed to get among the guns but were unable to bring them back. "The Fourteenth was almost alone in this slaughter pen," the regimental historian wrote, "the farther advance of the Fourteenth, or even its stand, mere wanton suicide."

"I think if McDowell had been in my lookout he would not have given the order."

ASSISTANT SURGEON EDWARD S. BARRETT

5TH MASSACHUSETTS INFANTRY, FRANKLIN'S BRIGADE

Barrett traveled to Washington with a supply of clothing for the soldiers of the 5th Massachusetts and accompanied them on the campaign. Perched in a persimmon tree, he had a panoramic view of the fight for Henry House Hill. By the time the men of the 5th reached Manassas, less than two weeks remained of their term of service.

When the commander of the 14th Brooklyn fell wounded, Lieutenant Colonel Edward B. Fowler (left) led the unit in the final stages of the engagement. "Leaving the battlefield of Bull Run was not a retreat or a falling back," he recalled, "it was a stampede." A year later Fowler was severely wounded at Second Manassas.

The Ellsworth Zouaves and the Fourteenth New York Regiment were ordered to the support of this battery. I watched this advance with intense interest, for I felt it was a hazardous movement, it being far in advance of our main line, and I could see from my tree-top a considerable body of cavalry and infantry directly in their front, and on their left, partially concealed by the woods, and I think if McDowell had been in my lookout he would not have given the order.

The Zouaves presented a beautiful appearance as they marched behind the artillery; their showy scarlet uniform and their perfect marching I well remember. It was supposed that the Zouaves would stand fire, and only sought a good opportunity to avenge the murder of Ellsworth. But scarcely had the battery halted and fired, before the enemy opened upon them with their partially concealed artillery and a terrific fire of infantry, and our artillery were driven back pell-mell through the ranks of the Zouaves, many of their men and horses being killed. The Zouaves stood their ground, firing in lines, then falling on their faces to load. Their ranks were becoming thinned, yet they would not retire. Suddenly the rebel fire ceased, when out from the low pines dashed Stewart's cavalry, and charged with uplifted sabres upon the broken ranks of the Zouaves. The Zouaves resisted this onset as best they could. After firing their guns, too sorely pressed to load, they clubbed their muskets. It was a grand *melée;* cannoniers, rebel cavalry, and Zouaves. I could see the horses rearing, sabres glistening, and revolvers flashing; the only approach to a hand to hand conflict on the field that day.

Recently transferred from the 71st New York Infantry to the 14th Brooklyn, Second Lieutenant Benjamin D. Phillips was among the 142 casualties sustained by that colorfully clad unit at Manassas. Disabilities from Phillips' leg wounds prevented him from returning to field duty, and he was mustered out in January 1862.

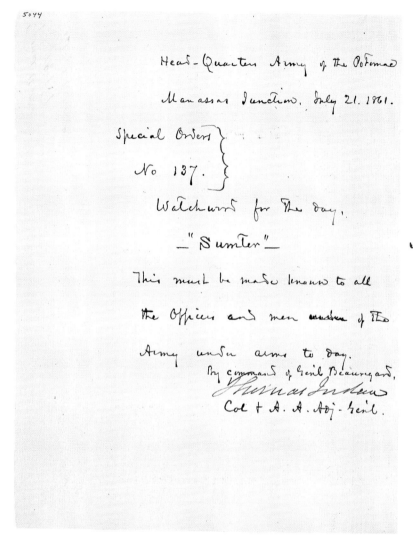

Beauregard feared that in battle his regiments might inadvertently fire upon one another or hold off firing on the enemy because their uniforms had no standard pattern or color and their national flags were similar looking. On July 21 Colonel Thomas Jordan, his acting assistant adjutant general, issued a special order instructing all troops to use the watchword "Sumter" as a form of identification.

PRIVATE JOHN O. CASLER
33D VIRGINIA INFANTRY, JACKSON'S BRIGADE

After J. E. B. Stuart's cavalry charge the New York Fire Zouaves re-formed and again advanced toward their unseen foe. It was most likely the Zouaves—rather than the 14th Brooklyn, as Casler supposed—that blundered into the waiting ranks of the 33d Virginia. The New Yorkers were routed, and the Virginians overran the two guns of Griffin's battery that had unlimbered opposite the Confederate left flank. A Union counterattack reclaimed the cannon, but only briefly.

That morning we had been given a signal to use in time of battle, to distinguish friend from foe, which was to throw the right hand to the forehead, palm outward, and say, "Sumter." When this regiment (which was the 14th Brooklyn, N.Y.), appeared in view Colonel Cummings gave the signal, and it was returned by one of the officers, but how they got it was a mystery. So, when the scattering shots were fired by some of our regiment, Colonel Cummings exclaimed: "Cease firing, you are firing on friends!" and the volley came from them at the same time, and I know I remarked, "Friends, hell! That looks like it."

Colonel Cummings, seeing his mistake, and also seeing a battery of artillery taking position and unlimbering, in close proximity and in a place where it could enfilade our troops, determined to capture it before it could do any damage. I don't think he had any orders from any superior officer, but took the responsibility on himself. Then came the command: "Attention! Forward march! Charge bayonets! Double quick!" and away we went, sweeping everything before us; but the enemy broke and fled.

We were soon in possession of the guns, killed nearly all the horses, and a great portion of the men were killed or wounded; and we were none too soon, for one minute more and four guns would have belched forth into our ranks, carrying death and destruction, and perhaps been able to have held their position. As it was, the guns were rendered useless, and were not used any more that day, although we had to give them up temporarily.

We were halted, and one of my company, Thomas Furlough, who had belonged to the artillery in the Mexican war, threw down his musket and said: "Boys, let's turn the guns on them." That was the last sentence that ever passed his lips, for just then he was shot dead.

LIEUTENANT SAMUEL J. C. MOORE

2D VIRGINIA INFANTRY, JACKSON'S BRIGADE

The Rebels on Henry House Hill also suffered their share of blunders and failures of nerve, as Moore recalled in a postwar memoir. When the 33d Virginia launched its unauthorized assault, Colonel James W. Allen failed to provide support to Cummings' unit, and both commands were savaged by a cross fire from the 14th Brooklyn.

Shouting, "Come on boys quick, and we can whip them!" 17-year-old VMI cadet Charles Norris (above) led the 27th Virginia against Ricketts' battery. Moments later he was struck and killed by a Yankee bullet or shell fragment, the mark of which is visible on the left shoulder of Norris' cadet jacket (right).

The two guns thus advanced towards our left flank were supported by the Brooklyn Regiment, known as "Lincoln's pet lambs", perhaps the best fighting men McDowell had in the field, the representatives of the lowest class of a City population. Col. Cummin's Regiment had orders to charge upon their Battery, which they did and succeeded in taking the pieces, but were in their turn charged by the Brooklyn Zouaves, who were too strong for them and drove them back in confusion. Col. Allen was earnestly entreated to support Cummins in this charge, but he refused to do so, upon the ground that his orders were to hold his position, which orders, however, were not obeyed at a later period of the fight, as you will see after a while. The result was that Cummin's men driven back by the Zouaves could not form again on our left, but retreated behind us, thus leaving our left flank exposed, which was taken advantage of by the Zouaves who came up on our left and open a brisk fire down the whole length of our line—thus were we exposed to a crossfire, in fact to a treble fire, viz. the battery in our front, that on our left, somewhat in front, and the infantry on our flank. By a sudden wheel to the left we might have removed ourselves from the range of the Cannons in front, and by a brisk charge we could have routed the Zouaves & taken the two guns on our left—thus holding our position and covering the 2nd Regiment with glory—this could have been done too, I am satisfied, with a loss no greater than we suffered—but to do it required promptness and courage in our Colonel, neither of which qualities, I regret to say, was exhibited by him in a great degree in the trying emergency I have described. Standing a while like one bewildered, Col. Allen called out in my hearing "fall back fall back, men"—a most unmilitary order, and given in such a way as to render confusion inevitable—in fact the nature of the ground, and of a very close pine thicket just behind us, rendered it impossible to form a line after having fallen back 5 paces. It is a fact which cannot be disputed that from this time the Col. lost all command over himself, and behaved more like a child than a man at one time shedding tears & at another excusing himself on the ground that he could not see all the time, however, keeping on the opposite side of the hill from the enemy. Lt Col. Lackland, though he had been prostrated with sickness for a long time, rallied part of the Regiment & took it gallantly forward, charging & taking the two cannons on our left—and Major Botts too behaved with courage & coolness.

COLONEL WILLIAM SMITH

49TH VIRGINIA INFANTRY, COCKE'S BRIGADE

At 63 one of the oldest Confederate field officers, "Extra Billy" Smith had been a Virginia governor and four-term congressman before taking up arms. Leaving his position on Bull Run, Smith marched for the sound of the guns, gathering stragglers as he went. His timely arrival on Henry House Hill was crucial to the Rebel victory.

Shortly after this bloody strife began, looking to my left, I saw a heavy mass of the enemy advancing from the direction of the Sudley and Manassas road, on a line parallel with and equidistant between my line of battle and the Henry house. For a moment I thought I must be doubled up, but had resolved to stand my ground, cost what it might, when, to my great relief, the Sixth North Carolina, Colonel Fisher, and the Second Mississippi, Colonel Falkner, came up from the direction of the Lewis house, and formed in much confusion

on my left, relieving me, however, in a great degree from my perilous position. I had three times stopped these regiments as previously described, and now they came up so opportunely to my relief that it almost seemed to be an act of Providence. By the time they had formed in tolerable order, the enemy nearly covered their front without seeming to have discovered them. Being on my extreme left, one of the North Carolinians, recognizing me, called to me from his ranks: "That is the enemy; shall we fire?" I replied: "Don't be in a hurry; don't fire upon friends." At the instant a puff of wind spread out the Federal flag, and I added, "There is no mistake; give them h——l, boys!" thus giving orders most strangely to a regiment which was not under my command to begin the fight. The enemy was soon scattered and disappeared from the field. I have not been able, after much investigation, to discover his name or number. Lieutenant-Colonel Lightfoot, of the Sixth North Carolina, claims that his regiment united with us in one of the charges on the enemy's guns and to have suffered severely. It was on this charge, I presume, that Colonel Fisher was killed, as he fell some one hundred and fifty yards in advance of his original line of battle. When driven back from the enemy's guns neither the North Carolinians nor Mississippians remained to renew the charge, but incontinently left the field.

Torn in later fighting, the flag of the 6th North Carolina—one of Johnston's regiments—was carried into action on Henry House Hill, where the regiment helped shore up the wavering Rebel left. Colonel C. F. Fisher was killed while leading the Tar Heels in an unsuccessful effort to capture the Yankee batteries.

FIRST SERGEANT JOSIAS R. KING
1ST MINNESOTA INFANTRY, FRANKLIN'S BRIGADE

The appearance of fresh Confederate troops on their right flank further demoralized battered Yankee regiments, as King recalled in a postwar lecture. At the outbreak of war King was working as a surveyor in Minnesota and went to the front from that state. He later served as regimental adjutant and as an officer on the staff of General Alfred Sully. In 1863 King accompanied Sully to the West to suppress a bloody Sioux uprising in Minnesota and the Dakota Territory.

When his skirmish line came in sight from out of the woods, and was discovered by our men, exclamations came from all around: "Who the hell are those fellows over yonder." It only required about a minute to find out who they were, as the Brigade line of battle emerged from this wood, which was from 200 to 250 yards away. Then the circus began. Cries of "Fall in"! "Fall in men"! "Where is the 14th Brooklyn?" "Where is the 69th New York?" Meanwhile the Confederates were approaching. An attempt had been made to rally the men, and form a line regardless of regiments, but every one was giving orders, and pandemonium reigned supreme. The enemy had now approached within a hundred yards and poured a volley into this howling mob; it was then "Skiddoo," every man for himself and the devil take the hindmost.

received the severe fire of the enemy, returned it with spirit, and advanced delivering its fire. This regiment is uniformed in gray cloth, almost identical with that of the great bulk of the secession army, and when the regiment fell into confusion and retreated toward the road there was an universal cry that they were being fired on by our own men. The regiment rallied again, passed the brow of the hill a second time, but was again repulsed in disorder.

By this time the New York Seventy-ninth had closed up, and in like manner it was ordered to cross the brow of the hill and drive the enemy from cover. It was impossible to get a good view of this ground. In it there was one battery of artillery, which poured an incessant fire upon our advancing columns, and the ground was very irregular, with small clusters of pines, affording shelter, of which the enemy took good advantage. The fire or rifles and musketry was very severe. The Seventy-ninth, headed by its colonel (Cameron), charged across the hill, and for a short time the contest was severe. They rallied several times under fire, but finally broke and gained the cover of the hill.

This left the field open to the New York Sixty-ninth, Colonel Corcoran, who in his turn led his regiment over the crest, and had in full open view the ground so severely contested. The firing was very severe, and the roar of cannon, muskets, and rifles incessant. It was manifest the enemy was here in great force, far superior to us at that point. The Sixty-ninth held the ground for some times, but finally fell back in disorder.

COLONEL WILLIAM T. SHERMAN
BRIGADE COMMANDER, TYLER'S DIVISION

A lean and grizzled Ohioan who would end up second only to Grant in the hierarchy of successful Union generals, Sherman had his first opportunity for field command at Manassas, where his brigade sustained more casualties than any comparable Federal unit. But his decision to commit his regiments to the attack one at a time proved unfortunate. Each charge was repulsed in turn, and the shaken survivors of earlier attacks demoralized those who followed.

Before reaching the crest of this hill the roadway was worn deep enough to afford shelter, and I kept the several regiments in it as long as possible; but when the Wisconsin Second was abreast of the enemy, by order of Major Wadsworth, of General McDowell's staff, I ordered it to leave the roadway by the left flank, and to attack the enemy. This regiment ascended to the brow of the hill steadily,

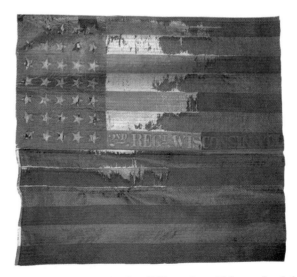

This national color was borne by the 2d Wisconsin, which spearheaded Sherman's assault. Later in the war the regiment became part of the famed Iron Brigade.

Rebel Triumph, Yankee Debacle

As the battle thundered on through the long, hot afternoon, General Johnston did the crucial work of hurrying regiments from the rear to reinforce and extend the battered Confederate line. The 18th and 28th Virginia Infantries, led by Colonel Philip St. George Cocke, marched to Jackson's threatened left, followed by Brigadier General Milledge L. Bonham's 2d and 6th South Carolina, then the brigade of Colonel Jubal A. Early.

Also rushing to Jackson's aid was a last, late-arriving brigade from Johnston's own Shenandoah army commanded by Brigadier General Edmund Kirby Smith, which had reached Manassas Junction by train about noon. Kirby Smith immediately double-timed the troops toward the sound of firing and, passing Johnston's command post at the Lewis house, got his orders. "Take them to the front," Johnston yelled. "Go where the fire is hottest."

Rude planks set in swampy ground mark the graves of Yankee soldiers in a photograph that was taken by a Northerner in the fall of 1862. Most dead Federals at First Manassas were hastily interred by the victorious Confederates in shallow mass graves.

Kirby Smith rushed his men to Bald Hill on the Rebel far left. Early's brigade moved still farther left to Chinn Ridge. As Kirby Smith's brigade approached the battle line about 4:00 p.m., he was wounded. But Colonel Arnold Elzey, taking command, quickly sent the troops smashing through a woods to the front, where they leveled a raking fire at Colonel Oliver Howard's brigade of New Englanders, then mounted an all-out charge.

The sudden attack, backed by musket fire and artillery fire from Early's brigade and from Jeb Stuart's troopers, sent Howard's Maine and Vermont regiments into disarray. After a brief but disorganized stand, Howard's men fell rapidly back across Young's Branch. Within minutes the entire right wing of General McDowell's army had begun to melt away.

Sensing victory, Beauregard ordered an assault by his entire line. With unearthly yells, the Rebels stormed down Henry House Hill, scattering the already disorganized Union regiments. By 4:30 the Federal center had dissolved, thousands of troops sullenly walking back toward the Warrenton Pike and Bull Run. "The men," wrote one of McDowell's aides, "seemed to be seized simultaneously by the conviction that it was no use to do anything more and they might as well start home." Streams of beaten men trudged back across Sudley Ford or went straight for Centreville by way of fords nearer the Stone Bridge, many discarding their gear—muskets, packs, cartridge boxes—as they retreated.

At first Beauregard sent troops and artillery charging on the heels of the fleeing Federals, Early's men dogging Howard's survivors, Stuart's cavalry pursuing the main body. Johnston for his part ordered Longstreet's brigade to cross Bull Run and close the escape route through Centreville. But then Beauregard, alarmed by a rumor that a fresh Federal attack had somehow threatened the Confederate right rear, halted all pursuit. By the time the rumor was proved false it was 7:00 and too late for his bone-weary troops to go on. Nor was there any pursuit of the thoroughly beaten Yankees the next day, as downpours turned the roads into quagmires.

Unharried, the Federal troops slogged back down the roads to Washington, as did the crowds of civilians—now as terrified and miserable as the most frightened of the soldiers—who had followed the army westward to see the great show. Amid the equipment captured by the Confederates, which included 27 cannon, 500 muskets, and a whopping 500,000 rounds of ammunition, were some ladies' slippers and even a parasol or two.

McDowell, judging his army too disorganized and dispirited for any more fighting, gave up any idea of making a stand at Centreville or anywhere else. After forming a reasonably effective rear guard along the pike, he also headed for the army's camps around Washington.

The scene there as the first troops dragged themselves back into the city on July 22 was grim indeed. The men were "baffled, humiliated, panic-struck," wrote Walt Whitman, then a reporter for the *Brooklyn Standard,* as well as "worn, hungry, haggard, blister'd in the feet." Where, Whitman wondered in sorrow, "are the vaunts, and the proud boasts with which you went forth? Where are your banners and your bands of music?"

For the Federals this clash on the banks of Bull Run was a profoundly demoralizing defeat, and a costly one in men lost. The fighting had been extraordinarily vicious, considering the soldiers' inexperience. Union casualties included only 470 known dead, but also 1,071 wounded and 1,793 "missing"—these latter being presumed captured or killed—for a total of about 3,000. Confederate losses were also heavy: 387 dead, 1,582 wounded, and 13 missing. Almost one-fourth of all Rebel casualties were from Jackson's regiments, which had fought with the dogged fury of their leader throughout the entire violent afternoon.

Inevitably the defeat cost McDowell his command. His scheme of attack on the exposed Confederate left had, in fact, been excellent. Bull Run, later wrote that exceedingly stern critic William Tecumseh Sherman, "was one of the best-planned battles of the war." But its execution—particularly the poor planning that led to slow, time-wasting marches and McDowell's own failure to press his great advantage during that long noontime delay—had been wretched.

On July 25, just four days after the battle, General in Chief Winfield Scott tapped George McClellan to take over the disorganized and downcast Union army skulking in and around Washington and see what miracles of reorganization and reinvigoration he could accomplish. This task matched McClellan's chief talents, and he would perform prodigies of regrouping, training, outfitting, and inspiring the defeated army. Unfortunately, he also learned a lesson—all too well, it turned out—from McDowell's experience. That general had complained repeatedly before setting out for Manassas that the army was too green to fight a big battle, though in the end the main problem had been that McDowell was too green to manage one. In the event, McClellan would subsequently drive President Lincoln, the Congress, and the high command nearly mad with his refusal to venture forth until he thought his force, now renamed the Army of the Potomac, was in such perfect order and had such an overwhelming advantage in numbers that it could not be defeated.

In the Confederate states, rejoicing over the Bull Run victory went on for weeks. Beauregard, the hero of Sumter, was lionized again as a born-again Napoleon. He was promoted to full general the day after the battle by President Davis—although General Johnston, in breaking free of his entanglement with Patterson's Federals in the Shenandoah Valley, speeding his reinforcements to Manassas, and repeatedly deploying them to the right place at the right time during the battle, had done far more than Beauregard to win it.

But after an initial optimistic expectation that the Yankees had been stopped cold and Southern independence assured, the people of the South soon came to a painful realization: The battle's size and ferocity meant that there would only be more such bloodbaths in the future.

The same harsh truth, along with waves of anger and indignation, spread through the North. If we "be not cast down and discouraged by this reverse," wrote one citizen, "we shall flog these scoundrels and traitors all the more bitterly before we are done with them." Echoed one soldier: "I shall see the thing played out or die in the attempt."

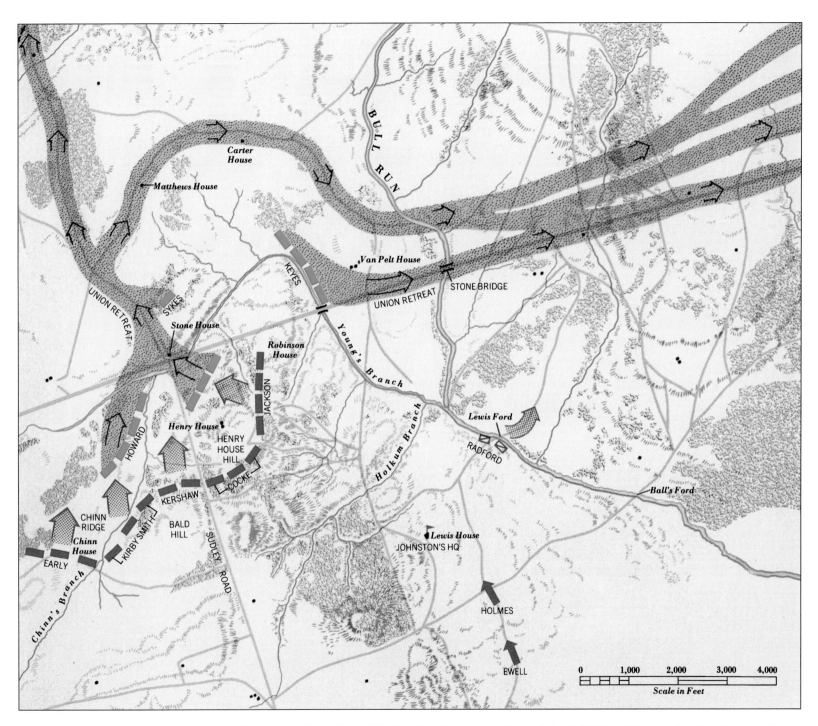

During the afternoon, while a fierce battle raged for control of Henry House Hill, Rebel reinforcements rushed to the battlefield from Manassas Junction. Beauregard deployed reserves to Jackson's left, sending others to Bald Hill and Chinn Ridge. By about 4:30 an attack up Chinn Ridge by fresh troops of Kirby Smith and Early routed Howard's Federal brigade, and the Yankees began to retreat. A general advance ordered by Beauregard sent most of McDowell's force streaming off the field in disorder.

PRIVATE RANDOLPH MCKIM

1st Maryland (C.S.) Infantry Battalion, Smith's Brigade

McKim joined the Southern cause, displeasing his Unionist father. The 19-year-old wrote: "You need not be alarmed about me; there is some danger in case of battle, but very little; the Yankees cannot shoot." McKim would soon discover that marksmanship scarcely mattered when massed troops were firing.

We had orders to cast off our knapsacks that we might march unimpeded to the field. Leaving them in a pile by the roadside under a small guard, we were soon marching at the double quick for Manassas. Our pulses beat more quickly than our feet, as we passed on, the sounds of battle waxing nearer and nearer every moment. It was a severe test of endurance, for the field was six miles away, and the heat of that July day was very exhausting. The weather had been very dry, and the dust rose in clouds around us, as we double-quicked on—so thick was it that I distinctly remember I could not see my file-leader.

We were by and by near enough to hear the rattle of the musketry, and soon we began to meet the wounded coming off the field in streams, some limping along, some on stretchers borne by their comrades. Stern work was evidently right ahead of us, and it did not steady our nerves for our first battle to be told, as the wounded told us, especially those whose wounds were slight, that it was going very badly with our men at the front. At length the dreadful six-mile double-quick march was over, and the firing line was right in front of us. Some few— very few—had dropped out exhausted. All of us were nearly spent with the heat and the dust and the killing pace; and a brief halt was made to get breath, moisten our lips from the canteens, and prepare for the charge. I remember how poor "Sell" Brogden, panting and exhausted, turned to me and asked for a drink of water from my canteen. I had scarcely a swallow left, but he was so much worse off than I, and his appeal was so piteous, that I gave him the last drop. . . .

I remember that after the first rush, when a brief pause came, some of us dashed down to a tiny little brook for a mouthful of water—only to find the water tinged with blood. Nevertheless not a few stooped and lapped it up where it was clearest.

BRIGADIER GENERAL EDMUND KIRBY SMITH

Brigade Commander, Army of the Shenandoah

Kirby Smith rushed his troops into the fight against Howard's Federals. A West Point graduate and Mexican War veteran, he was wounded almost immediately and was succeeded by Colonel Arnold Elzey. While recovering at Lynchburg, the general met the woman he would marry two months later.

From Manassas Junction my men had gone at double-quick; for the last mile or two the road was filled with fugitives going to the rear. Most of them had thrown away their arms, and so great was their demoralization they could not be rallied. With my staff we drove them off the road in advance of our column, so as not to intimidate the men who were advancing at double-quick and cheering. I galloped ahead, with my staff, and found Gen. Johnston, who ordered me to halt my column and form a line in the rear. I begged Gen. Johnston to let me take my command to the front, telling him of their enthusiasm, and that they would redeem the fight. He replied: "Take them to the front; it is our left that is driven back; but the ground is new to me, and I cannot direct you exactly." Putting spurs to my horse, I joined my column, and, taking the firing as a guide, I moved at a double-quick so as to bring my command on the flank of the enemy's victorious column. As I came into position I found a Carolina regiment deploying and taking position. I was shot almost immediately and carried senseless to the rear, but I believe it was the appearance of these fresh troops on the enemy's flank which occasioned the panic and flight.

PRIVATE GEORGE H. WESTON
1ST MARYLAND (C.S.) INFANTRY BATTALION, SMITH'S BRIGADE

Weston found himself amid furious fire as his unit hastened at a double-quick march to the front, ordered to reinforce the Confederate left west of Henry House Hill. Led by the 1st Maryland's own Colonel Arnold Elzey, the brigade struck at the exposed right flank of Howard's brigade, putting the Federals to rout. The staccato, present-tense style with which Weston recalls his part in the fighting suggests that he wrote his account immediately after the battle.

Our Col says boys there's work for you the rally cry is Sumpter the sign of recognition the back of your hand to your hats, forward quick march & we did march up to our Knees in dust & looking savage to Keep up our spirits 11 1/2 a.m. Stop for a moment to fill our canteens with muddy watter & off again can now distinctly hear the musketry & rifle shots thick & fast. Courier after courier riding up to hurry us on—with Men we want you for God Sake. hurry up Double quick march & off we start in a run & now we meet the straglers & wounded of our side. falling back but cannot see the Enemy Come on Baltimore they are driving us hard—close up—double quick. What

Regt is that? Col. Elzeys Marylanders—Hury up boys, even the wounded stop to hurry us on to avenge them, with an oath, as we skirt the edge of a thicket we hear an Alabamna & South Carolina Regt has been cut to peices & lost all their officers. Just here a large Shell bursts on our flank & explodes within 20 yards of us, look round but none of us hurt & now whiz-whiz-comnes the round shot right over our heads you cant help dodging to save your life. And up rides Col Elzeys says take the extreme left, the Enemy are trying to outflank us. & he getting in our rear File left, double quick march. another shell plous the earth from under a whole platoon of cavalry immediately in front of us without hurting a single one, man or horse now a shell explodes about the centre of our c.o. (Co A) & with a countenance I shall never forget & the expression oh my God poor Jno Berryman falls on his back & Wm Codd limps from the line into the woods, but we cant stop. a volley from the right in ambush & Gen Smith falls from his horse badly wounded. We now deploy into line, the Va's on the left., our boys in the Centre & Tennesse on the right, we forward straight on until the fire is so severe we are ordered to fall upon our face there we lay for 10 min. with the balls whisteling over our heads like nothing I ever heard before—the minnié balls comes so close you think every one is going to strike you.

This banner was bestowed on the 1st Maryland (C.S.) Infantry at Manassas after being carried through Union lines by a Miss Hattie Cary. Its flagstaff would later be adorned with a deer's tail to commemorate a victory by the 1st Maryland over the Pennsylvania Bucktails in the Shenandoah Valley in 1862.

SERGEANT URBAN A. WOODBURY
2D VERMONT INFANTRY, HOWARD'S BRIGADE

A native of Elmore, Vermont, Woodbury was mustered in a month before the Manassas battle. The wound that he suffered as his regiment advanced cost him his right arm. Woodbury was taken prisoner in the battle, paroled in early October, and discharged two weeks later because of his wounds. He later reenlisted in the 11th Vermont and was commissioned a captain. After the war Woodbury was elected mayor of Burlington and then lieutenant governor of Vermont.

As we came nearer the field we saw the Second Rhode Island Regiment resting beside the road, with arms stacked. Some of their boys called to us as we passed them. "We have been in and had a hack at the Rebs and now it is your turn." At that place we left the road, which was bordered with trees, and emerged into the open field. We were soon discovered by the enemy, who opened fire upon us with solid shot and, as we advanced farther, with shell and musketry. I did not see a man of our regiment leave the ranks, though there was some ducking of heads when a shot or shell came unusually near.

"In the twinkling of an eye I was transformed from an athlete to a pensioner."

We were the extreme right of our army. We went on to the field by the right flank, marching at quick time, but as we came under a hotter fire our pace was quickened to the double quick. We soon began to descend the hill to the Warrenton pike, beyond which the enemy who were firing upon us were situated.

Heavy firing was heard soon at the Henry house—to our left and front. A portion at least of the Fourteenth Brooklyn was retiring to our left, and Rickett's Battery was flying to the rear upon our right. The

idea of retreat or defeat had not entered our minds at that time. We thought, I did, at least, that the retiring battery and troops were going back after more ammunition or to make room for fresh troops.

While marching at double quick down the slope at trail arms, at the head of my company, which was next to the color guard, I was hit in the right arm, near the shoulder, by a piece of a shell, which passed across my breast and whirled around and fell to the ground. In the twinkling of an eye I was transformed from an athlete to a pensioner.

PRIVATE ALFRED E. DOBY

2D SOUTH CAROLINA INFANTRY, BONHAM'S BRIGADE

Led by Colonel Joseph B. Kershaw, the men of the 2d South Carolina moved to support Jackson on Henry House Hill, where Doby had his first experience of the horrors of war. A week after the battle Doby paused to write of his part in the fray and of his efforts to tend to the body of a fallen comrade. When Kershaw was promoted to brigadier general, Doby served on his staff.

Poor little Willie Hardy was killed during the engagement. He was shot down by a concealed foe while gallantly performing his duty. He was shot with a pistol, the ball passing through the neck, severing the main artery; he lived but a moment. I did not observe him when he fell on account of his being under cover of the woods, where he was conducting Col Preston's Regt but a friend told me of his death immediately afterwards, whereupon I went to obtain his body. When I found it, all covered with blood, his face disfigured, his eyes rolled in a gaze of death, I momentarly shuddered. I was almost paralyzed. I looked upon him for a few moments, then dismounting put him upon little Swannanoa which was standing near his body when I found it, but finding that I could not carry his body that way, I took it upon my shoulders and bore it several hundred yards to a place of safety. Good Heavens, Lizzie, my back was actually saturated with his blood. Never had I such feelings before, my own person stained with the blood of my dear little comrade. I covered his body with a few bushes, and again entered battle, not dreaming that I too might possibly meet in a few moments the same sad fate. But a something above seemed to have thrown an arm of protection around me and I went through unhurt; one ball passed through my coat, but did not touch the skin.

Sergeant Thomas J. Randolph, aide to Philip St. G. Cocke, was commended for "signal service" by Beauregard. Randolph arrived on the field with two of Cocke's regiments, the vanguard of 7,000 fresh troops rushing to Henry House Hill. He was killed in September 1862 at the Battle of South Mountain. His father was mayor of Vicksburg, Mississippi, which would later be the site of a major battle.

This painting by Captain James Hope of the 2d Vermont shows Maine and Vermont regiments of Oliver O. Howard's brigade charging up Henry House Hill, in virtually the last Union offensive action of the battle, to recover the lost guns of Ricketts' and other Yankee batteries. Edmund Kirby Smith's brigade, commanded by Arnold Elzey, flanked and turned back the New Englanders.

PRIVATE DAVID E. JOHNSTON

7TH VIRGINIA INFANTRY, EARLY'S BRIGADE

Johnston, a native of Pearisburg, Virginia, went through the fighting at Manassas untouched but was later wounded at Williamsburg. Wounded again at Gettysburg, Johnston was captured and held at Point Lookout, Maryland, but released in 1865. He returned home to practice law and became a circuit court judge before being elected to the U.S. House of Representatives.

*E*merging into an open field two hundred yards from Bull Run, by a movement by the right flank, we were in line advancing towards the stream, the banks of which were covered with timber, the opposite bank sloping from the stream, high and precipitous. Within one hundred yards of the stream, from the opposite bank the enemy poured into our ranks, or rather at us, a volley of musketry, which, thanks to his bad marksmanship, went high, doing little or no damage, but causing us, by common impulse, as is usual with soldiers in their first battle, to fall flat on the ground, and down we went. On the side next the enemy, in front of Isaac Hare, was John Q. Martin, who spring over Ike, leaving him next the enemy. Ike, with a curse and threatening gesture, compelled Martin to resume his former position. The men of the regiment were immediately upon their feet. As they rose, Lieutenant Squires, whose section of artillery had unlimbered immediately in our rear, gave the command, "Fire!" which command, being mistaken by our men for that of our own officer, caused us to let fly a terrific volley at the enemy in the woods in our front, and this was followed by a rush with fixed bayonets for the stream, behind which the enemy was posted, forcing him to retreat in confusion, leaving his dead and wounded, knapsacks, haversacks, hat and part of his small arms.

Corporal William L. Paxton of the 4th Virginia, his countenance captured in this prewar ambrotype, was struck through the heart by a cannonball at Manassas. Scarcely a month earlier, the 22-year-old Paxton had graduated from Washington College (now Washington and Lee University) and enlisted with former classmates in the Liberty Hall Volunteers, named for the dormitory in which many had lived. The Volunteers became Company I and fought in the 4th Virginia until Appomattox.

"Defeat was the best thing that could have happened to us; for it humbled us and made us make better preparations which led in time to a final victory."

COLONEL OLIVER O. HOWARD
BRIGADE COMMANDER, HEINTZELMAN'S DIVISION

Howard, shown here in a photograph taken before he lost an arm at Fair Oaks in 1862, describes the slow unraveling of the Federal line, which may have begun with a misconstrued order from him. His attempt to pull one regiment out of line to reposition it may have been taken as an order to retreat, triggering a general withdrawal.

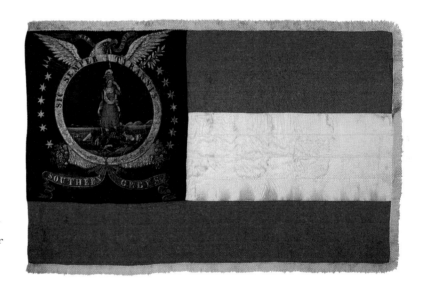

This banner, believed to be the only Confederate colors ever made from a U.S. flag, was carried at Manassas by the Southern Greys, a militia unit that became Company C, 10th Virginia. It was hidden for the rest of the war and later restored.

When under the orders to retire behind the crest and form, those who were left began quietly to retreat. They would not halt. They saw no army on our side, only irregular masses of men without order. One captain . . . walked for some time by my horse and shed tears because he no longer had any command. "They will not stay together; they will not obey me," he said. So the panic began everywhere. Some officers plead and threatened; surgeons pointed to the wounded and begged, "For God's sake stop; don't leave us!" But nothing could influence our hosts now except such cries as—"The enemy is upon us! We shall all be taken!" My command there at Centreville was brought into fair order. It had, curiously enough, followed the route of the morning around the loop of seven miles. An old and experienced officer says that defeat was the best thing that could have happened to us; for it humbled us and made us make better preparations which led in time to a final victory.

After the complete break-up near the crossing of Bull Run, Heintz-elman, with his wounded arm in a sling, rode up and down, trying to restore order. He spoke to me sharply, and told me to reform my lines. He did the same to other brigade and regiment commanders. My brother, C. H. Howard, whenever I was disposed to relax my effort, said: "Do try again." Once we noticed the 18th Brooklyn marching in regular column as we all moved back on the Sudley road, some three or four companies reorganized and tramping handsomely. My brother said: "See there; let us try to form like that." So we did, but all in vain. One foolish cry, following a team of horses thundering along through our ranks—"The Black Horse Cavalry are upon us!"—sent the Brooklyn men and all others in disorder and into the neighboring woods.

PRIVATE GEORGE W. BAGBY
CLERK, STAFF, GENERAL PIERRE G. T. BEAUREGARD

Educated as a physician, Bagby preferred journalism. In April 1861 he joined the 11th Virginia but because of illness was assigned light clerical duty at Beauregard's headquarters. Discharged in September, Bagby continued to work for the Southern cause through his editorials in the Southern Literary Messenger, a Richmond publication.

COLONEL WILLIAM T. SHERMAN
BRIGADE COMMANDER, TYLER'S DIVISION

Sherman's command was already in disorder when the retreat began. As he withdrew across the Warrenton Turnpike, he could not make his soldiers halt. His "irregular square" formation was an attempt to form the traditional defense against what the fleeing Yankees feared most, an attack by the Rebels' dreaded "Black Horse Cavalry."

Unable longer to bear the suspense, I left important papers, etc., to take care of themselves, and set out for the battle-field, determined to go in and get rid of my fears and doubts by action. I reached the hill which I had so often visited in the morning, and paused awhile to look at some of our troops, who were rapidly moving from our right to our left. Just then—can I ever forget it?—there came, as it seemed, an instantaneous suppression of firing, and almost immediately a cheer went up and ran along the valley from end to end of our line. It meant victory—there was no mistaking the fact. I stood perfectly still, feeling no exultation whatever. An indescribable thankful sadness fell upon me, rooting me to the spot and plunging me into a deep reverie, which for a long time prevented me from seeing or hearing what went forward. Night had nearly fallen when I came to myself and started homeward. The road was filled with wounded men, their friends, and a few prisoners. I spoke kindly to the prisoners, and took in charge a badly wounded young man, carrying him to the hospital, from the back windows of which amputated legs and arms had already been thrown on the ground in a sickening pile.

On the ridge to the west we succeeded in partially reforming the regiments, but it was manifest they would not stand, and I directed Colonel Corcoran to move along the ridge to the rear, near the position where we had first formed the brigade. General McDowell was there in person, and used all possible efforts to reassure the men. By the active exertions of Colonel Corcoran we formed an irregular square against the cavalry, which were then seen to issue from the position from which we had been driven, and we began our retreat towards that ford of Bull Run by which we had approached the field of battle. There was no positive order to retreat, although for an hour it had been going on by the operation of the men themselves. The ranks were thin and irregular, and we found a stream of people strung from the hospital across Bull Run and far towards Centreville. After putting in motion the irregular square, I pushed forward to find Captain Ayres' battery. Crossing Bull Run, I sought it at its last position before the brigade crossed over, but it was not there; then, passing through the woods where in the morning we had first formed line, we approached the blacksmith-shop, but there found a detachment of the secession cavalry, and thence made a circuit, avoiding Cub Run Bridge, into Centreville, where I found General McDowell. From him I understood it was his purpose to rally the forces, and make a stand at Centreville. But, about 9 o'clock at night, I received, from General Tyler in person the order to continue the retreat to the Potomac.

CAPTAIN JAMES RORTY

69TH NEW YORK INFANTRY, SHERMAN'S BRIGADE

Born in Donegal, Ireland, in 1837, Rorty immigrated to New York in 1857 and became a leader in the Fenian Brotherhood, an Irish nationalist political organization. At Manassas he was captured with his colonel, Michael Corcoran, and imprisoned in Richmond. On September 18, 1861, Rorty and a companion escaped, making their way north. Wounded at Fredericksburg, Rorty recovered and returned to a posting in the artillery. He was killed at Gettysburg.

Again, when our attack failed, and the retreat began, Col Corcoran endeavored to cover it by forming his men in square, in which order it moved to the point at which we crossed Bull Run, where on account of the woods and the narrowness of the path down the bluffs that formed the west bank, it had to be reduced to a column. Sherman, who was in the square, told the men to get away as fast as they could as the enemy's cavalry were coming. This prevented Col. Corcoran from reforming the men in square on the other side of the Run, a movement which would have not only effectually repelled the enemy, but would also have covered the retreat of every battery lost subsequently. It was in his endeavors to remedy the disorder and straggling caused by this "license to run," that Col Corcoran (who, from the unfortunate and irreparable loss of Haggerty, and the absence of all his staff, was obliged to be somewhat in the rear) was cut off from the main body of the regiment, by the enemy's horse, and being able to rally only nine men, moved into a small house, to make a better defence, but was induced by some of his officers to surrender as resistance was hopeless. Meantime about half a dozen men had joined him at the house, of whose arrival he was ignorant. Trifling as the reinforcement was, he surrendered so reluctantly that I verily believe had he known of it he would not have surrendered without a desperate fight.

Colonel Michael Corcoran commanded the "Irish" 69th New York, one of the regiments that briefly took Henry House Hill about 3:00 p.m. He was later wounded and taken prisoner. The medal at right, issued by the Papal States, may have been lost by one of the men of the 69th, many of whom had served as papal soldiers.

CAPTAIN MILTON MCCOY

2D OHIO INFANTRY, SCHENCK'S BRIGADE

As the Federal withdrawal turned into a panic, McCoy noted—and later recounted with sarcasm—the stampede of civilians who had come out from Washington to watch the fun. McCoy, a three-month volunteer, escaped to rejoin his unit and reenlisted in August 1861. He was wounded in his left wrist and hand at Perryville in October 1862 and resigned his commission in March 1863.

Any one who witnessed it will not forget it to his dying day: the charge of the cavalry across the open field to the fence on the opposite site of the road—over it into the road, running their horses between the teams, wagons and caissons, with drawn sabers, to be followed by others, with firing of pistols; horses attached to wagons containing bridge timber running in every direction; timber unloading itself at every jump; caisson teams taking their own way out of the melee! The teams of the fine barouches with the Congressmen, where were they? . . . They had important business to transact at the seat of Government. Without witnessing such a scene, one cannot picture in his imagination one like it.

Many of the stragglers commenced an indiscriminate firing from a point on the road west of the hospital, near the stable and edge of woodland, which had the effect to check, in a measure, any movement of the cavalry down the Warrenton road, as no doubt was their intention.

I had crossed the road from the place I had the guard stationed, and got near the hospital yard fence. There was a caisson near by, over the rail of which I threw my blanket. I drew my pistol and took position alongside of one of the artillery horses; the driver had clambered off, as he was struck at by a cavalryman with his saber, and got to the head of his horse; an artilleryman jumped off the seat on the caisson as the horse was shot. All three of us were ranged alongside the near wheel horse: I in the middle, with my left hand holding to the harness. The two horses in the lead had got loose somehow and gone. The artilleryman to my left was shot in the shoulder, as it afterwards proved, and fell to the ground, hanging on to the rein of the horse; the horse being shot reared up, got his legs over the tongue, and we all fell in a heap, the horse lying on my left foot with his breeching around the heel of my boot. The artilleryman to the right fell on top of me. In my exertion to free myself, throwing him off, I fired my pistol. The ball must have taken effect in the back of the horse as his struggles somewhat freed my foot, all except the breeching. While in that position I had a view of cavalrymen riding between and around the teams running away, firing pistols, and striking with their sabers. Many persons were run over, and it was the belief, had not the cavalry met with the check at the hospital, they would have gone down the Warrenton road in the rear of our brigade.

Panic on the road between Bulls run & Centerville

This sketch portrays the latter stages of the Federal retreat from the Manassas battlefield. What started out as a disorganized but unhurried departure by demoralized individuals and units began changing into all-out flight when the Yankees were blocked by dead horses and destroyed wagons on the bridge over Cub Run, which had been shelled from Henry House Hill. Fear of being ridden down by Rebel cavalry intensified the panic, contributing to what came to be called the Great Skedaddle.

"We had been surprised, and the enemy was close upon us in large force."

PRIVATE OTHO S. LEE
1st Virginia Cavalry, Army of the Shenandoah

Lee, a native of Bel Air, Maryland, left his home in May 1861 to volunteer with the 8th Virginia Infantry, then mustering around Leesburg. Not liking the foot soldier's life, Lee and several friends from home transferred to Captain George R. Gaither's company of Maryland cavalry and were soon attached to the 1st Virginia. Lee remained with this regiment until the end of the war, serving part of the time as a courier at General Fitzhugh Lee's headquarters.

MAJOR HENRY J. HUNT
Battery M, 2d U.S. Artillery, Richardson's Brigade

A West Pointer, Hunt had seen service on the frontier and was twice breveted for gallantry in the Mexican War. On July 21, as part of the withdrawal of Richardson's brigade, Hunt's gunners opened fire on Rebel troops advancing along Bull Run, helping discourage a Confederate pursuit.

The sight on the road was wonderful to behold. Abandoned wagons, camp chests, ambulances and artillery wagons left behind by the fleeing Federals. Improvised tables had been set along the road with many delicacies spread on them, which had been left as arrayed. Occasionally one of my regiment would spring from his horse and seize something inviting and remount. I fancied some white sugar, with nothing to carry it in but my tin cup which I filled; but alas! in the course of the evening I found it had all disappeared except a small quantity; this was caused by the motion of my horse, as I, of course, had the tin strapped to my saddle.

We captured many prisoners and some citizens from Washington who had come from that city, they said, to see the fun, as they had been led to believe the Yankees would whip us in short order, and then they with the soldiers would have a jolification, but alas! "The plans of men and mice oft gan agle." I don't know whether this quotation from Burns is correct, but if not, it fits the case.

At Cub Run we were obliged to ford the stream; three or four pieces of artillery had blocked the bridge; each team had evidently tried to get through first, and consequently got jammed. The drivers cutting loose their horses, had made their escape with the teams for the present. Farther on, in a field on our left a regiment of cavalry was seen in line of battle on the far side of the field. Colonel Stuart immediately ordered the fence torn down and the regiment went over at a gallop, and formed to charge. But before we got near the enemy, they had disappeared. It appeared that each man of their imposing line of battle had turned suddenly to the rear and disappeared over the fence in their rear.

About 4 1/2 or 5 p.m., after the battle was apparently gained on the right, and whilst large reinforcements of infantry and cavalry were observed hurrying up from the direction of Manassas, a strong force of infantry and some cavalry, variously estimated at from 2,000 to 5,000 men in all, appeared on our left, approaching parallel to our front by the lateral openings into the great ravine on our flank. The infantry only was first seen, and as they approached without any apparent attempt at concealment, preceded by our skirmishers, they were supposed to be our own troops. As the numbers increased I rode down the ravine with my first sergeant to reconnoitre them. Some of our skirmishers stated that they had seen no troops; others said they were the 34th New Yorkers coming in. They carried no colors, and their numbers increasing to an alarming extent, I hurried back and changed the front of the battery, so as to command all the openings into the ravine, and the approaches to our position. Col. Davies, at the same time, detached a couple of companies into the ravine as skirmishers. The latter had scarcely deployed when a sharp rattle of musketry removed all doubts as to the character of the advancing troops. We had been surprised, and the enemy was close upon us in large force. Our infantry regiment had changed front with the battery, but unfortunately closed their intervals behind it. Precious time was now lost in getting them on our flanks. Had they remained in our rear, they would have been unnecessarily exposed to the fire directed on the battery; and in case of a determined charge for our capture, which I confidently expected, they would have been apt to fire through us, destroying men and horses, and crippling the guns. At length they were moved to the right and left, and ordered to lie down and await the approach of the enemy, who by this time were closing up in apparently overwhelming numbers. I now directed the gunners to prepare shrapnel and cannister shot, and in case the enemy persisted in his advance, not to lose time in sponging the pieces—for minutes were now of more value than arms—but to aim low, and pour in a rapid fire wherever the men were thickest or were seen advancing. The enemy having by this time completed his preparations, and driven in our skirmishers, now rushed forward and opened a heavy musketry fire on the battery; but from the shortness of range, or from aiming upwards as they ascended the ravine, their shots mostly passed over us. The command was then given to the battery to fire. Under the directions of Lieuts. Platt and Thompson, 2d artillery, and Edwards, 3d artillery, commanding sections, the most rapid, well-sustained, and destructive fire I have ever witnessed was now opened. The men took full advantage of the permission to omit sponging, yet no accident occurred from it. The guns were all of large calibre, two 20-pdr. Parrott rifle guns, and four light 12-pounders, and they swept the field with a perfect storm of cannister.

ALFRED ELY
U.S. Congressman, New York

Born in Connecticut, Ely practiced law in Rochester, New York, and was elected to Congress on the Republican ticket in 1859. He accompanied McDowell's army to witness the battle expected around Manassas, only to be captured during the Federal retreat. Ely was held in Richmond for six months before being exchanged. His party did not renominate him in 1862.

*I*t was while under the tree above mentioned that a company of infantry issued from the woods, marching in great haste, "double quick," with a military officer on horseback leading in advance. On arriving within about ten rods of the spot where I was standing, the company halted. Two officers then came forward to the tree and inquired who I was, and I told them my name was "Alfred Ely." "What State are you from?" "From the State of New York," I replied. "Are you connected in any way with the Government?" "Yes." "In what way, sir?" "A Representative in Congress." One of the officers, a captain, immediately seized me by the arm, and said that I was their prisoner, and took from me the pistol which I had that morning borrowed of Mr. Seth Green. He took nothing else. The officer repeatedly assured me that I should not be harmed, and behaved with kindness and courtesy. He took me to the colonel, sitting on horseback, and introduced me in these words: "Colonel, this is Mr. Ely, Representative in Congress from New York," to which the colonel, in a most angry tone, replied, drawing his pistol, and pointing it directly at my head, "G–d

Commander of the Union 5th Division, Dixon S. Miles (left) was assigned to create a diversion on the Rebel right. Later a drunken Miles ordered Richardson to withdraw his brigade from its position guarding a route of retreat along the road to Centreville. A court of inquiry found Miles culpable but declined to act.

d—n your white-livered soul! I'll blow your brains out on the spot." The captain and another officer rushed before the colonel, and prevented him from carrying out his threat, the former exclaiming: "Colonel, colonel, you must not shoot that pistol, he is our prisoner." The colonel immediately rode away, when the captain stated to me that he was ashamed of his colonel; that he was very much excited, and had been drinking.

The colonel alluded to above turned out to be Colonel E. B. C. Cash, of South Carolina, in command of a regiment from that State; the name of the more humane officer was Adjutant W. S. Mullins.

I was conducted, in company with about six hundred officers and men, all prisoners of war, on foot, that evening to Manassas, a distance of about seven miles from where I was arrested,—over the dustiest road that it was ever my fortune to travel. The dust, so dense that it might almost be cut with a knife, the weather dry, and no water to be had, my mouth became so parched that it seemed impossible for me to move my tongue. On the march, by the side of the road, a few of the soldiers' canteens were partly filled from dirty pools of water, and from one I took a draught which relieved me very considerably.

LIEUTENANT J. ALBERT MONROE
REYNOLDS' BATTERY, RHODE ISLAND ARTILLERY, BURNSIDE'S BRIGADE

Monroe helped organize Rhode Island's first field battery and was commissioned in June 1861. A survivor of hard fighting at Manassas, Monroe served with the Army of the Potomac until after the Battle of Antietam, when, with the rank of major, he was assigned to command the army's artillery training center at Camp Barry, outside Washington. By the war's end, Monroe, then a lieutenant colonel, had commanded the artillery brigades of both the II and IX Corps.

The bullets began to whistle uncomfortably thick, and I gave up the search for my horse, and rejoined the battery, then moving along the road in good order, in which condition it continued until the head of the column reached the foot of the hill at the base of which flowed what is known as Cub Run. Here was a bridge rendered impassable by the wrecks of several baggage wagons. In the ford at the left was an overturned siege gun, completely blocking up that passage, and the right ford was completely filled with troops and wag-

Published by the Illustrated London News, these sketches accompanied reports on the battle by the paper's special correspondent, William H. Russell. A veteran newsman who had covered the Crimean War, Russell was castigated in the North for his critical comments about Union generalship at Manassas.

The epitome of postbattle desolation, this scene shows the Sudley Ford over Catharpin Run near its junction with Bull Run. This ford was part of the route by which two divisions—the greater part of McDowell's attacking force—would fall upon the weak Confederate left flank. The structure on the hilltop is the Sudley Church, which began Sunday, July 21, with the usual worship service but soon was witness to the horror, pain, chaos, and death of a Civil War field hospital. Many wounded Union soldiers were left there untended when the Yankees retreated.

ons. Of course the leading team of the battery had to halt, and it was impossible to stop the rear carriages on the steep hill, so that the column became only a jumbled heap of horses, limbers, caissons and gun carriages. To add to the confusion, just at this moment a rebel battery in our rear opened fire, and it seemed as if every one of their shots came down into our very midst. The men immediately set to work taking the horses from their harnesses, after doing which they mounted upon them in the most lively manner. Some horses carried only a single passenger, others had on their backs doublets and some triplets. . . .

I forded the run on the right hand, or down stream side of the bridge.

Going up the hill after crossing, I overtook Captain Reynolds who crossed a little in advance of me, and just as I rode along side of him, a shot from the enemy's artillery struck the ground only a few feet from us. Unsophisticated as I was, I could not understand why they should continue to fire upon us when we were doing the best that we could to let them alone, and I said to Captain Reynolds, "What do you suppose they are trying to do?" His reply was a characteristic one: "They are trying to kill every mother's son of us; that is what they are trying to do," the truth of which was very forcibly impressed upon me as shot after shot came screeching after us in rapid succession.

SARAH EMMA EDMONDS
2D MICHIGAN INFANTRY, RICHARDSON'S BRIGADE

Disguised as a man, Edmonds enlisted in the 2d Michigan under the alias Frank Thompson. She remained with the regiment, mostly working as a hospital steward, until "Frank Thompson" deserted in 1863. Edmonds served throughout the rest of the war as a nurse for the U.S. Christian Commission. In 1865 she published a book in which she claimed to have spent the entire war as a female volunteer nurse. In 1882 she admitted her deception and was later granted a pension.

Mrs. B. and I made our way to the stone church around which we saw stacks of dead bodies piled up, and arms and legs were thrown together in heaps. But how shall I describe the scene within the church at that hour. Oh, there was suffering there which no pen can ever describe. One case I can never forget. It was that of a poor fellow whose legs were both broken above the knees, and from the knees to the thighs they were literally smashed to fragments. He was dying; but oh, what a death was that. He was insane, perfectly wild, and required two persons to hold him. Inflammation had set in, and was rapidly doing its work; death soon released him, and it was a relief to all present as well as to the poor sufferer. . . .

Our hearts and hands being fully occupied with such scenes as these, we thought of nothing else. We knew nothing of the true state of affairs outside, nor could we believe it possible when we learned that the whole army had retreated toward Washington, leaving the wounded in the hands of the enemy, and us, too, in rather an unpleasant situation. I could not believe the stern truth, and was determined to find out for myself. Consequently I went back to the heights where I had seen the troops stack their guns and throw themselves upon the ground at nightfall, but no troops were there. I thought then that they had merely changed their position, and that by going over the field I should certainly find them. I had not gone far before I saw a camp fire in the distance. Supposing that I had found a clue to the secret, I made all haste toward the fire; but as I drew near I saw but one solitary figure sitting by it, and that was the form of a female.

Upon going up to her I recognised her as one of the washerwomen of our army. . . . I soon found out that the poor creature had become insane. The excitement of battle had proved too much for her, and all my endeavors to persuade her to come with me were unavailing. I had no time to spare, for I was convinced that the army had really decamped.

CAPTAIN GEORGE M. FINCH
2D OHIO INFANTRY, SCHENCK'S BRIGADE

Soon after Fort Sumter, Finch joined the 2d Ohio and was appointed captain. After surviving Manassas, he reenlisted for three years. Assigned to the western theater, Finch fought at Perryville, Stones River, Chickamauga, and Chattanooga before resigning his commission in May 1864. He then accepted a commission as lieutenant colonel in the 137th Ohio and mustered out in August.

By eight o'clock Monday morning we reached our camp at Falls Church, twenty miles away. I have always denied that we ran a yard during this memorable and mortifying retreat, but cheerfully admit that we did some splendid heel and toe marching. When we reached our old camp I was utterly exhausted. My feet were swollen and inflamed, and I had a raging fever. I volunteered to take command of the invalid camp guard, who, under command of Sergeant Eckle, had been detailed to remain behind, in charge of all the stores, baggage, etc. My physical condition was such that I lost all interest in the "Black Horse Cavalry" or the Confederacy. I even saw my company march away, under command of the first lieutenant, to cross the Potomac, without a pang of regret. My indifference seemed to restore some measure of confidence to the well-nigh panic-stricken camp guard.

After a hearty meal, and six hours' sleep, I felt equal to the demands of the occasion. I sent the sergeant with an armed detail out into the road, with instructions to capture all the empty wagons returning from the front, that came that way. He soon had six or eight teamsters corraled. There was some terrific kicking by drivers as well as mules, accompanied by volleys of profanity. We soon had all the camp equipage, stores, knapsacks and baggage loaded, and about 4 P.M. we took up our march for Fort Corcoran at the Virginia end of the Chain Bridge. There I reported to General Sherman, who had assumed command at that point. It had been raining hard all day and the soft roads were fearfully muddy. Truly the surroundings were discouraging, from every point of view. When General Sherman told me that no one could cross without a pass, and none would be granted for that day, at least, I suppose he saw a look of disappointment on my face. With that brusque manner that was peculiar to him, and a sort of dry humor that seemed almost malicious at such a time, General Sherman said: "Ever been whipped before, Captain?" "Not since I left school!" was my reply. "Well, Captain, it's my private opinion, publicly expressed, that it's a d—— disagreeable thing to be whipped."

"During the forenoon Washington gets all over motley with these defeated soldiers—queer-looking objects, strange eyes and faces, drench'd (the steady rain drizzles on all day) and fearfully worn, hungry, haggard."

WALT WHITMAN
POET

Whitman had already published his monumental Leaves of Grass to mixed critical reaction when the outbreak of the war absorbed all of his energies. In 1861, briefly visiting Washington as a correspondent for the Brooklyn Standard, Whitman witnessed the return of the broken Federal army from Manassas. He would come to Washington again in 1862 as a volunteer nurse, and in 1865 he was appointed to a clerkship in the Department of the Interior. In that year he published a collection of war poetry entitled Drum Taps.

cover'd return'd soldiers there (will they never end?) move by; but nothing said, no comments; (half our lookers-on secesh of the most venomous kind—they say nothing; but the devil snickers in their faces.) During the forenoon Washington gets all over motley with these defeated soldiers—queer-looking objects, strange eyes and faces, drench'd (the steady rain drizzles on all day) and fearfully worn, hungry, haggard, blister'd in the feet. Good people (but not over-many of them either,) hurry up something for their grub. They put wash-kettles on the fire, for soup, for coffee. They set tables on the sidewalks—wagon-loads of bread are purchased, swiftly cut in stout chunks. Here are two aged ladies, beautiful, the first in the city for culture and charm, they stand with store of eating and drink at an improvis'd table of rough plank, and give food, and have the store replenish'd from their house every half-hour all that day; and there in the rain they stand, active, silent, white-hair'd and give food, though the tears stream down their cheeks, almost without intermission the whole time. Amid the deep excitement, crowds and motion, and desperate eagerness, it seems strange to see many, very many of the soldiers sleeping—in the midst of all, sleeping sound. They drop down anywhere, on the steps of houses, up close by the basements or fences, on the sidewalks, aside on some vacant lot, and deeply sleep.

The sun rises, but shines not. The men appear, at first sparsely and shame-faced enough, the thicker, in the streets of Washington—appear in Pennsylvania Avenue, and on the steps and basement entrances. They come along in disorderly mobs, some in squads, stragglers, companies. Occasionally, a rare regiment, in perfect order, with its officers (some gaps, dead, the true braves,) marching in silence, with lowered faces, stern, weary to sinking, all black and dirty, but every man with his musket. . . .

 . . . The sidewalks of Pennsylvania Avenue, Fourteenth Street, &c, were jammed with citizens, darkies, clerks, everybody, lookers-on; women in the windows, curious expressions from faces, as those swarms of dirt-

This drum, belonging originally to a Federal infantry regiment, became a trophy of the 17th Virginia at Manassas. The Virginians covered the Federal eagle decorating the drum with black paint and used the instrument themselves from then on.

PRIVATE OTHO S. LEE
1ST VIRGINIA CAVALRY, ARMY OF THE SHENANDOAH

The day after the battle the Confederate army set about the task of burying the dead and recovering abandoned equipment. Lee recounted an instance of a Confederate recognizing the body of a friend, an artillery officer, among the Union dead. Lee also visited the Henry house, called Spring Hill Farm by the family, where Judith Henry and her son and daughter had taken refuge during the battle.

Bright and early after partaking of a slight repast, we were allowed to go over the battlefield where many of our men assisted in removing and burying the dead. Long trenches were dug and the dead wrapped in their blankets and buried. On going over the field with a comrade he suddenly halted, and gazing at a dead Federal officer, said, "Why there is my old friend, Dug Ramsay from Washington." He had known him in Washington and he proved to be an officer in the Federal artillery. Many of our own dead were still on the battlefield, one of them in particular I noticed. A cannon ball or shell had taken off all of his head except his lower jaw which remained, his chin whiskers being preserved intact. As I said before, it had rained the night before, and the effect of the rain on the dead made them have a horrible appearance.

I came across a Federal Soldier lying on the bank of a small ravine where some of his comrades no doubt had laid him. He was shot through the head by a minnie ball piercing his forehead. He was not dead but dying, he could not speak, but motioned as if he wanted water. I dismounted and placed my canteen to his lips, but he could not swallow, though his lips were made moist, and he soon after expired.

I then rode over to the Henry house where Mrs. Henry had been killed during the battle. I saw her dead body in the bed where she had been killed, with her family around her. She was very ill when the battle commenced and could not be moved. During the battle a grape shot pierced the house and passed through her body, killing her instantly.

Recovered from the Henry house, this purse of carpet-style fabric bore the initials J. H. on the inside flap, indicating that it belonged to Judith Henry. Mrs. Henry, too ill to be moved to safety, was struck by shell fragments while lying in bed and became the only civilian fatality of the battle.

PRIVATE CLEMENT D. FISHBURNE
ROCKBRIDGE ARTILLERY, VIRGINIA, JACKSON'S BRIGADE

A graduate of Washington College, Fishburne taught in Christiansburg, Virginia, before earning a master's degree from his alma mater and becoming a professor of mathematics at Davidson College in 1854. He was attending law school at the University of Virginia when he volunteered with the Rockbridge Artillery in June 1861. Fishburne ended the war as an officer in the Ordnance Department.

Some of our men got permission to go back to the field, and they returned to us loaded with canteens, haversacks well filled with "hardtack" and oil cloth and woollen blankets. Others went with a horse or two and came back supplied with many luxuries which we had never known. Among the plunder brought to us were large tarpaulins used to cover the guns and caissons of the celebrated Rickett Battery which we had knocked into uselessness. We went into camp very near to the Lewis House, and had our suppers, for the most part, from the haversacks of the enemy. We slept, as usual, in the open air, for we had no tents and had had none up to that time. During [the next] . . . day we were called to bury young Davidson, a private in a Rockbridge Infantry Company. We had nothing to dig a grave with—our battery not being supplied with spades as batteries usually are—but we got axes, stones and such things as we could and made a grave wherein we layed him, enshrouded in the old blanket in which he was lying, and coffined with barrel staves, which we layed over his body. It was a sad scene—this rainy dreary day after the victory—a band of soldiers, some of them personally unknown to the poor fellow laying away his body in this ignoble grave.

Published a few weeks after the battle, this sketch shows the grim work of taking the wounded from the field. Although this scene accurately depicts Union troops caring for their suffering comrades, once the Federal withdrawal began late in the afternoon, many hundreds of wounded Yankees were left lying in the field to be tended to by the victorious Rebels. The grisly task of burying the dead of both sides also fell to the Confederates, as they alone held the field at battle's end.

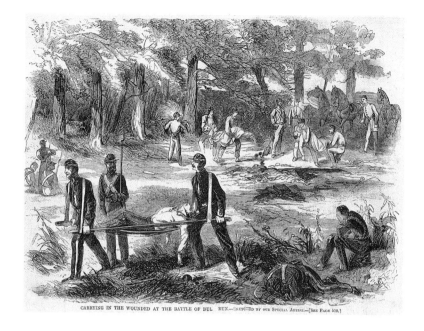

CARRYING IN THE WOUNDED AT THE BATTLE OF BUL RUN.—SKETCHED BY OUR SPECIAL ARTIST.—[SEE PAGE 530.]

EDWARD TAYLOE
RESIDENT OF VIRGINIA

As news of the outcome at Manassas spread, there was rejoicing throughout the Confederacy. On August 2, 12 days after the battle, Tayloe, a farmer in King George County, Virginia, wrote to his sister, Olivia, of Washington, D.C. Tayloe, who had two sons in the army, was ready to believe the wildest rumors of Northern perfidy. He viewed the Confederate victory as the justification of the South's secession and the opening of a second American Revolution.

God has helped us with a glorious unparraled victory. We cannot doubt that it is His work thro' the feable instruments which accomplished it. Hardly otherwise could a "Grand Army," of 53,000 men, under the immediate command of the greatest Captain of the age, have been beat back and routed by a force of 35,000 of which only 15,000 were actually engaged. What a just retribution upon those who brought with them 30,000 handcuffs to manacle us rebels! No rightminded person, be he Northern as well as Southern, can do otherwise than rejoice at the defeat of the hosts of an insatiate despot, aiming to subjugate people of his own race, who are claiming to exercise the right guaranteed to us in the Declaration of Independence— that governments are instituted among men, deriving their just powers from the *consent of the governed,* "to secure life, liberty, the pursuit of happiness," and "that, whenever *any form* of govt becomes destructive of these ends, *it is the right of the people* to alter or to *abolish* it, & to in-

stitute a new government, laying its foundation on such principles, and organizing its powers in such form, as to them shall *seem most likely to effect their safety & happiness."* The Bill of Rights of Virginia, coeval with its Constitution & older than the Constitution of the U.S., guarantees the same rights to us; and these have never been surrendered, *nor will they be* until the extermination of the race of Southern men. Can any rightminded person of the North entertain a purpose so savage? All such must rejoice, I say, at the victory now near Manassas Junction —and must rejoice yet more if it should be followed, as it ought to be by the blessing of peace.

Two of our sons marched 35 miles on the day of the battle, & reached the Junction at sundown too late, of course, to participate in it. They witnessed a large part of its horrors. It is likely that two of George's sons & his son in law were in the fight, and came out unscathed. The overpowering numbers of the enemy made the result doubtful for some hours, & must have crushed us but for the heroic stubbornness of men fighting for their homes, wives, children & brethren. "When Greek meets Greek, then comes the tug of war." So was it near Manassas Junction. What a stigma upon the 19th century, upon the Republican Party of the North, and *all its people,* that such a battle should be fought at all! And yet we see in the Northern papers that it is to be fought again and again! Well, let them come—We shall be still better prepared for them.

LIZZIE DEAN
RESIDENT OF SOUTH CAROLINA

For Southerners, news of the triumph also brought apprehension. On July 23 Lizzie Dean wrote from her home in Limestone Springs to her brother, Corporal Edward C. Dean, who had fought with the 5th South Carolina. Though the North's technological advantages enabled news to travel faster there, the absence of established systems for notifying loved ones of battle casualties meant that those waiting at home suffered long periods of uncertainty.

I sit down to write a letter, little knowing whether you will ever see it, whether you are still living and well, or wounded and sick, or even worse, have been slumbering in death for hours and even days, oh my dear Bud you can scarcely imagine my feeling since last night when the news came of the awful battle of Sunday the twentieth. I felt as I heard the words "numbers slaughtered on both sides" that I had seen you and bid you Farewell for the last time. Can it be so? The short unsatisfactory dispatch to the papers leaves us in doubt whether you or the enemy are victorious, and worse still leaves us in doubt as to the fate of those we hold dear on earth. We can only hope against hope. Next to those in real danger in Va, I feel anxious about our poor Mother. How she must have suffered to-day! Oh! my dear Bud, you little know and indeed we knew not ourselves how much we love you, how great a blank there would be in this world to us if you were gone. Will you not while striving to do the part of a brave defender of his country, at the same time remember the loved ones at home and for their sakes be prudent and careful of your life.

I tremble to think of the bullets whizzing around you and the cannon balls flying past you in their path of death, and for all I know one of them may have prostrated forever my noble, darling brother. I can scarcely bear the idea for a moment, the tears blind my eyes, and despair almost overpowers me.

Our Merciful Fathers hand has been seen in our Cause all through the past and may we not trust him this time? Surely his mercy is not spent, and he will deliver us safely from the hands of our enemies!

I try to imagine you as being well and strong as you read this letter, but my thoughts *will* take me with it to a hospital and on a rude uncomfortable bed is my dear brother suffering in all the agony of body and mind of a wounded soldier far from Mother and sisters. I pray the first picture may be the true one and that the last may *never* occur.

Having little direct news of the battle, this Southern newspaper carried Northern reports of the Confederate victory. A consequence of the dearth of information was that Southerners could read in detail about Yankee dead and wounded while having to wait in agonized ignorance to learn the fate of their own loved ones.

"It was either the mistake or the generosity of our brave enemy that saved us. I am disposed to believe that it was the latter."

PRIVATE JAMES GILLETTE
71ST NEW YORK STATE MILITIA, BURNSIDE'S BRIGADE

Gillette, a 22-year-old from New York City, joined the 71st New York as an engineer in May 1861. Captured by Confederate cavalry during the Federal retreat across Bull Run, he was sent to Richmond as a prisoner of war. On August 8 he sent a letter to his parents assuring them that he was safe and well treated and attributing to the Rebels a nobler attitude toward their enemy than they themselves might have claimed. Despite his concerns, he was paroled in January 1862.

*I*t is my opinion that *it was not the fault of our generals and officers that the enemy did not* make our precipitate retreat a scene of carnage the story of which but few would have remained to relate. It was either the mistake or the generosity of our brave enemy that saved us. I am disposed to believe that it was the latter.

Dr. Burns rec'd a telegram from you some days ago but was unable to answer save by letter. He called on me on the day succeeding my arrival and stated with regret his inability to accomplish anything in the way of obtaining a parole or a change of quarters. He has since called and brought a number of books from his library. They were highly acceptable to all of us.

I am convinced from what I have seen and heard, that our release is soley dependant upon the action of the powers at Washington.

The community here are willing—nay anxious for an exchange, thus far their desires and ours have been without relief, as Government has refused with an unwavering negative all applications on our behalf coming from the authorities here. I am loth to believe it possible or even probable that we are to be ignored untill the termination of the war. Our friends will not suffer it. Our gov'mt cannot be so ungenerous. Many of us are now citizens our term of service having expired—in some instances—at dates previous to the day of our capture. In one case, a man forfeits the sum of $1500.00 by his unforeseen and prolonged detention from home; in another, that of a student, he is thrown back a year in his

course, by inability to be present at the commencement of the term; many are *utterly ruined* in business by this untoward event. Their loyalty & willingness to remain in their gov'mts service a few days longer than the oath called for has cost them dearly.

Surely such facts as these super added to the domestic misery already occasioned, demands an immediate exchange of prisoners.

Humanity dictates *frequent exchanges*. Much of the horror of war would be saved by weekly exchange of prisoners. I believe this was the custom in the Crimea. Mortality is ever great among captives. It is not certain in my mind but that the uncertainty of imprisonment is productive of more actual misery & misfortune than serious wounds rec'd upon the field of battle.

The extract from newspapers stating the total of killed, wounded, & prisoners as 1806 in no is far behind the actual facts. In one regiment alone where it is stated that but one is missing—I have visual proof that no less than thirty are now under guard in this city. Our regimental loss is stated at 58. I have a list of thirty five not known in N.Y. or if known, suppressed.

My health is good. We have plenty to eat, and are treated in every way as well as circumstances will permit. Our safety depends on the treatment given prisoners in hands of Genl Scott—so *dont hang the privateers* unless you are willing we should be similarly treated.

We are in strong hopes of a speedy release. But *without hope* what would a prisoner live on? It is the hope of ultimate freedom that keeps him alive, by giving him something to *live for.* . . .

We are in the hands of a generous people and if our government will exhibit the same desire for an exchange as do the people here, we will soon be restored to our families and friends.

Men of the 11th New York and the 79th New York Highlanders (bottom) are held prisoner at Castle Pinckney, in Charleston, South Carolina, guarded by Charleston Zouave Cadets. Of more than 1,800 Federal soldiers listed as missing at Manassas, many ended up as prisoners of war in scattered locations throughout the South.

GLOSSARY

barouche—A four-wheeled carriage with the driver's seat high in front, two double seats inside facing each other, and a folding cover over the backseat.

bivouac—A temporary encampment, or to camp out for the night.

breastwork—A temporary fortification, usually of earth and about chest high, over which a soldier could fire.

buck and ball—A round of ammunition consisting of a bullet and three buckshot.

caisson—A cart with large chests for carrying artillery ammunition; connected to a horse-drawn limber when moved.

canister—A tin can containing lead or iron balls that scattered when fired from a cannon.

case shot—*Case shot* properly refers to shrapnel or spherical case. The term was often used mistakenly to refer to any artillery projectile in which numerous metal balls or pieces were bound or encased together. See also *shrapnel.*

change front—To alter the direction a body of troops faces in order to deliver or defend against an attack.

color company—The center company of a regiment in line of battle, which included the color guard and carried the regimental flags or colors.

commissary—The department or officer responsible for the acquisition, transportation, and issue of rations. Also a slang term for government-issue whiskey.

double-quick—A trotting pace.

dragoons—Originally, mounted infantry or heavy cavalry. In the United States the first two regiments of mounted troops in the Regular Army bore this traditional title.

echelon—A staggered or stairsteplike formation of parallel units of troops.

embrasure—An opening in a wall of a fortification through which cannon was fired.

enfilade—Gunfire that rakes an enemy line lengthwise, or the position allowing such firing.

forage—To search for and acquire provisions from nonmilitary sources. To soldiers of the Civil War it often meant, simply, stealing.

furlough—A leave of absence from duty granted to a soldier.

garrison—A military post, especially a permanent one. Also, the act of manning such a post and the soldiers who serve there.

havelock—A cloth cover for a kepi that hung down in back to shield the neck from the sun. Named for British general Sir Henry Havelock, whose troops wore such covers during the Sepoy Mutiny in India.

haversack—A shoulder bag, usually strapped over the right shoulder to rest on the left hip, for carrying personal items and rations.

hollow square—A formation with four lines of infantry facing outward in four directions to create a square. With fixed bayonets this was the standard defensive formation to protect against attack by cavalry.

howitzer—A short-barreled artillery piece that fired its projectile in a relatively high trajectory.

limber—A two-wheeled, horse-drawn vehicle to which a gun carriage or a caisson was attached.

long roll—A sustained drumroll used as the signal to take arms and fall immediately into ranks.

masked battery—Any concealed or camouflaged battery of artillery.

Minié ball—The standard bullet-shaped projectile fired from the rifled muskets of the time. Designed by French army officers Henri-Gustave Delvigne and Claude-Étienne Minié, the bullet's hollow base expanded, forcing its sides into the grooves, or rifling, of the barrel. This caused the bullet to spiral in flight, giv-ing it greater range and accuracy. Appears as minie, minnie, and minni.

musket—A smoothbore, muzzleloading shoulder arm.

parole—The pledge of a soldier released after being captured by the enemy that he would not take up arms again until he had been properly exchanged.

picket—One or more soldiers on guard to protect the larger unit from surprise attack.

prolonge—A stout rope on a gun carriage that allowed soldiers to maneuver an artillery piece over short distances without having to attach it to a limber.

rammer—An artillerist's tool used to force the powder charge and projectile down the barrel of a gun and seat them firmly in the breech.

ration—A specified allotment of food for one person (or animal) per day. The amounts and nature of rations varied by time and place throughout the war. *Rations* may also refer simply to any food provided by the army.

round shot—A solid, spherical artillery projectile.

secesh—A slang term for secessionist.

shotted guns—Artillery pieces fully loaded with powder and shot, as opposed to those used for signal or celebratory firings, which contained powder only.

shrapnel—An artillery projectile in the form of a hollow sphere filled with metal balls packed around an explosive charge. Developed by British general Henry Shrapnel during the Napoleonic Wars, it was used as an antipersonnel weapon. Also called spherical case.

skirmisher—A soldier sent in advance of the main body of troops to scout out and probe the enemy's position. Also, one who participated in a skirmish, a small fight usually incidental to the main action.

solid shot—A solid artillery projectile, oblong for rifled pieces and spherical for smooth-bores, used primarily against fortifications and matériel.

spherical case—See *shrapnel*.

spike—To render a piece of artillery unservice-able by driving a metal spike into the vent.

vent—A small hole in the breech of a weapon through which a spark travels to ignite the powder charge and fire the piece.

Zouaves—Regiments, both Union and Confederate, that modeled themselves after the origi-nal Zouaves of French Colonial Algeria. Known for spectacular uniforms featuring bright col-ors—usually reds and blues—baggy trousers, gaiters, short and open jackets, and a turban or fez, they specialized in precision drill and load-ing and firing muskets from the prone position.

ACKNOWLEDGMENTS

The editors wish to thank the following for their valuable assistance in the preparation of this volume: Eva-Maria Ahladas, Museum of the Confederacy, Richmond; James Baughman, U.S. Army Military History Institute, Carlisle Barracks, Pa.; Elizabeth Bilderbach, University of South Carolina, Columbia; Laura Young Bost, University of Texas Press, Austin; James Burgess, Manassas National Battlefield Park, Manassas, Va.; Robert Cayson, Alabama Department of Archives and History, Montgomery; Pam Cheney, U.S. Army Military History Institute, Carlisle Barracks, Pa.; Emily Cromwell, Chrysler Museum of Art, Norfolk, Va.; Paul M. Culp Jr., Sam Houston State University, Huntsville, Tex.; Christina M. Deane, University of Virginia Library, Charlottesville; Noah Dennen, Woburn, Mass.; Susan G. Drinan, Atwater Kent Museum, Philadelphia; Jane Duggan, Boston Public Library; Barbara Gill, Historical Society of Berks County, Reading, Pa.; Jeff Goldman, Maryland Historical Society, Baltimore; Randy W. Hackenburg, U.S. Army Military History Institute, Carlisle Barracks, Pa.; Bill Irwin, Duke University, Durham, N.C.; Mary Ison and Staff, Library of Congress, Washington, D.C.; Norma J. Johnson, Greenwood Publishing Group, Westport, Conn.; Janie C. Morris, Duke University, Durham, N.C.; Emily Murphy, Maryland State Archives, Annapolis; RoseAnn O'Canas, High Impact Photography, Baltimore; Susan Otto, Milwaukee Public Museum; Rosy Rash, Lynchburg Museum, Lynchburg, Va.; Teresa Roane, Valentine Museum, Richmond; Richard Roberts, Connecticut State Library, Hartford; Irene Roughton, Chrysler Museum of Art, Norfolk, Va.; Ann Sindelar, Western Reserve Historical Society, Cleveland; Mary L. Sluskonis, Museum of Fine Arts, Boston; Joanna L. Smith, Stonewall Jackson Foundation, Lexington, Va.; Dr. Richard Sommers, U.S. Army Military History Institute, Carlisle Barracks, Pa.; Greg Starbuck, Savannah; Philip J. Weimerskirch, Providence Public Library; John White, University of North Carolina at Chapel Hill; Michael J. Winey, U.S. Army Military History Institute, Carlisle Barracks, Pa.

mond, photographed by Larry Sherer. 51: Courtesy Brian Pohanka. 52: Library of Congress, Waud #824. 53: From *A Duryee Zouave*, by Thomas P. Southwick, privately published, (c)1930, Elizabeth M. Southwick; courtesy Walt Brown Jr., copied by Henry Mintz. 54: Courtesy Smith-McDowell House Museum, Asheville, N.C., copied by Henry Mintz. 55: Courtesy Brian Pohanka. 56: Museum of Fine Arts, Boston. 59: Frank and Marie-Thérèse Wood Print Collections, Alexandria, Va. 60: Courtesy Brian Pohanka. 61: *Stonewall Jackson's Way*, by John W. Wayland, McClure, Staunton, Va., 1940. 62, 63: Museum of the Confederacy, Richmond, photographed by Katherine Wetzel; Frank and Marie-Thérèse Wood Print Collections, Alexandria, Va. 64: Library of Congress, Neg. No. LC-USZ62-10260. 66: MASS-MOLLUS/USAMHI, copied by A. Pierce Bounds; Meserve Collection of Mathew Brady negatives, National Portrait Gallery, Smithsonian Institution, Washington, D.C./Art Resource, N.Y. 67: Frank and Marie-Thérèse Wood Print Collections, Alexandria, Va. 68: Frank and Marie-Thérèse Wood Print Collections, Alexandria, Va.; courtesy collection of William A. Turner. 70: Private collection, copied by Evan H. Sheppard—West Virginia and Regional History Collection, West Virginia University Libraries, Morgantown. 71: Frank and Marie-Thérèse Wood Print Collections, Alexandria, Va. 72: Print Collection, Miriam and Ira D. Wallach Division of Art, Prints and Photographs, New York Public Library, Astor, Lenox and Tilden Foundations. 73: Private collection, copied by Evan H. Sheppard. 74: From *Battles and Leaders of the Civil War*, Vol. 1, published by Century, 1884. 77, 78: Map by Walter W. Roberts. 80: From *The Civil War Letters of First Lieutenant James B. Thomas, Adjutant, 107th Pennsylvania Volunteers*, edited by Mary Warner Thomas and Richard A. Sauers, Butternut and Blue, 1995, copied by Philip Brandt George—courtesy Maryland Historical Society, Baltimore. 81: Museum of Fine Arts, Boston—Milwaukee Public Museum. 82: Special Collections Library, Duke University, Durham, N.C.; Greg Starbuck—Museum of the Confederacy, Richmond, photographed by Larry Sherer; Special Collections Library, Duke University, Durham, N.C. 83: Library of Congress, Neg. No. LC-B8184-10658. 84: Library of Congress. 85, 86: USAMHI, copied by A. Pierce Bounds. 87: MASS-MOLLUS/USAMHI, copied by A. Pierce Bounds. 88, 89: Courtesy Kirk Denkler, copied by Evan H. Sheppard—Manassas National Battlefield Park, Va., photographed by Michael Latil (2). 90: Lee-Fendall House Museum, Alexandria, Va. 91: MASS-MOLLUS/USAMHI, copied by A. Pierce Bounds; Library of Congress, Neg. No. LC-B8172-6429. 92: Alabama Department of Archives and History, Montgomery. 93: Cook Collection, The Valentine Museum, Richmond. 94: Library of Con-

gress. 95: Library of Congress, Neg. No. LC-B8184-4099. 96: MASS-MOLLUS/USAMHI, copied by A. Pierce Bounds. 98: Courtesy Lynchburg Museum System, Va.; courtesy Collection of William A. Turner. 99: MASS-MOLLUS/USAMHI, copied by A. Pierce Bounds. 100: State Archives, Connecticut State Library, PG85, copied by Gus Johnson. 101: Courtesy Collection of William A. Turner—Frank and Marie-Thérèse Wood Print Collections, Alexandria, Va. 102: Don Troiani Collection, copied by Larry Sherer. 103: Courtesy William B. Styple, photographed by Jim Geutzman. 104: Courtesy South Caroliniana Library, University of South Carolina, Columbia—Robert A. Quinn Collection, photo at USAMHI, copied by A. Pierce Bounds. 105: MASS-MOLLUS/USAMHI, copied by A. Pierce Bounds. 106: Courtesy Brian Pohanka—Museum of the Confederacy, Richmond, photographed by Larry Sherer. 107: Alma Y. Carroll, photo at USAMHI, copied by A. Pierce Bounds. 108: Library of Congress, Waud #717. 109: From *Four Brothers in Blue*, by Robert Goldthwaite Carter, University of Texas Press, Austin, 1978, copied by Philip Brandt George—Manassas National Battlefield Park, Va., photographed by Michael Latil. 111: Map by Walter W. Roberts. 112: From *The Confederate General*, Vol. 2, edited by William C. Davis, National Historical Society, 1991, copied by Philip Brandt George; South Carolina Confederate Relic Room and Museum, Columbia, photographed by Larry Sherer. 113: Library of Congress, Neg. No. LC-B813-6770. 114: Roger D. Hunt Collection at USAMHI, copied by A. Pierce Bounds; MASS-MOLLUS/USAMHI, copied by A. Pierce Bounds. 115: Courtesy South Caroliniana Library, University of South Carolina, Columbia. 116: James B. Vicksburg Collection, photo at USAMHI, copied by A. Pierce Bounds—MASS-MOLLUS/USAMHI, copied by A. Pierce Bounds. 117: MASS-MOLLUS/USAMHI, copied by A. Pierce Bounds; from *Confederate Veteran*, Vol. 22, August, 1914, copied by Richard Baumgartner. 118: Museum of the Confederacy, Richmond, photographed by Larry Sherer. 119: MASS-MOLLUS/USAMHI, copied by A. Pierce Bounds. 120: Courtesy Doug Bast/Boonsborough Museum of History, copied by Larry Sherer; courtesy Collection of William A. Turner. 122: Courtesy Stonewall Jackson Foundation, Lexington, Va.; Virginia Military Institute Museum, Virginia Military Institute, Lexington, Va., photographed by Larry Sherer. 123: MASS-MOLLUS/USAMHI, copied by A. Pierce Bounds. 124: Library of Congress, Neg. No. LC-B8172-1373. 125: Patrick L. Chandler, photo at USAMHI, copied by A. Pierce Bounds—courtesy Colin J. S. Thomas Jr. 126: Museum of the Confederacy, Richmond, photographed by Larry Sherer—Manassas National Battlefield Park, Va., photographed by Michael Latil. 127: MASS-MOLLUS/USAMHI,

copied by A. Pierce Bounds. 128: James W. Crowell Collection, photo at USAMHI, copied by A. Pierce Bounds. 129: Museum of the Confederacy, Richmond, Va., photographed by Larry Sherer; courtesy Collection of William A. Turner—Mrs. S. P. Herron Collection, photo at USAMHI, copied by A. Pierce Bounds. 130: From *Battles and Leaders of the Civil War*, Vol. 1, published by Century, 1884. 131: Division of Military and Naval Affairs, NYS Adjutant General's Office, Albany, N.Y., copied by A. Pierce Bounds. 132: Courtesy South Caroliniana Library, University of South Carolina, Columbia. 133: Courtesy Ben Ritter; courtesy Charles Robert Norris III and Charles Robert Norris IV, on loan to Manassas National Battlefield Park, Va. (coat photographed by Michael Latil). 134: MASS-MOLLUS/USAMHI, copied by Philip Brandt George; North Carolina Museum of History, Raleigh. 135: Wisconsin Veterans Museum, Madison. 136: MASS-MOLLUS/USAMHI, copied by A. Pierce Bounds. 139: Map by Walter W. Roberts. 140: From *A Soldier's Recollections: Leaves from the Diary of a Young Confederate*, by Randolph H. McKim, published by Longmans, Green, New York, 1910; Private collection, copied by Evan H. Sheppard. 141: Courtesy Maryland State Archives, Annapolis. 142: Courtesy Dr. Larry Freeman, American Life Foundation, photographed by Lon Mattoon. 143: Old Courthouse Museum, Vicksburg, Miss., copied by Henry Mintz. 144: From *The Story of a Confederate Boy in the Civil War*, by David E. Johnston, Glass & Prudhomme, Portland, Oreg., 1914—Manassas National Battlefield Park, Va., photographed by Michael Latil. 145: MASS-MOLLUS/USAMHI, copied by A. Pierce Bounds; New Market Battlefield State Historical Park, Hall of Valor Museum, New Market, Va., photographed by Larry Sherer. 146: From *The Old Virginia Gentleman and Other Sketches*, by George W. Bagby, Dietz Press, Richmond, 1938, copied by Philip Brandt George; MASS-MOLLUS/USAMHI, copied by A. Pierce Bounds. 147: MASS-MOLLUS/USAMHI, copied by A. Pierce Bounds; Museum of the Confederacy, Richmond, photographed by Larry Sherer. 148: Museum of Fine Arts, Boston. 149: Library of Congress, copied by Philip Brandt George. 150: From *Divided We Fought: A Pictorial History of the War, 1861-1865*, published by Macmillan, New York, 1956—Western Reserve Historical Society, Cleveland. 151: Frank and Marie-Thérèse Wood Print Collections, Alexandria, Va. 152: Library of Congress, Neg. No. LC-B8171-314. 154: Library of Congress, Neg. No. LC-USZ62-8678—Private collection, photographed by Evan H. Sheppard. 155: Manassas National Battlefield Park, Va., photographed by Michael Latil. 156: Frank and Marie-Thérèse Wood Print Collections, Alexandria, Va. 157: Special Collections, University of Virginia Library. 159: Library of Congress, Neg. No. LC-B8184-4375.

BIBLIOGRAPHY

BOOKS

Alexander, Edward Porter. *Fighting for the Confederacy*. Ed. by Gary W. Gallagher. Chapel Hill: University of North Carolina Press, 1989.

Bagby, George W. *The Old Virginia Gentleman and Other Sketches*. Ed. by Ellen M. Bagby. Richmond: Dietz Press, 1938.

Baker, Henry H. *A Reminiscent Story of the Great Civil War*. New Orleans: Ruskin Press, 1911.

Barclay, Ted. *Ted Barclay, Liberty Hall Volunteers: Letters from the Stonewall Brigade (1861-1864)*. Ed. by Charles W. Turner. Berryville, Va.: Rockbridge, 1992.

Barrett, Edwin S. *What I Saw at Bull Run: An Address*. Boston: Beacon Press, 1886.

Battles and Leaders of the Civil War (Vol. 1). Ed. by Robert Underwood Johnson and Clarence Clough Buel. New York: Thomas Yoseloff, 1956.

Blackford, William W. *War Years with Jeb Stuart*. New York: Charles Scribner's Sons, 1945.

"Carleton." *Stories of Our Soldiers*. Boston: Journal Newspaper, 1893.

Carter, Robert Goldthwaite. *Four Brothers in Blue*. Austin: University of Texas Press, 1978.

Casler, John O. *Four Years in the Stonewall Brigade*. Dayton: Morningside Bookshop, 1971.

Chittenden, Lucius E. *Invisible Siege*. San Diego, Calif.: Americana Exchange Press, 1969.

Clark, Walter. *Histories of the Several Regiments and Battalions from North Carolina* (Vol. 1). Wendell, N.C.: Broadfoot's Bookmark, 1982 (reprint of 1901 edition).

Cohen, Stan. *The Civil War in West Virginia: A Pictorial History*. Charleston, W.Va.: Pictorial Histories, 1982.

Coles, Robert T. *From Huntsville to Appomattox: R. T. Coles's History of 4th Regiment, Alabama Volunteer Infantry, C.S.A., Army of Northern Virginia*. Ed. by Jeffrey D. Stocker. Knoxville: University of Tennessee Press, 1996.

Comings, Harrison H. *Personal Reminiscences of Co. E, N.Y. Fire Zouaves*. Malden, Mass.: J. G. Tilden, 1886.

The Confederate General (6 vols.). Ed. by William C. Davis. Harrisburg, Pa.: National Historical Society, 1991.

Dannett, Sylvia G. L., ed. and comp. *Noble Women of the North*. New York: Thomas Yoseloff, 1959.

Davenport, Alfred. *Camp and Field Life of the Fifth New York Volunteer Infantry*. New York: Dick and Fitzgerald, 1879.

Davis, William C. *Battle at Bull Run*. Baton Rouge: Louisiana State University Press, 1977.

Dennis, John B. "March of the Sixth Massachusetts through Baltimore." In *Civil War Sketches and Incidents: Papers Read by Companions of the Commandery of the State of Nebraska, Military Order of the Loyal Legion of the United States* (Vol. 1). Wilmington, N.C.: Broadfoot, 1992.

Ely, Alfred. *Journal of Alfred Ely*. Ed. by Charles Lanman. New York: D. Appleton, 1862.

Finch, George M. "The Boys of '61." In *G. A. R. War Papers* (Vol. 1). Cincinnati: Fred C. Jones Post, No. 401, 1891.

"The First Regiment (N. C.) Volunteers." In *Southern Historical Society Papers* (Vol. 19). Ed. by. R. A. Brock. Wilmington, N.C.: Broadfoot, 1990 (reprint of 1891 edition).

Frobel, Anne S. *The Civil War Diary of Anne S. Frobel*. McLean, Va.: EPM, 1992.

Goree, Thomas J. *Longstreet's Aide*. Ed. by Thomas W. Cutrer. Charlottesville: University Press of Virginia, 1995.

Hall, H. Seymour. "A Volunteer at the First Bull Run." In *War Talks in Kansas: A Series of Papers Read before the Kansas Commandery of the Military Order of the Loyal Legion of the United States*. Wilmington, N.C.: Broadfoot, 1992 (reprint of 1906 edition).

Hall, James E. *The Diary of a Confederate Soldier*. Ed. by Ruth Woods Dayton. Philippi, W.Va.: private printing, 1961.

Haynes, Martin A. *History of the Second Regiment, New Hampshire Volunteers: Its Camps, Marches and Battles*. Manchester, N.H.: Charles F. Livingston, 1865.

Hennessy, John. *The First Battle of Manassas: An End to Innocence, July 18-21, 1861*. Lynchburg, Va.: H. E. Howard, 1989.

Hudgins, Robert S., II. *Recollections of an Old Dominion Dragoon: The Civil War Experiences of Sgt. Robert S. Hudgins II, Company B, 3rd Virginia Cavalry*. Ed. by Garland C. Hudgins and Richard B. Kleese. Orange, Va.: Publisher's Press, 1993.

Hunt, Gaillard, comp. *Israel, Elihu and Cadwallader Washburn*. New York: Macmillan, 1925.

Ingraham, Charles A. *Elmer E. Ellsworth and the Zouaves of '61*. Chicago: University of Chicago Press, 1925.

Johnson, Charles F. *The Long Roll*. East Aurora, N.Y.: Roycrofters, 1911.

Johnston, David E. *The Story of a Confederate Boy in the Civil War*. Portland, Oreg.: Glass & Prudhomme, 1914.

King, Josias R. "The Battle of Bull Run." In *Glimpses of the Nation's Struggle: Papers Read before the Minnesota Commandery of the Military Order of the Loyal Legion of the United States, January, 1903-1908*. Wilmington, N.C.: Broadfoot, 1992 (reprint of 1909 edition).

Knox, Edward B. "The Capture of Alexandria and the Death of Ellsworth." In *Military Essays and Recollections* (Vol. 2). Wilmington, N.C.: Broadfoot, 1992 (reprint of 1894 edition).

Krick, Robert K. *Lee's Colonels*. Dayton: Morningside, 1992.

Lyster, Henry F. "Recollections of the Bull Run Campaign." In *War Papers: Being Papers Read before the Commandery of the State of Michigan, Military Order of the*

Loyal Legion of the United States (Vol. 1). Wilmington, N.C.: Broadfoot, 1993 (reprint of 1888 edition).

McGuire, Judith W. *Diary of a Southern Refugee during the War, by a Lady of Virginia*. Lincoln: University of Nebraska Press, 1995.

McKim, Randolph H. *A Soldier's Recollections*. New York: Longmans, Green, 1910.

Marvel, William, comp. *Biographical Sketches of the Contributors to the Military Order of the Loyal Legion of the United States*. Wilmington, N.C.: Broadfoot, 1995.

Mast, Greg. *State Troops and Volunteers: A Photographic Record of North Carolina's Civil War Soldiers* (Vol. 1). Raleigh: North Carolina Division of Archives and History, 1995.

Milhollen, Hirst D., Milton Kaplan, and Hulen Stuart. *Divided We Fought: A Pictorial History of the War, 1861-1865*. New York: Macmillan, 1956.

Moe, Richard. *The Last Full Measure: The Life and Death of the First Minnesota Volunteers*. New York: Henry Holt, 1993.

Monroe, J. Albert. "The Rhode Island Artillery at the First Battle of Bull Run." In *Personal Narratives of the Battles of the Rebellion*. Wilmington, N.C.: Broadfoot, 1993 (reprint of 1878 edition).

Parker, Daingerfield. "The Battalion of Regular Infantry at the First Battle of Bull Run." In *Military Order of the Loyal Legion of the United States, Commandery of the District of Columbia*. Wilmington, N.C.: Broadfoot, 1993.

Patrick, Rembert W. *Jefferson Davis and His Cabinet*. Baton Rouge: Louisiana State University Press, 1944.

Post, Lydia Minturn, ed. *Soldiers' Letters: From Camp, Battle-Field and Prison*. New York: Bunce & Huntington, 1865.

The Rebellion Record: A Diary of American Events (Vol. 2). Ed. by Frank Moore. New York: D. Van Nostrand, 1866.

Richmond Howitzers in the War. Gaithersburg, Md.: Butternut Press, n.d. (reprint of 1891 edition).

Sherman, William Tecumseh. *Memoirs of General William T. Sherman*. Westport, Conn.: Greenwood Press, 1957.

Small, Abner R. *The Road to Richmond*. Ed. by Harold Adams Small. Berkeley: University of California Press, 1939.

Smith, James Power. *With Stonewall Jackson in the Army of Northern Virginia*. Gaithersburg, Md.: Zullo and Van Sickle Books, 1982.

Smith, William. "Reminiscences of the First Battle of Manassas." In *Southern Historical Society Papers* (Vol. 10). Wilmington, N.C.: Broadfoot, 1990.

Southwick, Thomas P. *A Duryee Zouave*. Brookneal, Va.: Patrick A. Schroeder, 1995.

Staples, Horatio. "Reminiscences of Bull Run." In *War Papers: Read before the Commandery of the State of Maine, Military Order of the Loyal Legion of the United States* (Vol. 3). Wilmington, N.C.: Broadfoot, 1992 (reprint of 1908 edition).

Thomas, James B. *The Civil War Letters of First Lieutenant James B. Thomas, Adjutant, 107th Pennsylvania Volunteers.* Ed. by Mary Warner Thomas and Richard A. Sauers. Baltimore: Butternut and Blue, 1995.

Turner, William A. *Even More Confederate Faces.* Orange, Va.: Moss Publications, 1983.

United States Army. *Official Army Register of the Volunteer Force of the United States Army: For the Years 1861, '62, '63, '64, '65* (Vols. 1, 3, 5, 6, 7). Gaithersburg, Md.: Olde Soldier Books, 1987 (reprint of 1865 edition).

United States Navy. *Official Records of the Union and Confederate Navies in the War of the Rebellion* (Series 1, Vol. 4). Washington, D.C.: Government Printing Office, 1896.

United States War Department. *The War of the Rebellion: A Compilation of the Official Records of the Union and Confederate Armies* (Series 1, Vol. 51, 2 parts). Washington, D.C.: Government Printing Office, 1897.

Warfield, Edgar. *A Confederate Soldier's Memoirs.* Richmond: Masonic Home Press, 1936.

Whitman, Walt. *The Complete Writings of Walt Whitman.* New York: G. P. Putnam's Sons, 1902.

Wise, George. *History of the Seventeenth Virginia Infantry, C.S.A.* Baltimore: Kelly, Piet, 1870.

Woodbury, Augustus. *The Second Rhode Island Regiment.* Providence: Valpey, Angell, 1875.

PERIODICALS

Buck, Nina Kirby-Smith. " 'Blucher of the Day' at Manassas." *Confederate Veteran,* Vol. 7, 1899.

Coxe, John. "The Battle of First Manassas." *Confederate Veteran,* Vol. 23, 1915.

"Florence." Published letter. *Southern Magazine* (Baltimore), May 1874.

Gordon, Eben. "On Bull Run's Field." *National Tribune* (Washington, D.C.), February 8, 1894.

Hagy, P. S. "The Laurel Hill Retreat in 1861." *Confederate Veteran,* Vol. 24, 1915.

Hains, Peter C. "The First Gun at Bull Run." *Cosmopolitan,* Vol. 51, 1911.

Howard, O. O. "Battle of Bull Run." *National Tribune* (Washington, D.C.), November 29, 1883.

Huske, Benjamin R. "More Terrible Than Victory." *Civil War Times,* October 1981.

McCoy, Milton. "First Bull Run: Experiences of an Ohio Three Months' Man." *National Tribune* (Washington, D.C.), October 30, 1884.

Rorty, James. Letters. *Irish American* (New York), December 7, 14, 1861.

Sonderman, John G. "First Bull Run." *National Tribune* (Washington, D.C.), July 2, 1896.

Thatcher, Orville D. "1st Minn. at Bull Run." *National Tribune* (Washington, D.C.), June 3, 1886.

Thorpe, Wallace W. "Big Bethel." *National Tribune* (Washington, D.C.), November 8, 1883.

OTHER SOURCES

Barnsley, George Scarborough. Papers, 1860-1866. Chapel Hill: University of North Carolina Library, Southern Historical Collection.

Beauregard, Pierre G. T. Letter, July 13, 1861. Durham, N.C.: Duke University, Special Collections Library.

Coble, Eli S.:
Civil War reminiscences, papers, and letters. Raleigh: North Carolina Department of Archives and History. "Reminiscences by E. S. Coble of 'The Dixie Boys.' " Unpublished manuscript, Mss. #16. Greensboro, N.C.: Greensboro Historical Museum.

Connor, James. Letter, July 22, 1861. Columbia: South Caroliniana Library.

Dean, Lizzie. Letter, July 23, 1861, from the Lewis Leigh Collection. Carlisle Barracks, Pa.: U.S. Army Military History Institute.

Doby, Alfred. Letter, July 25, 1861. Columbia: South Caroliniana Library.

Duffy, Edward S. Diary, n.d. Richmond: Virginia Historical Society.

Freeman, S. D. Papers, n.d. Washington, D.C.: Library of Congress, Manuscript Division.

Gillette, James J. Letter, August 8, 1861. Washington, D.C.: Library of Congress, Manuscript Division.

Grant, Robert. Letter, July 21, 1861. Manassas, Va.: Manassas National Battlefield Park.

Habersham, Richard A. Letter, July 26, 1861. Washington, D.C.: Library of Congress, Manuscript Division.

Harris, William C. Letter, June 11, 1861, from the Alonzo Choen Collection. Durham, N.C.: Duke University, Special Collections Library.

Hill, John Lyon. Diary, from the Doubleday/Catton Papers. Washington, D.C.: Library of Congress, Manuscript Division.

Hotchkiss, Jedediah. Papers, 1861-1864. Washington, D.C.: Library of Congress, Manuscript Division.

Hudson, James G. Diary. Montgomery: Alabama Department of Archives and History.

Hunt, Henry J. "Report of Light Battery M, Second Artillery, U.S.A., under Command of Major Henry J. Hunt." Report, July 25, 1861, from the Polk, Brown and Ewell Family Papers #605. Chapel Hill: University of North Carolina Library, Southern Historical Collection.

Hunter, Alexander. Memoirs, n.d. Richmond: Virginia Historical Society.

Hutson, Charles W. Letter, July 22, 1861. Chapel Hill: University of North Carolina Library, Southern Historical Collection.

Kirby, Reynold Marvin. Letter, June 11, 1861. Staunton, Va.: Mary Baldwin Alumnae Association.

Lee, Otho Scott. "Reminiscences of Four Years Service in the Confederate Army." Unpublished manuscript, n.d. Manassas, Va.: Manassas National Battlefield Park.

Leib, Charles. "Nine Months in the Quartermaster's Department." Unpublished manuscript, 1862, from the Doubleday/Catton Papers. Washington, D.C.: Library of Congress, Manuscript Division.

McClellan, George B. Proclamation, May 26, 1861, from the Frederick West Lander Papers. Washington, D.C.: Library of Congress, Manuscript Division.

Meagher, Francis F. "Last Days of the 69th in Virginia." Unpublished manuscript, n.d., from the Doubleday/Catton Papers. Washington, D.C.: Library of Congress, Manuscript Division.

Melloy, George. Letter, June 11, 1861. Carlisle Barracks, Pa.: U.S. Army Military History Institute.

Moore, Samuel J. C. Papers, 1847-1937. Chapel Hill: University of North Carolina Library, Southern Historical Collection.

Poe, Orlando M. Papers. Washington, D.C.: Library of Congress, Manuscript Division.

Pollack, Curtis C. Letter, April 28, 1861. Carlisle Barracks, Pa.: U.S. Army Military History Institute.

Reid, John C. Journal, n.d. Manassas, Va.: Manassas National Battlefield Park.

Ritter, Henry. Letter, July 23, 1861. Manassas, Va.: Manassas National Battlefield Park.

Taliaferro, William B. Letter, July 20, 1861, from the Doubleday/Catton Papers. Washington, D.C.: Library of Congress, Manuscript Division.

Tayloe, Edward. Letter, August 2, 1861. Charlottesville: University of Virginia Library, Manuscripts Department.

Weir, James E. Letter, June 12, 1861. Private collection.

Weston, George Harry. Diary, n.d. Durham, N.C.: Duke University, Special Collections Library.

Wheeler, Henry C. Letter, May 17, 1903, from the Douglas Southall Freeman Papers. Washington, D.C.: Library of Congress, Manuscript Division.

Wight, Charles Copland. "Recollections of Charles Copland Wight, 1841-1897." Unpublished manuscript, n.d., from the Wight Papers. Richmond: Virginia Historical Society.

Wilkinson, Gilbert D. Diary. Savannah: Greg Starbuck Collection.

INDEX

TIME® Time-Life Books is a
LIFE division of Time Life Inc.
BOOKS

TIME LIFE INC.
PRESIDENT and CEO: George Artandi

TIME-LIFE BOOKS
PRESIDENT: Stephen R. Frary
PUBLISHER/MANAGING EDITOR: Neil Kagan

VOICES OF THE CIVIL WAR

MARKETING DIRECTOR: Pamela R. Farrell

FIRST MANASSAS

EDITOR: Paul Mathless
Deputy Editors: Harris J. Andrews (principal), Kirk Denkler,
Philip Brandt George
Design Director: Barbara M. Sheppard
Art Director: Ellen L. Pattisall
Associate Editor/Research and Writing: Gemma Slack
Senior Copyeditor: Judith Klein
Picture Coordinator: Lisa Groseclose
Editorial Assistant: Christine Higgins

Initial Series Design: Studio A

Special Contributors: Brian Pohanka, Dana B. Shoaf, David S.
Thomson (text); Paul Birkhead, Connie Contreras, Charles
F. Cooney, Steve Hill, Robert Lee Hodge, Grady Howell,
Susan V. Kelly, Henry Mintz, Dana B. Shoaf (research); Roy
Nanovic (index).

Correspondent: Christina Lieberman (New York)

Director of Finance: Christopher Hearing
Director of Book Production: Marjann Caldwell
Director of Publishing Technology: Betsi McGrath
Director of Photography and Research: John Conrad Weiser
Director of Editorial Administration: Barbara Levitt
Production Manager: Marlene Zack
Quality Assurance Manager: James King
Chief Librarian: Louise D. Forstall

First printing. Printed in U.S.A.
School and library distribution by Time-Life Education,
P.O. Box 85026, Richmond, Virginia 23285-5026.

TIME-LIFE is a trademark of Time Warner Inc. U.S.A.

Library of Congress Cataloging-in-Publication Data
First Manassas / by the editors of Time-Life Books.
    p. cm.—(Voices of the Civil War)
    Includes bibliographical references (p.   ) and index.
    ISBN 0-7835-4712-9
    I. Bull Run, 1st Battle of, Va., 1861.
    I. Time-Life Books. II. Series.
E472.18.F49 1997
973.7'31—dc21   97-19101
                                                           CIP